May your lemons
be transformed
into something oh
so sweet! Bernard

# lemonade

## inspired by actual events

# bernard L. dillard

Published by BerNerd Publishing.

Visit us at www.bernarddillard.com

ISBN-10:  0615696112

EAN-13:  978-0615696119

in

celebration

of

vicky,

dwayne, jr.,

and

takeva

and

to

those

who

learned

how

to

use

their

hinds'

feet!

# preface

I t was 9:02 AM on a chilly morning in November of 2009. I sat in my apartment on 138th Street and Lenox Avenue in Harlem, pondering the direction of my life while staring at the clock. A few paces from Abyssinian Baptist Church, I lay in my bed on the sixth floor, happy because I had recently moved from the first floor in the same building thanks to my upstairs neighbor, who had transformed her own apartment into a gym. She decided she'd jump hard and long on a trampoline in her unit at any time of day or night. In hindsight, I guess it was funny. Who actually has the audacity to go through with such a plan and ignore what most would deem as common sense with respect to communal living conditions? Then, I soon remembered the proverb that reminded me what common sense ain't to most people and took it in stride. Subconsciously, it was probably at this point that I decided that my life would no more be a reactionary thing. I would try not to act in response to how others acted, which was a tall order, living in Harlem or New York period for that matter. But it was at least a goal.

As I sat at the edge of the bed on that morning, I booted my laptop, opened a blank document, and started typing. I had no idea when enough would be enough or when too much would be too much. All I knew was that I wouldn't wait until something *made* me write. In my mind, I had overcome quite a bit without holding up the I-overcame-the-most trophy. But I knew I had something to say perhaps to inspire and encourage others, especially menfolk, who had conquered much and still had much to conquer. I was sure there were others who have had to endure much more than I, but I knew my story was unique in its own right and could be at least a source of empathy for someone else, a mirror into which others could stare and see a glimpse of themselves for the purpose of enduring. With this resolve, however, came a bit of angst. By right, this was my life and these were my successes and scars. I really didn't have to share them with or reveal them to anyone. I had concluded, nevertheless, that this entire project was just my making sense of my own life, a therapy of sorts. This was my telling myself my own story from my own perspective. It was *my* life. So I made a resolve to tell it and present it from *my* vantage point.

Hence, *Lemonade* is inspired by actual events that transpired in my life. It is what I know and recall. I clarified some details through interviews and discussions to help jog my memory. Most names have been changed to secure anonymity. People who read it will know who they are, but at least some thoughtfulness has been given with respect to names to protect whomever from whatever. What was more important to me was not the *who* but the *how*. I wanted to share how I made it through. The overall mission of this work primarily was to help me work though my own feelings concerning my past. Second, if this work were able to inspire and help the proverbial "one person," then it really was worth the time and effort expended to make this project come to life.

Finally, the reader should be advised that *Lemonade* contains some strong language and some adult content. I thought briefly about altering these aspects of the book. I decided, however, that eliminating the realness and rawness of these aspects would eliminate the realness and rawness of my experiences. The purpose for which I chose to write would have indeed been defeated. What would have resulted would have been an innocuous, watered-down, simple version of my life. As most writers attempt to do, I generally strove to write from the perspective of the fly on the wall. Since this is a treatment about the happenings concerning me, the fly occasionally flew down and became a part of the action. Outside of his own speaking and participation, though, the fly simply conveyed what he saw, smelled, heard, and felt, often shamefacedly so.

And so here's to all of you who don't just move because of the trampoline-jumpers out there. In the grand scope of things, you move because moving is just the right thing to do.

And now, I present to you . . . *Lemonade*. Take a sip!

And after six days Jesus taketh with him Peter,

and James, and John, and leadeth them

up into an high mountain . . .

*Saint Mark 9:2*

# table o'contents

# lemonade

# still okay

It was March, and she had taken out a loan from the bank for $7,000 to get the shingles on the roof fixed. She had always been a self-starter and took it upon herself to use her own credit and good name to get things moving. No need to wait for him. They were partners working toward one goal and one mission. Plus, she herself was tired of watching the water leak into the house and vowed this was the time to settle the problem once and for all. He didn't know that she planned to do this, so he had to be elated when she gave him the money and told him to handle it. After about a month, there was no word on how things were progressing, so she thought she'd ask.

"Dwayne, so when the people supposed to come and fix the roof?" She yelled it since he was in the back room. She was finishing up with dinner and had been feeling a little sick because of her condition. There was no response. Maybe he didn't hear her, so she decided to make her way back to the bedroom and inquire again. "Have you heard anything about when the people are going to come to fix the shingles?"

He hesitated and confessed, "Oh, well I actually used it to buy some speakers and equipment for the group." He was a member of a singing group, and he had made major purchases for it as opposed to using the money to fix the roof. Perhaps he planned on fixing the roof when money from gigs started rolling in. Right now, the investment in the equipment was more important than some dumb roof.

"You used the money to buy what? I know I didn't hear what I think I heard. I gave you the money 'cause I thought you would be on top of it and get stuff going on the roof, not use it for no damn group. Why can't they use they own money?" She knew that $7,000 was no chump change.

"Damn, Vicky, it'll get done when it get done. I didn't know it was a time limit to get it fixed." He was trying to outfox the fox.

"Yeah, well it's leaking all in TaKeva's room when it rains. It's April, and you know what they say about rain in April. It needs to get fixed before then or at least they need to start on it." She was unsuccessful at trying to lighten the mood.

"Well damn, I didn't know you were gone ride me like a horse until I got it fixed." He turned off the lights in the half-bath and started to walk past her, but she cut him off and continued.

"It ain't got nothin' to do with ridin' nobody. And why you damn gotta cuss and get an attitude about it? You would think you would be happy that I took it upon myself to give you the money to have it done. You can say damn, then I can say damn too, shit!" She had inched closer to his face.

"Vicky, move back. I'm going to the kitchen. I ain't got time for this."

"Move back hell. You act like you ain't 'posed to be responsible and answer to nobody. You wouldn't be actin' like that if it was yo' money. So you need to let me know when it's gone get fixed or start giving me the money back so I can get on it." Now virtually in his face, she was almost yelling. "Be a damn man!"

So he became one. Without warning, he struck her in the stomach, perhaps because he couldn't deal with having been caught. She fell backward and bumped up against the dresser drawer, and he continued toward the kitchen. A little shocked, she tried to regain her balance and composure, lifted her shirt, and did her own self-examination. Thankfully, in her mind, there would be no need to go to the doctor. No miscarriage.

She hadn't lost me. I was still in there, and I was still okay.

# stay in your lane

aking my entrance into the world through Durham, North Carolina seemed somewhat anticlimactic for me. When people used to ask me where I was from, I generally hesitated and tried to figure out how I could make Durham hip. I always wished I could say I was from L.A. or New York or Paris or somewhere else that was considered the right place to be born. So I'd always say something like, "I'm from the Dirty South," hoping they'd accept that as a good-enough response. Almost invariably, they would require more details.

"Oh, okay, so you're from Atlanta?"

"Naw, not quite, more north."

"Really, where?"

"I'm from North Carolina."

"Oh, okay, the Charlotte area?"

"Naw, not quite. Raleigh-Durham."

At least I'd figure they knew where that was because of the major airport at RDU or the Research Triangle area. Then, they would go on and on and on about Raleigh since most of them knew it was the capital. And then they would talk about Charlotte, the Atlanta of North Carolina. They elaborated none about Durham, my stomping ground. I eventually discovered how to connect with most of those who inquired as to my beginnings. Most people were basketball fans and seemed to know about the leading teams in college. So once I let them know that I was born at Duke University Hospital, they made some connection, although faint.

"Oh yeah, Duke. Is that where Duke is, in Durham?"

"Yep. Duke Blue Devils. Durham, North Carolina."

"Well, I'm actually a Tar Heel fan." They often had to get that in.

"Alright. That's cool. No love lost."

I had lost again. Failed in my mission to make my hometown stand out over others. After moving to other areas, I'd discover that it was not all that bad. It seems as though the more north I lived, the sexier that the ladies thought my southern accent was. So I learned to embrace where I was from and all that came with it.

I am told when I arrived home from the hospital, TaKeva, my sister, quickly expressed her disapproval. Up to that moment, she was the youngest and was used to basking in the glory that came along with such a title. At three years old, she was full of wit and voiced her opinion in a way that was convincing, at least to herself. The conversation between my mother and her was somewhat comical, but my mother was a master at making TaKeva feel as though what she said had merit.

"Who is this?"

"Say 'Hello' to Bernard, TaKeva. This is your baby brother," my mother responded while beaming with joy.

"Baby brotha? But I already have a brotha."

"Yeah, well now you have another one."

"But what if I don't want another one?"

"Well, it's a little bit too late now, TaKeva. He's already here. Isn't he a cute little thing?"

"But nobody axed me if I wanted another brotha. If someone woulda axed me, maybe I woulda said I wanted a sister. Or nothin' else. It's not fair."

"Well, TaKeva, just be happy for right now. You'll get to know him and you all will be best friends."

"Well, is he gone be my fren or my brotha?"

"If you're lucky, TaKeva, he'll be both."

"How can he be bof? Brothas can't be frens."

"Keva, never mind. You'll understand what I'm saying later as you get older."

"Well, nobody still didn't ax me if I wanted another nothin', brotha or sista."

It was no winning with TaKeva. She was always going to find a way to make sure her argument was the most sound and persuasive. As usual, my mother just let Keva, a chopped version of her name, feel like she had the upper hand, just for the sake of peace for everyone around. So that was my first day at home. Not the best welcome party, but it sufficed.

To the grown-ups, I was a cutie. But what newbie is not? I had a reputation of grabbing the hair of anyone who wanted to hold the "new baby." I scratched something awful, too. My mother had to stay close because whoever was holding me was going to want to give me back to her with the quickness. And of course, my mother would end up apologizing to whomever managed to be the victim of my scratches. She didn't know why I did that.

To my two siblings, I was just another occupant in the house whose mouth had to be fed. The runt of the litter. Nothing special. Nothing cute. Just one of them. I shared a room with my brother, Dwayne, Jr. He was seven years my senior. My father gave him the nickname, Dimpo, because he had a deep set of dimples. And I still struggle to figure out how he ended up so dark-skinned, much darker than my mother and my father. I wasn't charmed at all, though. We did what brothers do: fought like dogs. I think this is where my sense of courage and resolve came from. If at one, I could stand up to an eight-year old, then I was good to go. Even if I got beat up, which is what generally happened, I kept coming back. I think I was fearless.

Around four, I got the typical big-brother christening. Dwayne loved apples, but apparently apples didn't love him back. We were chilling, playing, and lying in the bed watching TV, and all I remember was that he hurried up and placed the covers over my head and trapped me inside. As I wrestled to get out, I couldn't hold back the screaming and the tears, not because I was claustrophobic but because the smell that I had to contend with honestly seemed like it came from an animal. The pungency of his farts, especially the silent ones, wreaked havoc in my little bitty world. It literally smelled like something crawled up inside him and died. Once I got free, I would charge him with all my might, snot everywhere, eyes burning. The smug smile on his face said it all as he held me at arm's length while I swatted. No matter how feisty I was, he was still older, stronger, stinkier.

But things managed to work themselves out in the home between us, Dwayne, Keva, and me. My father and mother never tried to change our personalities. Dwayne, with his unspoken confidence and understood authority. Keva, with her stubborn nature and final say-so. Me, with my fighter instinct and need to challenge all semblance of power and authority. We were far from the Brady bunch, but we found our own familial rhythm and managed to gel as a unit.

My mother, Vicky Alston, was a country girl, the second oldest of nine. If you thought Durham was obscure, take a journey to where she was from. Moncure. Around the Pittsboro area. The town had one bank and one post office. She was born on July 23. She had begun making waves early, becoming the first woman in her town to drive a school bus. She always thought she could do what the guys did. Hell, who were they to think that a woman couldn't do what they could do, and why couldn't she be the one who did it? That's how she thought. Never took down to anyone. She was a precursor to Dwayne. In charge. A precursor to Keva. Stubborn in her own right. My precursor. A fighter. She later moved to Durham after high school to attend college at North Carolina Central University. She had a little more motivation to do so, after she had met my father, Dwayne, at a homecoming church service in Pittsboro.

She played the piano and organ there at the church, where her father was the pastor. Hortense Alston was his name. A smooth, debonair man who had charisma for days. He had that wavy hair, that good hair. He must have had Indian in his family. Or so we always thought. We as kids didn't worry about asking about the details of who he was. He wasn't concerned about us that much, so we didn't give him the time of day. I don't even remember sitting on his lap as a kid, and I never can recall a conversation between us. I'm sure I managed to swindle gum and candy out of him as a lad, but no interaction with him sticks out as being life-changing. He had caught the eye of and hooked up with Sue Slade, the classy and composed diva, who was also from Moncure. Together, they had made a spitfire of a daughter in Vicky, who was indeed her own person, with her own fiery personality.

A smooth operator in his own right, Hortense couldn't shake a stick at my father, Dwayne, Sr. As a very young kid, I always was impressed with his pride in providing for his family. He was a strapping guy, who was an ex-high jumper with huge calves like Popeye. Like most of the men in our family, his hairline had started receding in his twenties. I guess this was true because the men on his mother's side had similar receding going on. Or at least that's what I learned concerning that phenomenon in biology class. Genes were something else.

There were times that I couldn't wait to leave from our family restaurant at closing with him. At four, I knew I was going to take part in a special privilege that only my father could make happen for me on our way home.

"Here, take this rag and wipe off the table," he encouraged.

"Like this?"

"Boy, you gotta wipe the whole table. You ain't doing nothing but just wiping in one spot. I keep telling you that. See, watch me."

"Okay, let me do it."

"Okay, but you can't just keep wiping in one spot. Here. Look." He was demonstrating.

"Okay, I can do it." I grabbed the rag back from him.

I climbed up on the chair and finished the task as I wiped the table semi-clean. Of course, I started playing and put my dirty finger on the wet table, doodling through the wetness and defeating the purpose. Plus, the rag smelled of bootleg bleach.

"Boy, you just . . ." He breathed a sigh of impatience, grabbed the rag and hurriedly righted my wrong.

"Alright, Bernie Wernie, that about does it. Ready to roll?"

"Yep," knowing what that eventually implied.

He whisked me off the chair and did that airplane thing. "Vrooooom!" I didn't have sense enough to be scared. It must have been a mile high from the ceiling to the floor, but it didn't bother me one bit because I was in sure hands. I laughed a lot of different laughs, which made him laugh. But this was only the beginning.

"Okay, get your stuff. We gotta lock up."

"M'kay."

I grabbed my empty book bag. Even back then, I championed the idea of coming off scholarly. I went outside and stepped down the two stairs leading away from the door. I heard the familiar snap of the locked door, signifying that another day's work of my father had been done. He said something, but I had already blocked him out because there, in front of me, was my four-wheel passion. The light blue van.

It was terribly cold, so we both jogged to the van. Well, I think I was actually running at full speed. We got to the driver's side. He knew as well as I what the ritual was. He opened the door. During this time, people around there didn't lock their doors, car doors or even doors at home. They just didn't. When he swung the door open, he hoisted me up and let me stand between the driver's seat and the passenger's seat until he sat down and got settled. Once started, the van had to idle for a good five minutes. Soon, he shifted his eyes over to me while his face remained straight ahead, as if he were up to something mischievous.

"You ready?"

"Yep."

"You sure?"

"Uh huh."

"You ready, Freddy?" Whatever that meant.

"Yeah," as I got more impatient.

Soon, it was on. He lifted me from my standing position and placed me in the driver's seat, along with him. He had to scoot back a little so my little booty could fit on the seat. I witnessed the orange indicator go from P to R and felt his right leg rise slightly from the brake. As was customary, his hands fell by his side. I did my best to concentrate with all my might. I started turning the wheel to the right so that we could go left. He hit the brake, and I saw the orange peg go from R to D and felt the foot-and-leg transition again. We were on our way home.

As we maneuvered out of the restaurant parking lot, he hit the gas pedal and told me to concentrate. We were on the actual road. I never really saw that much traffic. On occasion, there were cars in their own lane coming toward us from the other direction. He told me not to look at their lights and to just pay attention to the lane I was in. My hands gripped steady at three and nine o'clock, and my feet swung back and forth together and then separately. Five mph. Ten. Fifteen. No more than twenty. For the entire way home, he controlled the gas and the brake, and I the wheel. Without regard for any police who may have been patrolling the area, he wielded his fatherly authority. Thank God no cops came along because I'm sure he would have gotten the book thrown at him, twice. But I didn't care. To me, this was the freest I had ever felt. There we were, a team, making our way home.

"Be careful," he admonished. "Stay in between the white lines."

"M'kay." I wished he would just let me do this.

"Good job, man. There you go."

"I'm doin' pretty good, ain't I."

"Yeah, you're doing real good."

Left turn on Griffin Road. Street more narrow. Focus. Then a right on McIntosh. The road snaked down the hill then back left. Cars parked in the street, so he slowed down.

"Don't hit the cars. Stay on the road."

*Hell, you only going five miles an hour.* Well, that's what I wanted to say. "Okay." That's what actually came out.

On up the street, up the hill, bear to the right a little. Make the right on South Dakota Way. Right into the driveway. Stop. Finished.

"Good job, jughead."

"That was fun! Can we do it again tomorrow?"

"We'll see, Bernard." That meant yes.

When I walked in the house, I got ready to hit the sack. Mama was finishing up the dishes. Of course, Dwayne, Jr. and Keva were already home and had already gotten ready for bed. They made sure before the night was over that they managed to say whatever was necessary to get on my nerves, but as far as I was concerned, I had a daddy shield around me. He hadn't let *them* take the wheel. I knew they would never understand the bond between the baby boy and his father. After a couple of hits between Dwayne, Jr. and me, we bid adieu to that night.

# one last wave

The kids in the hood always made their own sense of entertainment. We didn't have Wiis and all the other advanced technological gadgets, but it was fine by us. The most we had was Atari. If you were really ahead of the pack, you had Nintendo. But for the most part, we collectively made up our own games. Red light, green light. Mother May I. Two square. Four square. We raced in the middle of the street and learned how to dodge cars when they came. And the most famous of them all, Hide and Go Get, an adaptation of Hide and Go Seek. I especially recall one time we played when I was about seven.

All the boys had to start counting and the girls had to hide. Of course, we all peeked to see where the girl we liked went running to.

". . . seven, eight, nine, ten. Ready or not, here we come."

Then we took off to go see if we could find the girls. Once they spotted us getting closer, they ran for dear life to touch the tree in our yard, which was the base. Touched it? Safe. Caught before you made it to the tree? Tossed on the grass and dry humped by the boy who caught you. I still remember the first time I finally caught Yandi, who was just one year older than I. As I was reveling in the spoils, totally clueless as to what I was supposed to be doing while I had her under me, Dwayne, Jr., Lydell, Mal, and the rest of their cronies came over and started laughing.

Lydell seemed to be the most entertained by my lack of knowledge in this regard. "Look, y'all. He suffocatin' Yandi. He just layin' on top o' her. He'n movin' or nothin'." All the older guys laughed hysterically. Dwayne picked me up by my shirt to give Yandi some breathing room and told me I didn't know what to do with it. Poor Yandi finally got up and started brushing the grass-and-weeds mixture out of her thick hair. Her embarrassment was more for me than for herself. We all finally called it quits and headed inside since the street lights were beginning to flicker on, our cue to wrap up playtime and prepare for dinner.

For the most part, though, the neighborhood was cool, typical, no bells and whistles. Nice, decent neighbors. Average families who went through the predictable maze of life like little rats. All the yards kept up, grass shrubs nice and cut. Everybody speaking to everybody. Asking how school was, how work was. Talking about what they were going to make for dinner that night. Normal stuff.

"Hey, Vicky," blurted Marjorie. I swear, she saw everything from her window. She stayed diagonally from us, right on the corner. She was the neighborhood watch all by herself. She always used to go get her morning newspaper in her robe and slippers. She knew how to take the *house* out of house shoes. And she always managed to catch us on our way out of the door as the day started with Dwayne, Jr. and Keva on their way to catch the bus and with me on my way to Ms. Williamson's, my babysitter. As normal, she had seen my mother and me head for the car.

"Hey, girl. How you doing over there?" My mother spoke back.

"Girl, me and Jefferson doing just fine." I always wondered why wives always called their husbands by their last name. "With him, it's always work, work, work. I tell you, I don't know who he married to more, me or his dern job."

"Well, just be happy he got one, girl. You don't work, you don't eat."

"I know that's right! How y'all doin'?"

"Doin' good, chile, can't complain."

Indeed, she was right. Both my father and mother worked at IBM in Research Triangle Park. At this time, it wasn't a necessity that you had to have some fancy business degree from Duke or Carolina. You just had to be a conscientious and driven employee. Seems like almost everybody in Durham made their way to RTP to make the money and head back into the city to their own communities. My father would later quit this job and work full time at the family restaurant, but at the time, both of them made money hand over fist. They had a joint account that they both put money into and just enjoyed the luxury of living. They had paid their dues, both having some close tie with being from rural and country areas but now were devouring their piece of the American pie. As most older people say, they were living high on the hog. And Marjorie Jefferson loved being neighbors with my mom and dad, for theirs was a story of being upwardly mobile.

"Good morning, Mr. Bernard." Mrs. Jefferson loved including me in the morning conversation.

"Hey."

"You look mighty handsome this morning."

Silence.

She turned to Vicky, "Girl, he gettin' bigger and bigger every time I see him." I wasn't sure why she said that because she made sure she made a way to see me every day as we came out the house. I know I wasn't growing that quickly. Just words to fill time and space, I guess.

"Yeah, girl. My little man smart as a whip. He readin' already and he'n nothin' but three. Ms. Williamson doin' a real good job with him."

"What?! Girl, he readin' already?"

"Mm hmm."

"Bernard, that's very good. I didn't know you could read. Most kids around your age are still learning their ABCs, and here you go readin' already."

Silence as I played with the car door handle.

"Well, girl, we gotta get outa here. I gotta drop off Mr. Bernard and get to work."

"Okay. Well y'all have a good one. See y'all later. Bye, Bernard."

"Bye."

So in a nutshell, that was the neighborhood, at least the part of it where our house was. As the youngest, I got extra special treatment by those in the area. It just so happened that I wasn't just the youngest in my home, but I was one of the youngest kids in the surrounding host of homes. Consequently, I was the recipient of many an outfit outgrown by the veteran teens. It wasn't atypical for me to wind up in the living rooms of many of the households as I tried on skinny polyester pants, wool sweaters that scratched the hell out of my flesh, and penny loafers that still had the penny in them. It took hours to try these clothes on, but you couldn't tell me that I wasn't a special kid. I'm not sure if the neighbors rallied around me and looked out for my well-being because of what they would later find out. Either way, I didn't care. In my mind, I was getting free stuff. Point blank.

"Okay now, Bernie, slip on these pants," said Mrs. Phillips. She had two older boys a couple of houses down and across the street. Her husband was so friendly and smoked a pipe. I didn't know how he could stand that smell. He probably just did it just to occupy time. They always called me Bernie.

"Oh man, these are nice," I marveled.

"Turn around," she inspected the fit.

"What are these? Wranglers? Whoa, they are nice."

"Bo, go get some dress socks so he can try on these shoes," she yelled to one of her sons.

"Alright. Here." Bo returned with a sly smile as if he were giving away some in-the-way trash.

"Man, these fit real good," I grinned.

"Well. They fit well," she corrected me. "Take care of these clothes, and make sure Vicky washes them. We washed them already, but it won't hurt to wash 'em again. You want an apple?"

"Yes, ma'am."

"Here."

"Thank you, Mrs. Phillips."

"Mm hmm. Can you carry these home? It's quite a lot of stuff."

"Yes, ma'am." Where did she think I was going? It was just a house away across the street. "Okay, be careful crossing the street."

"Kay. Thanks again."

Her older boys snickered because of how stupid the clothes looked on me and how happy they were to get rid of them. Besides, I was scary slim, super skinny. Even wife beaters were baggy on me. To me, though, the clothes were high-fashion whether they fit me exactly or not. By the time the fitting was over, I was walking with a huge black hefty bag full of garb that I was proud of. I hugged it and proceeded home, trying not to stumble along the way. And I wolfed down the Granny Smith simultaneously. Mrs. Phillips kept eyeing me all the way home, like I was going to get lost or shot or run over in that little short walk. She leaned on the side of the door and talked to her husband as she eyed me like a hawk.

"I feel sort of bad for that child, honey," she stated to the pipe smoker. They had knowledge of something that was thought to be so secretive. And it was something that I kept smiling through each day and night.

"Yeah, me too a little bit. I think he'll be alright, though. He'll make it. He got a pretty strong mind."

"Well, he needs one livin' in there."

In hindsight, I didn't realize that the village was in the process of raising me. God had his own way of providing for me through others. It wasn't much, but the neighborhood hand-me-downs were, in fact, provision and sustenance, however homely they were. It wasn't just the clothes because some of the same neighbors who gave me clothes and apples scolded and corrected me. They were literally helping to raise me, teaching me some sense of values and responsibility. In spite of what Mrs. Phillips and the other neighbors knew, they cleverly kept me focused and steered me in a direction pointing toward better. Their mission was intentional. Their method, non-intrusive but effective.

I turned around one last time before going inside to see if she was still looking. Yep.

One last wave from both of us.

# two lions

aturdays in the neighborhood were typical. Seems like during the summer, everybody was outside cutting their grass by nine o'clock in the morning. And the smell of the cut grass used to slide into Dwayne's and my room through the window like an angel in the wind. Nothing like the smell of freshly cut grass. My father was already up and at work at the restaurant before I got up. My mother would wake Keva up and try to dress her while Dwayne and I slept. She wanted to sneak Keva out with her on Saturday mornings to go to the mall and McDonald's and Payless and Kroger and wherever else my little mind drummed up. Almost always, as they were sneaking toward the front door, I would come out in my pajama onesie that had the plastic bottoms attached underneath so that my feet couldn't be seen. Mama and Keva would try to be extra quiet as they grabbed their purses and walked closer to the door.

They would prepare for their typical, secret Saturday morning journey. After rubbing a wad of grease in Keva's thick hair and brushing it, my mother quickly put it into three doo-doo ponytails. They were tiptoeing as they glided closer to the door. They thought they were talking low. No such thing with Keva.

"TaKeva, get your jacket," mama whispered.

"Okay. I got it."

"Shhhhhh!"

"So where we goin'?"

"Out."

"Out where?"

"Keva, be quiet. Just come on. You'll see when we get there."

"Ma, do I need my hat?"

"Girl, stop talkin' so loud."

"Do I need my hat?" she still unsuccessfully attempted to whisper.

"Yes, just bring it just in case."

"Ma, I'm hongry."

"We gone stop and pick up something while we out."

"Where, at McDonald's?"

"If you be good and if you stop talkin' so loud now, yeah."

"Ma, where y'all going?" I startled her, as I would make my inquiry right as they made it to the front door.

"Damn!" grunted my mother. "We not going nowhere far. We'll be right back."

"I wanna go!"

"No, Bernard, go back to bed. We'll be right back."

"But I wanna go!" I started a tantrum that was rivaled by few. I couldn't imagine my mother just up and leaving me, even for a few hours. I was her baby boy. And she was taking Keva out for the spoiled treatment. I didn't want to hear anything about any stupid mother and daughter bonding, how mothers loved doing the prissy things with their little girls. To my mother, Keva was a little mother in the making. Yada yada yada. Whatever. I wanted to go too.

"Bernard, no! Keva, get in the car."

"I wanna go!" I looked for some clothes that I could put on in a hurry.

"No, we'll be right back." I heard the door open and then close and then lock.

"NO! I'M GOING TOO!" I didn't have a key to get out. So I climbed on a chair and just banged on the door window and watched them buckle up. I yelled at the top of my lungs that I wanted to go. Screaming. Watery eyes. The grey Chrysler backed up as I watched in horror. How could they leave me? As precious as I was.

I stormed back into the room and lay in the bed, crying and yelling. I still couldn't process why and how they decided to go without me.

"Will you please shut up?!" I had awakened Dwayne, Jr. He understood that he had to babysit until they got back. With him, it just meant he could pester me to no end and control the TV channels.

"You shut up!"

"Just go back to sleep and stop acting like a big baby," he jabbed.

"You shut up and go back to sleep!"

He got up and went to the bathroom. I could hear the steady waterfall. And then a pause. And then more of the waterfall, then tinkles. He was back in the room and back to bed. "You do this every Saturday."

"So what! Shut up!"

Almost instantly, he fell back asleep. I don't know how anybody twelve could go back to sleep so quickly after he had just peed. Or maybe he was just acting like it so I would leave him alone. It worked. Since I couldn't go back to sleep, I went to the living room and turned on the television after I got my Fruit Loops. I needed someone to counsel me until I could get it together because I refused to believe that those other two could go on an excursion without me. And my doctors were just a click away, and I knew which channel. There they were, my Saturday morning counselors. Tom and Jerry.

Cartoons like those were different than the ones today. Neither Tom nor Jerry said a word. You had to observe what they did, piece together the plot, and find the humor in it. Soon, my tears dried up, and I found myself laughing at their stupid antics. It didn't even register to me how Tom could get electrocuted, stabbed, drowned, and the like and still show up for the next scene. All to try to catch some sneaky mouse. Thank goodness for progress, though. I hadn't realized at the time how subliminal some of the messages were in a few of the episodes. Like that faceless, big Aunt Jemima type who appeared on occasion. From what I remember seeing, she is one of the only ones who spoke words in any of the episodes. But when she did, it was horrendous.

She had given Tom the task of keeping it quiet around the house, and Jerry decided he would attempt to make as much noise as possible. Jerry won often, creating painstaking commotion and upsetting Aunt Jemima's rest. Tom would have one more chance to keep things peaceful and noise-free, and this character type would voice in no uncertain terms her intention.

"Tom, let me tell you some'm!" as if the cat really understood. "I work sun up tuh sun down and I ain't got no's time to be in here lis'nin' to all this mess. I tell you, if I gots to come back in here one more times, it's gone be out for you. You heah me, out, O—U—W—T, out."

She had just spelled "out" incorrectly to a huge audience of Saturday morning kids whose parents were either sleep or gone with their daughters out on morning excursions without their son. Thankfully, I knew better.

"It's O—U—T stupo!" I yelled at the tube. "They can't even spell on cartoons." Little did I know that it was probably intentional. All we have to

17

contend with nowadays are cartoons where protagonists simply stab the next guy or gal, decapitate them, or maim their opponent some other way during those coveted Saturday morning slots. Progress. Yay.

Finished the Fruit Loops. Turn up the bowl and drink the dirty milk. After a few more hours of cartoons, I heard the car pulling in the driveway. I started getting mad all over again. Two car doors slammed and Keva came in and took right to it. The goal was to push my buttons and let me know what I missed, and she rarely ever failed.

"We had fun!"

"Where y'all go?"

"We went everywhere."

"Ma, I don't see why I couldn't go." My anger returned. "I wanna go to McDonald's too."

"No, I'm getting ready to cook."

"I don't want none of that stuff. I want McDonald's. You always taking Keva somewhere and leaving us here."

As if Dwayne, Jr. really cared. Better for him to have the house to himself with relative peace and quiet. But with me, it was the principle. Fair was fair. And I was going to speak out about it. Me and my activist self.

Other than that, though, Saturdays were pretty predictable. Wake up. Check. Throw tantrum. Check. Fight siblings. Check. Play outside with kids. Check. Eat, eat, eat. Check, check, check. Watch TV. Check. Endure hellified guitar lessons with John P. Kee's brother, Wayne. Check. Very exciting for a five-year old. Until one Saturday night, things in my world started on a course of change that would eventually impact me significantly.

Saturday nights were not a big deal, per se. We all just wound down from a regular ebb and flow of the day's events. We'd ready for bed and just retire to our rooms and find some way to entertain ourselves, which boiled down to watching TV. On this night, my father had come in from working at the restaurant. He was beat. Nothing, though, was as comforting to hear him come through the door. It brought some sense of finality to my day and offered a feeling of protection.

We kids didn't pay any mind to his arrival for the most part. We just knew things would be okay overall when he got home. Dwayne and I laughed, argued, fought, and made up, all within the course of five minutes. And of course, no night was complete with me unless I barged into Keva's room and tap-danced on her last nerve until she would yell for me to get out.

As long as we heard the settling muffle of a conversation between mom and dad, we paid them no attention. We could hear the monotone banter and tune them out unless they told us to quiet down and go to sleep. One night, the settling muffle became clear. They were talking in their bedroom, right next to Dwayne's and mine.

"That Keva is something else. We went out this morning, and dat girl know she talk a mile a minute. And ain't nobody gone get nothin' pass Mr. Bernard. He sholl know how to argue and get his point across. He must gone be a lawyer. And I don't think Dwayne, Jr. said two words today. He so quiet." My mother was bragging on us while at the same time venting to my father about our personalities.

"Mm hmm. They something else." My father agreed but only tersely. Not really a man of many words at night.

"I tell you the truth. Oh yeah, I went by CCB this morning, and more money was missing than I thought." My mother was asking my father about her trip to the bank when she and Keva went out on their regular Saturday morning excursion.

"Really?"

"Mm hmm. You take any extra money out?"

"I don't know. I can't remember."

"Can't remember?" My mother was playing but my father didn't take it that way.

"Damn, Vicky! Who you? The damn money patrol?" He misinterpreted my mother's joke and was getting aggravated. But my mother was a leo. She was not to be shrugged off, playing or not.

"Hell yeah, I guess I am the damn money patrol. If we gone take extra money out, we just need to let the other one know. I can say damn too, shit!" My father was a leo too. They were born on the same day. Of the same year. They literally had the same birthday. Enough said. Two leos. And in some people's minds, this similarity was all the explanation that was needed. They were, in fact, two lions. They got louder.

"Vicky, whatever. Ain't nobody got time to be talkin' 'bout no damn money tonight. Damn, we ain't broke."

"It don't matter that we ain't broke. That ain't the point. And if to-night ain't the time to talk about it, tell me when is."

What had started out as light and simple banter had escalated to a serious shouting match. I'm sure this wasn't the first time they had a disagreement, but this seemed different. Now was the first time that I heard Charlie Brown's teacher speak distinctly. Maybe I was just overreacting since I was so young. Arguments in our home couldn't get but so heated. We were a regular family in North Carolina. No thrills, no fame, no fortune. Just a regular family. This was surely a joke, I rationalized. They loved each other and us too much. So why was my stomach getting tight all of a sudden? Like a bundle of nervous energy gathering in my tiny stomach. Dwayne, Keva, and I argued, but I thought that was what we were supposed to do. I didn't think mom and dad would follow our lead. I stopped pestering Dwayne, got back in my bed, laid back, and hoped the arguing would soon stop. It didn't.

"You can talk about it tonight all you want to. But you mind as well be talking to that wall 'cause I'm finished talkin' bout it."

"The hell you is! We both putting money in the account, and we both need to be accountable for it."

"Shit, Vicky, you just being difficult." He came out of his room and walked down the hall to the kitchen to get something to drink. She followed right behind him. The conversation became distant but still loud and clear. He slammed the frig door, angering her.

"Difficult? What make you think I'm being difficult just because I'm asking about what I got a right to ask about? Neither one of us just gone spend and not let the other know. And don't be slamming the damn frig door. The children back there trying to sleep."

I don't know how she thought the sound of a slamming refrigerator door could compare to what they were giving off. They both knew how to keep the argument going. Neither deferred to the other to call a truce. It was in their blood to keep it going. They somehow made it back to their bedroom and managed to get to bed. After about an hour and a half, I still lay in bed staring at the dark ceiling, still feeling the tight nervous ball in my stomach. I'm sure Dwayne was asleep. He could sleep through anything. I wonder what Keva was doing. She had a hard shell, so I'm sure it wasn't affecting her like it was affecting me.

Finally, it was all fine. There was silence. I had no inkling, though, that the confrontation they had on tonight would be one of the mildest the two of them would ever have.

I should have been grateful.

---
*five*
---

# mission five

s a child, it was pretty difficult for me to process the heated arguments between my mother and father. It may have been because I was close to both of them and couldn't understand why I couldn't keep peace between them. I think part of my problem was part of most kids' problem. I tended to think that it was my responsibility to keep them together. Or that it was my fault that they weren't getting along. Whatever the reason, I was hoping there would be some change. Much to my disappointment, though, the confrontations became more frequent and more violent. On one occasion, I recall my father coming in from work. The bickering always seemed to occur around this time. I can't remember why they were arguing this time, but I just remember the knots forming in my stomach whenever they started. The arguments seemed to escalate in their intensity.

"I'm tired of this shit," mama said. I didn't know what the *this* was that she was referring to, but obviously it was important enough to her.

Silence.

"Dwayne, you hear me talking? I said I'm tired of this shit."

"Damn, Vicky, how can I *not* hear you?" he retorted.

They kept it going and got louder and louder and louder. I could tell they were in each other's faces like two pit bulls. Nothing on TV mattered to me, and I couldn't distract myself by playing with some dumb toy. I couldn't act like it wasn't happening. I could feel tears welling up but fought them. I heard them walking, stopping, shouting, walking again. If they were in a pot of water, the water would be boiling over because they were indeed hot. I decided it was time that I came to the rescue. And what else does a five-year old do in a situation like this? I would have to save the day, sort of like how they did on cartoons.

21

*Mission One. Get reinforcement.*

"Dwayne, you hear them arguing. Go do something. Make them stop." This was my appeal to my big brother. He seemed like he always had the answer. So surely he could make magic happen here. I didn't realize he was probably just as scared. He was only twelve. But in my mind, he was a giant. He just sat on the bed, looking at the wall. "Dwayne, go make 'em stop!"

Realizing that he had little power to make anything happen, he barked back at me, "Just shut up and go sit down." I couldn't do that, especially now that I was hearing chairs in the kitchen scuff the floors and the dinner table being pushed. "You always trying to change something. Just sit down."

"You shut up!" By this time, I started getting upset and crying. I don't know if it had to do with the fact that I couldn't convince him to join my plan or because I myself felt helpless in the situation. And those knots in the stomach just wouldn't subside. So it was time to move on.

*Mission Two. Seek more backup.*

Keva's door was closed. I knocked. She didn't open it because the shouting was too loud. So I opened the door. "Close my door!" How could she say this? Didn't she hear the commotion? "I said close my door!" So I did so only after letting myself in.

"Keva, go tell them to stop." She ignored me. Looked through me like I was a ghost. She didn't say a word. "Keva, why you just sitting right here? Go make 'em stop." I hadn't really made the connection either that she was only eight. What was she really going to do? For some reason, I guess I never saw age or stature as hindrances to trying to make a change. In her mind, it was just best to stay out of the way and let the disturbance just take its course. But I persisted. "Keva, go do something." She said not one word. So it was all up to me.

*Mission Three. Be a hero and confront the assailants alone.*

I left Keva's room and left the door cracked by mistake. I heard it crash shut right after I left. She was so ruthless and stubborn. So it was just me. I walked slowly in the hallway toward the kitchen. I stuck close by the wall as

I walked, almost like I was using it as a shield. Almost to the kitchen. Pause right by the refrigerator. Move up slowly. Peek around the frig. I could see them, but I hadn't seen them quite like this before. They were different people. It was one thing to hear it in the back room, but it was another thing to be up close. I saw him point in her face. I saw her slam the cabinets. I saw him throw the spoon in the sink. Honestly, I had seen enough. It was time to make a move and make a difference. Fire away!

"Y'all stop!" I shouted to the top of my lungs. "Y'all stop!" The knots got tighter. I cried uncontrollably hoping that my dramatics would hit home. They kept shouting as if I weren't there. "Y-y-y'all stop!" My head was hurting from their yelling and my yelling too. "Y'all stop!" Then to my surprise, my father finally acknowledged my presence.

"Bernard, get on back to the back." He pointed to show me which direction to go, as though I didn't know where the back was. And they started right back going at it. After all of the suspense I had drummed up, I was no more than a gnat.

*Mission Four. Retreat.*

I turned around and left the kitchen with all the raucous behind me. No need to scale the wall. No heroics. Just walk. Pass Keva's room. Door still closed. Keep walking. More doors slamming. Keep walking. Arrive at retreat destination. Turn right. Dwayne, Jr. still sitting on bed. Looks at me like I'm crazy. He can't believe I went in the midst of flying bullets. Walk past his bed. Prepare for last mission.

*Mission Five. Pray.*

Even at a young age, I always prayed. It probably all started around the dinner table when I sang my prayers for the food. But at this point, I didn't care about food, and the dinner table was God knows where after having been pushed during all the fireworks. I figured if God were concerned about what I was eating, He would surely be concerned about what I was going through now. I just knelt by my bed. I'm sure I asked for the obvious. *Lord, make them stop!* A pause to hear if it worked. Still loud shouting. *Lord, make them stop!* More stomping and fussing. Dwayne no doubt thought I was off of my little rocker, but he just let me be me. No telling what he thought I was doing on my little knees. But somehow, I knew that even if this prayer wouldn't make them stop fighting, it would sort of hold my little mind together until they finished. Tears, tears, and more tears wetting up my sheets. I just kept praying. *Lord, make them stop!* Silence. Success.

But then I heard a smack. Someone was on the ground. I was hoping it was my father, but it wasn't.

Dwayne and Keva had managed to keep their spirits up fairly well. I took the arguments a little more personally, probably because I felt close to both parents and was the youngest. I internalized most of the arguments and struggled to make sense of the bitter disputes. I couldn't figure out why the nervousness in my stomach wouldn't go away. Even though living on South Dakota was no picnic, we somehow managed to find some way to smile or laugh through the house drama. In addition to the games we played in the community, we developed games within our own house. The ten-second TV absence rule was chief among them. A game primarily developed by Keva, this was our childish attempt to protect our channel-watching privileges if either of us wanted to watch different shows at the same time.

The rules were simple. If you left the living room for more than ten seconds, irrespective of why, you relinquished your ability to control what was watched. Whoever was in the room when ten seconds were up was now in control of the channels. Mostly, the battle was between Keva and me. Dwayne just thought he could come in and change the channels whenever he wanted. If you had to pee, you had better do it in ten seconds. If you wanted something to drink or eat, you had better get the drink first and then come back in the room and then go get the eats.

"Keva, I'm coming right back. I gotta go get a peanut butter spoon." I announced my intentions and left.

"Bye." She was glad and started counting out loud. This was her so-called way of being fair. "One, two, three, four, five, six, seven, eight, nine." She wasn't fair because her seconds really weren't seconds. By the time she got to nine, only four seconds had really passed. She didn't care. But I succeeded because my foot made it back in the living room at her count of nine. I was still in control of the channels. Soon, I had to use the bathroom.

"Keva, I gotta go to the bathroom."

"What you telling me for?"

"Keva, don't change the channel. I gotta go to the bathroom." I ran out.

"One, two, three, four, five, six, seven, eight, nine, ten."

There was no way I was going to get back into the living room before her version of ten seconds. I had barely pulled out my little wee-wee to let the fountain flow. She made me sick with the games she developed to benefit her. For some reason, the only time she seemed like she had to use the bathroom was when she was leaving the living room for good anyway and going to her room. Triflin'.

But nobody, including Dwayne, Jr., worried about any ten-second rule when our all-time favorite show came on. This was probably the only thirty-minute span when all of us managed to get along and keep the station on the same channel. We stayed glued to the set even during the commercials because there was no way on God's green earth that we were going to miss a moment of *Good Times*.

Somehow, I would always be in the living room right before it came on. "Y'all, *Good Times* comin' on." You could hear Keva and Dwayne rustling and making their way to the front. I had already gotten my good spot on the sofa. We all would try to catch the first note when it came on. There was no warning. Just the white words that popped up on the screen. We started singing and semi-dancing, even Dimpo himself. We couldn't wait to sing our version of what we thought were the lyrics.

| Our Version | Actual Lyrics |
|---|---|
| *Good Times.* | *Good Times.* |
| *Anytime you need a playmate.* | *Any time you meet a payment.* |
| *Good Times.* | *Good Times.* |
| *Anytime you need a friend.* | *Any time you meet a friend.* |
| *Good Times.* | *Good Times.* |
| *Anytime you need a wonder.* | *Any time you're out from under. Not gettin' hassled, not gettin' hustled.Not gettin' hassled, not gettin' hustled.* |
| *Keeping your hair above water.* | *Keepin' your head above water.* |
| *Making wuh-waves when you can.* | *Makin' a wave when you can.* |
| *Temporarily lay offs.* | *Temporary lay-offs.* |
| *Good Times.* | *Good Times.* |

| | |
|---|---|
| *Easy credit rip offs.* | *Easy credit rip-offs.* |
| *Good Times.* | *Good Times.* |
| *Shuckin' and survivin'.* | *Scratchin' and survivin'.* |
| *Good Times.* | *Good Times.* |
| *Hangin' in a crowd lie.* | *Hangin' in and jivin'.* |
| *Good Times.* | *Good Times.* |
| *Please be lucky we got 'em.* | *Ain't we lucky we got 'em?* |
| *Good Times.* | *Good Times.* |

At least our take was more creative.

Of course, we'd discover that some of our lyrics were utterly laughable. Why would anybody other than us put premium on appreciating the need for a playmate? Hangin' in a crowd lie? What on earth was that? Some people thought that this line was *Hangin' in a chow line*, but the creators of the song lyrics confirmed that the line was *Hangin' in and jivin'*. To us, though, our lyrics worked just fine. I think the African-American ladies would appreciate the line about keeping the hair from getting wet. We couldn't Google the lyrics like we do nowadays to find out if we were right. We just let our imaginations soar. These were our lyrics, and to us they were right.

We weren't art aficionados either, but we loved those paintings of the lanky people displayed when the show was coming on and going off. They were also the paintings that J.J. "painted" to show his artistic prowess. They had a cool, soulful, and mellow feel that oozed from the easel. I couldn't believe it when I discovered that the real-life painter of these images was Ernie Barnes, a gifted artist from where else? Durham, North Carolina. A homeboy. I even found out that we both graduated from Hillside High School, he much earlier than I, of course.

The most striking connection that existed with the show, though, was an eerie similarity to the cast of that show and my own family. Maybe this is why we identified with it so well.

J.J. was dark-skinned, tall and lanky, and so was Dwayne, Jr. Of course, both were named after their fathers. I often wondered how he got to be so dark when both of my parents were light brown. J.J. always tried to dominate his siblings through wit and his defense that he was older, thus allegedly making him wiser. This was often done to no avail. Dwayne, Jr. was just as obnoxious when it came to trying to wield his so-called authority. And I really couldn't get over how much he and J.J. looked alike.

Then there was spicy Thelma, a one-woman army who took down to no one. Just get her started and soon the sparks were flying. Her beauty was undeniable, and her tongue was sharp as a sword. She was a quick thinker who often stumped J.J. in his mental tracks. To this day, I am convinced that no one embodied the essence of Thelma more than Keva. Quick-witted, stubborn, set in her ways, grumpy, and beautiful. Keva would indeed grow up to be a pretty girl. She and Thelma had some of the same features. Light caramel skin, shorter hair, and that oval face. They looked very similar. Although Keva was not a dancer, she was athletic. She ran track and played basketball. Still, when I saw both, there were more similarities than differences.

Last but not least was the "militant midget" or so his father called him. Being the youngest, Michael always felt like he had something to prove. He was always voicing his opinion, whether it was asked for or not. Especially when it came to civil rights and justice, that black power, Black Panther type of stuff. He would often challenge his father through his intellect and try to get others to see from the right point of view. His. In addition to being as vocal as Michael was, I developed an appreciation for all things scholarly. Somehow, I devoured books and developed a strange knack for math. In my early photos, I even bore resemblance to him: the smaller, slanted eyes, the skin tone (I was much lighter as a child), the kinky, fro-like hair, small frame for my age. It was too weird.

Even my mother and father fit James, Sr. and Florida almost to a T. James was the loud father with the receding hairline at an early age. So was my father. He could definitely get loud, and he was balding early. I was sure this trait would skip me since it was reputedly reported to come from the mother's side of the family. Or so went the story. His mother's brothers had become bald early but my mother's brothers had full heads of hair. Both James and my father always seemed to work from sun up to sun down. Florida was nice, but you had better think twice if you thought her niceness was weakness. She was a woman who tried to instill in her children a moral code so that they could survive in a harsh world, a world that would not always look beyond their skin color to appreciate who they were. And Vicky was the same. Although she never tried to change our personalities, she tried her best to equip us with what we needed to make it, especially common sense. Pretty reserved, she made no waves. Cross her, however, and one would witness a formidable mean streak.

The unique oneness with the characters of the show made it overwhelmingly intriguing to us siblings, who watched faithfully each week. Theirs was a family struggle to survive in the tenements of Chicago. But through the screen, we saw us. It was like Chicago, North Carolina. For thirty minutes, the TV had become a mirror, and we stared in it like it was no tomorrow.

The episodes were quite memorable. Who could forget Janet Jackson's portrayal of an abused Penny? Chip Fields managed to enrage an entire African-American community as she channeled an explosive mother, who dealt with life by physically and emotionally mishandling her daughter. Then there was Florida's relentless determination to rescue Michael from the grips of a Chicago gang that he was forced to join. In an effort to get her son back, she actually took a solo journey into Warlord territory and wielded a bat on a few of the members. We all saw that there's no love like a mother's love when both mother and son were able to escape what so many youth fall prey to. Of course, this ending was somewhat farfetched, that a mother and son would come out of a situation like that unscathed. Nowadays, given the same circumstances, both Florida and Michael would have more than likely been carried away in body bags. That is, if the bodies would have ever been found.

Then there was that one episode that made our world stop. Dwayne, Keva, and I were up dancing with the Evans family and friends. They were about to move to Mississippi, where James, Sr. had gone to look for work so that he could move his family out of the ghetto. Everybody was reading telegrams that people had sent concerning their move to bigger and better. As Florida read hers, we were dumbfounded. "We regret to inform you that your husband, James Evans, was killed in an auto–mo– . . ." And in the midst of the silence, all we could hear was *Movin'* by Brass Construction playing in the background. The reality, though, was that the Evans family wasn't movin' anywhere. Like most families, they would have to pick up the pieces and try to find the silver lining in those clouds. Words couldn't describe how paralyzed we felt as we just stood and stared at the TV. Their world was crumbling right before our eyes. And since the TV screen was our mirror, what did that mean about ours? It almost felt as if someone had punched me right in the gut. Here was a family struggling to move forward and always seemed to have the rug snatched from under them just as they got some sense of sure footing.

As I got older, I would come to learn that there were standing rumors about John Amos' dissatisfaction with how J.J. was being portrayed as an illiterate buffoon, who worked at the local chicken shack and had no real substance. Although Esther Rolle had been a bit more verbal about her disenchantment with J.J.'s depiction, the ax had fallen on Amos. Consequently, CBS failed to renew his contract, or at least this was the rumor. Much to the chagrin of fans, writers eventually wrote Rolle out but invited her back. The absence of the father, however, hit home for a lot of children viewers since many were struggling themselves to survive without their own fathers in the home. Or the father was physically present but emotionally absent, giving undue amounts of attention to the workplace or other side flings.

But *Good Times*, which probably should have been called *Bad Times,* given what it seems like the family kept experiencing, helped my siblings and me get a feel for viewing life through the eyes of children who were fighting to make it. Maybe this was to us what *The Brady Bunch* was to our white counterparts. Even though we didn't live in a ghetto, we still had to deal with much of the peer pressure that played out on the show. At the time, though, we took it for what it was, just a show that allowed us to get along in a civilized manner for a good thirty minutes. After that, it was back to normal, back to the same in-house bickering between three headstrong kids.

# turn off the beans!

The night after the physical altercation in the kitchen, a new world opened up to me as a child. My make-believe world of cartoons and everything nice gave way to a more sobering sense of reality. Things wouldn't quite be the same, and I had better get used to it if I were to survive. Apparently, the next day, my mother had decided to stay at her brother Quincy's to get herself together from the night before. Maybe she had a bruise she didn't want us to see. That night, my father had made dinner and all the children sat around the table quietly eating. My father decided to eat in his room but visited the kitchen to get something he was missing, like hot sauce or his beer. When he walked in, I couldn't help but notice a changed man. This wasn't the man whom I initially knew. The caring, doting father. This wasn't the man who sat me on his lap and let me drive the big blue machine home after work hours. He was indeed different. So I could do nothing when he walked into the kitchen but stare at him. Everywhere he moved, my eyes followed him. I didn't even realize how obvious it was that I had stopped eating and sized him up.

"Bernard, why you staring at me like that? You got a problem?" he grumbled. Silence. I told myself just to look down and start back eating my corn and string beans. I ate some bread but didn't really taste it. The knots in my stomach were coming back and seemed to tighten up whenever he got around me. I didn't realize it, but I started staring at him again. "I said why you staring at me like that?" Silence. Then he walked back to his room. If I had a gun, I would have shot him. More than anything, I guess I was trying to process this shift, this new dad, and how to make it in this new world. All I knew was that whereas most children were excited when their father came home from work, I was anxious, nervous, and angry whenever his car arrived home now. The clinched fist in my stomach always informed me that the bond my father and I had would probably never be the same again.

Sadly, many of the nights of arguing and fighting in our home became more of the norm rather than the exception. Peace in the home was more of a farfetched wish instead of a reality. On average, every other night gave way to more and more drama. Somehow, the nice, quiet house in Ocean Heights had become a scene for World War III. Nowadays, I try to convince myself that it couldn't have been that bad. After all, I wasn't homeless. I didn't live in the impoverished communities of South African Soweto townships. There weren't any flies buzzing around my mouth from the lack of food. Even still, all I knew as a kid was that this constant lack of peace and incessant fighting hurt me and was tearing me down, which is often the struggle for children growing up in these types of households in America. Since there may not be obvious outward indications that something in the home has gone awry, other family members may not realize the deleterious effect it has on children and their ability to cope. At six, it's hard to process such situations without counseling and tell yourself that in the grand scheme of things, what you are going through is probably minor. The knots in my stomach said differently. Children process violence in the home in their own way. They carry stress in ways that adults do not seem to understand. I had stopped eliciting the help of Dwayne, Jr. and Keva. I always found myself on my knees against my bed, believing that God would create peace out of this chaos.

Who cares what they were arguing over, really? It didn't seem to matter. It always seemed to get to a point beyond human reason. Both were feisty, and neither would take down. They had started up again, and the next thing I knew, mama had gotten hit in the eye. I'm sure she got some blows in but managed to make her way across the street to Marjorie's house. Apparently, she'd had enough for the night and decided to get while the getting was good. He didn't worry about chasing her.

She ran to Marjorie's door. "Marjorie, open up! It's me, Vicky. Dat crazy ass fool done hit me in my eye." She held her eye as Marjorie let her in with understandable concern.

"Lord, have mercy, girl. Get in here. What in the world?" She opened the freezer and grabbed some frozen peas. "Put this on it." Her husband was in the back sleep. "Just sit here, and relax."

"Girl, lemme see me the phone. I'm calling the damn cops." This was it for mama. She was now taking action. She dialed 911 and explained that an officer needed to be sent to our residence. "Yeah, my damn husband just hit me. I'm at a neighbor's house now. I'll go back across the street when y'all get here." She gave the address and waited.

The operator was on top of it. "Okay, ma'am. We're sending a unit out now. Just hold tight."

The blue and red lights spiraled as they pulled up into our driveway. I didn't know exactly how to react or what was about to happen. I know I had heard my father leave about ten minutes earlier. He sped off and left us there, assuming that my mother would return eventually. Maybe he knew her well. She had to be up to something because this was the first time she'd gone to seek help at a neighbor's house. And something was definitely the thing she was up to.

"Officer, he's in here somewhere. I need to press charges and get a restraining order on his ass. Dwayne, where you at?" She was back from across the street and was livid. We kids were somewhat dazed. All we wanted was sleep, but terror was thick in the air. Why were the cops here? Were they going to split up our family? This was one of my greatest fears, that we'd be split up and made to fend for ourselves, a group home or something.

"D-Daddy g-gone." I'd throw my two cents in.

"Well ma'am, we can't press any charges without him being here." The officer did his best to explain police protocol. But my mother wasn't hearing it.

"He somewhere out here. Now, I know y'all can find him if y'all want to." She was accepting no lame excuse from some doughnut-eating, coffee-sipping fat man in a uniform.

"Ma'am, why don't you get your children, and I'll take y'all to a nearby hotel so y'all can be safe." My mother didn't have a car yet and decided that she wasn't staying in that house that night. Anything could have gone down.

She went back over to Marjorie's to let her know where we were going. "They gone take me and the kids to the hotel downtown so we can stay there. We'll be alright."

"Here, Vicky, take this." Marjorie handed her $17 so we could have something to eat for the night. My mother didn't have any cash on her. "Y'all be safe."

"Thank you, girl." My mother ran back to the house and asked the cop to help her with getting us in the squad car. She locked the door of the home and hopped into the passenger's side. This was beyond new for us. Who was this stranger driving us to God knows where? I resorted to what I knew. I tried to pray to God the best way I knew how. *Lord, please help us.*

We arrived at the hotel and grabbed our stuff. "Dwayne, y'all come on." She barked out orders, and we knew better than to complain about anything. We entered and waited for further instructions.

"Hello, ma'am. These people need a little help." The officer was speaking to the lady at the front desk. "They're having a tough situation and will need to stay here for a while 'til they can get on their feet again." That was nice. The doughnut-eater had a heart.

The lady got my mom's information and gave us the key to the room. She let us stay as long as we wanted without charging us. Maybe it was my puppy-dog eyes that convinced her to do so. Maybe it was the prayer. At this point, I didn't care what the reason was. We'd have a week of peace, real peace. We could be kids again. We ran all over that hotel, swam in the pool, and didn't have to worry about cleaning up our room. My mom seemed peaceful too. The happiest I'd seen her in a while. We kids hadn't thought of where my father had gone and didn't care. He was better out of the picture. We had disappeared, and so had he. We found safety in the kindness of a policeman and a no-named hotel clerk. He had avoided the cops by finding safety where most men tend to retreat in times of uncertainty, fear, and, anger: his mother's house.

That was probably one of the final times my mother put up with my father and all of the bickering and physical violence that came along with him. She decided she would take Dwayne, Keva, and me and move in with Uncle Quincy. Uncle Q was cool. A Vietnam Vet, he always managed to say something that kept us laughing. Well, at least Dwayne, Jr. and me. Nothing was cracking Keva's shell. In hindsight, I am rather surprised at how functional he remained in society. The stories I've heard concerning how some Vets cope post-war make me have great respect for Uncle Q and his ability to get back into the normal flow of life. In many ways, he was sort of like the first version of my father, always joking, helping us not to think about life too seriously. In his own uncanny way, he always kept me grounded by never letting me forget the time once when my mother had to change my diaper. As the diaper came off and the aroma filled the room, Uncle Q took notice and realized that "dat baby's doo-doo flat as a damn pancake, Vicky." Leave it to Uncle Q to say it how he wanted to say it, often to make the hearers erupt in a good laugh.

So on our way over to his apartment, we just sat quietly while listening to my mother and her tirade. "Shit! Dwayne must think I'm damn crazy! Acting like he done lost his damn mind! I'm getting away from his crazy ass!" We children were glad we were going over Uncle Q's, and Keva and I tried to strike up some semblance of a conversation.

"Bernard, move over!" she barked.

"W-W-Whut you mean, m-m-move over? I c-c-can't," I responded.

She tried to process what I said and why I said it the way that I did.

"Why you talkin' like dat?" she coldly inquired.

"T-talkin' l-like w-whut?" I tried to figure out what she meant.

"Why you saying your words like that?"

"I-I-I 'on't n-n-know."

"Well slide over. You crushin' me."

I hadn't the slightest inkling what she was referring to. What did she mean, *Why was I talking like that?* Talking like what? Granted, I never really paused when I spoke. But it was no big deal. Or that's what I thought. In actuality, the knot in my stomach was taking its toll. It was revealing itself as a stuttering problem. I hadn't even noticed a change in my speech. Even after Keva brought it to my attention, I didn't see what the big deal was. I discovered that whatever this animal was, it seemed to have a mind of its own. Sometimes, it would affect me. Other times, it wouldn't. It was totally unpredictable. It seemed to affect me more when my stress level was high. Funny. Talking about stress at such a young age.

"Ma, why Bernard talkin' like dat?" Keva was quick to ask.

"Girl, talkin' like what?" My mother was still having a conversation with herself and was not interested in any distractions as she processed her next move.

"He startin' and stoppin'."

"'Cause he crazy." Dwayne thought he'd chime in. He and Keva started laughing.

"He alright. He just need to take his time and talk. Bernard, just take your time and talk." Mama looked at me through the rear view mirror while setting her Newport ablaze with the car lighter. "Just take your time and talk when you speak." She continued smoking, cracked the window, and went back to engaging in her self-dialogue. I took note of how the smoke snaked out the window.

Maybe nobody at the time, not even me, realized how the instability was beginning to affect me. More and more, I fought this animal, struggling to convey whatever it was that I was trying to say. But for now, I didn't care. I just wanted to see what Uncle Q was up to.

As we pulled into Colony Manor, my mother swerved through the apartment roads like she was in NASCAR. The force of the movement caused my weight to shift onto Keva. She helped me gain my balance by angrily shoving me back off of her. Then, my weight shifted to Dwayne, who responded as Keva did. We snaked through the winding roads and got to Uncle Q's apartment building. We finally leaped out and walked upstairs. I was squashed in the middle in the back, so I was the last one out on the driver's side in the back. "Bernard, close the door." My mother reminded me after I forgot to shut it. We climbed the three flights of outside stairs and walked to Uncle Q's door. I also held on to the top of the railing when I walked. Looking down, I was always scared that the walkway would collapse. Before we knew it, Uncle Q was opening the door, thanks to mama's banging. You would have thought it would have fallen as hard as she knocked.

"Hey, what's up? What y'all doing here?" Uncle Q was excited but a little shocked. If there were cell phones back then, I'm sure my mother would have called. It was good that he didn't have company because that would have been too weird, with us just showing up out of nowhere. The only time he saw all of us together was at some family function, like a Thanksgiving or Christmas dinner or some slow-paced, gut-wrenching family reunion, where everybody was trying to act brand new. This day, though, was a regular day. No holiday, no gifts, no sweet potato pie. Just a regular day.

"Quincy, that damn Dwayne, Sr. done lost his damn mind!" She didn't feel the need to go into specifics. "He just ain't the same person. He just triflin'. We need to stay over here for a little while." Uncle Q knew she wouldn't make up such drama. As far back as I could remember, he never spoke evil of my father. He just gave support to his older sister and her children. That was interesting. His door was always open to us. They kept talking while we kids just settled in, adapted, and tried to make the best of it. Our comfort zone was just finding the nearest working TV and watching show after show until Uncle Q would make his way over to us and start joking.

"Well if it ain't the three stooges," Uncle Q started in. It didn't take me long to laugh. I was waiting for his avalanche of jokes.

"S-stooges? W-what's s-stooges?" I wanted to know.

"Boy, you ain't heard of those funny silly white people on TV called the three stooges? One of 'em be hittin' the other two upside their noggins. One of 'em fat and be running all around the place. You ain't never heard of them?"

"Naw," and I fell out laughing. It was the way he said it and imitated how the three stooges apparently acted. "Uncle Q-Q, you c-crazy!"

"And what you over here doing, Ms. Meany?" He looked over at Keva, who had that permanent frown on her face and uttered not a word. Of course, she stared at the TV, acting like Uncle Q didn't exist. That was a shame. Looking at Uncle Q's TV and ignoring Uncle Q. If I were him, I would have turned it off and saw how she liked those apples. But again, that was just Keva's personality. She had a mind that was all her own, and he let her be her. "Well I'm just gon' leave you alone so you can watch your little TV show, Ms. Meany."

"And look at you, D.J., you messin' around and gettin' all tall on me. You just gettin' lanky." He was one of the few who called Dwayne, Jr. by that name. "You still trying to play tennis?" He didn't wait for an answer. "I'm gone have to take you out on that court and show you a thing or too. I bet I can hit that ball wherever I want and have you runnin' all over the place. You think you can beat me? And how is school? You doin' good in school? How old you now, 'bout twelve? It's 'bout time for you to get ready for high school soon, ain't it? And you better be keepin' your grades up. You got a girlfriend yet?"

Confused and not knowing which question he should answer, Dwayne just said, "Yeah." At present, he was just thirsty and wanted something to drink and to rest. After navigating the kitchen and avoiding the roach that was here or there, he quenched his thirst with whatever was in the frig and got comfortable.

But that was just Uncle Q. He had personality for days. Always trying to find a way to keep us children happy and help us not really think about what was really going on. We stayed over a few days and just made due. We hung out with a lot of the children in the neighborhood. It wasn't too hard to make new friends. Dwayne met a lot of friends, and I shadowed him, much to his disapproval, but things worked out. It helped that it was summertime too, so there was no worry about going to school and the like. But realistically, my mother knew we couldn't just move in with her brother. He was good to let us stay for a few days, but ultimately we weren't his responsibility. At long last, the inevitable was obvious. We'd have to leave Uncle Q's and head back home to God knows what.

After we moved back, we kids just braced ourselves for the unknown element in the Dillard household. Our name was respected in the community because of our restaurant business, but here we were, going through hell while everybody thought we were the Cosbys. The arguing and fighting between the two adults in the home were becoming the standard rule. And it took the most insignificant act to trigger a melee. Neither of them was known to defer to the other. To them, it didn't seem like it was about peace. It was about ego, and in their mind, they weren't about to be weak and let the other one win. So the yelling continued as did the violence. The hitting too. No signs of peace seemed to exist. I tried hard to understand how an otherwise gentle man could put his hands on a woman. Maybe we kids were the reason they were having problems. I did keep leaving my toys in the wrong place, and Dwayne always had his shoes in the living room. Or maybe it was the way we were always at each other's throats. In fact, we *were* always arguing with each other. Keva and I were forever at odds and were perhaps causing much of the tension between mama and daddy. Or maybe it was Dwayne's and Keva's grades in school so far. They weren't the worst but they weren't the best. I would make sure I'd always get good grades to help ease the tension so they wouldn't fight. I had tried to rationalize the bitter situation that was before me through my simple mind. And to me, it was cut and dry. Be and do good. That way, they would be proud of the kids and not fight. Simple.

On top of what we kids were doing to cause the problem, maybe mama should have stopped nagging him? That was it. Didn't she know he worked long hours? She was known to take an argument to the $n$th degree and not let it rest. Or maybe he was just unhappy with the relationship and was too old-fashioned to seek help and go to marriage counseling. After all, admitting to needing counseling was a sign of weakness. Just go ahead and choose the civil option by duking it out. Or maybe it was his penned-up anger toward his own father, who allegedly said he'd send him away to Lincoln University in Pennsylvania after high school graduation, only to renege on the promise and keep him close by to work at the family business. Whatever the reason, it couldn't have just been the fact that he himself was unhappy and not being responsible for his own actions.

The communication between them seemed to dissipate. The only communication that existed was in the form of tirades. My mother would wait in the living room to discuss things sensibly with him when he got in from work, and he'd walk right past her and head for the bedroom. By the time night came, more tensions grew and arguments continued to ensue. And me, in all of my confusion, continued to think I'd make a difference by trying to play mediator and yell at both of them until my head pounded in anguish. Of course, the refrain was for me to "get my ass back to the back" and to stay out of grown folks' business. And off I went, to my room, falling to my knees and asking God to help them stop. A predictable sequence of events.

One incident seemed to be the straw that broke the camel's back when it came to her willingness to endure the stress of the marriage. She was never afraid to challenge or confront him concerning being a man and doing what was right. Whenever the opportunity presented itself, she was right on it, especially now. We had just come through the drive-thru at Hardee's. We were starving and eating our hearts out. Soon, we kids in the back were stunned at what we saw and heard.

"I know I ain't seein' what the hell I think I'm seein'." Somehow, she had spotted a van that was just like my father's blue van, the van that I had driven while sitting in my father's lap. It was the van that symbolized for me a sense of family, protection, and love. There it was parked at some apartment building. "That's Dwayne, Sr.'s van." She was sure. I wasn't hungry anymore. That menacing fist was forming again in my stomach, and it felt like I had to throw up.

"N-nuh uh m-mama. That ain't d-daddy v-van." I was hoping that it wasn't. I just wanted to go home and avoid all conflict, but avoidance was not my mother's nature. She drove into the parking lot and parked right beside the van. She got out of the car and went straight to the door in front of where the van was parked. It was a tough neighborhood, and I was so scared that I was shaking. Keva and Dwayne, Jr. were silent, too. None of us were eating anymore. My mother was a bull, and she had started charging. To this day, I have no idea about how she knew which apartment to go to. She started banging on the door with her fist. The door opened slightly and I caught a glimpse of Denise's face. I was relieved because the face was familiar. She was one of the workers at the family restaurant. I almost rolled down the window and shouted, "Hey Denise." But I didn't, and I'm glad I made that decision. I know my mother would have beaten me down.

"Denise, open this damn doe, girl. I know Dwayne in here. You better open this damn doe." My mother was ruthless. She was loud. She was a country girl who was not afraid to fight. Surely, if she had gone toe to toe with my father, she was not afraid to whip up on Denise. And I was watching all of it like it was an HBO special.

"Hey, Vicky, naw he ain't in here. How's it going?" She was acting so pleasantly. She always gave me quarters when I was at the restaurant so I could play back-to-back games of Ms. Pacman. I had gotten so good that I could get to the levels where the ghosts didn't change colors anymore after the power-pellet was eaten.

"Denise don't play with me, bitch! This is Dwayne's van. Tell him to bring his sorry ass out here right now!" About this time, my five-year old eyes witnessed something that was a little confusing. The door had opened a bit more in the verbal exchange, and I saw my father dart across the hall. I was hoping my mother didn't. Unfortunately, she did. Before I knew it, my mother had punched Denise so hard in the face that I myself became stunned. She tried to fight back, but this was my mother. Once she got in that zone, that was all she wrote. She had tunnel vision. Even if you got some licks in, you had better cripple or maim her because she was always coming back to let you know that she was not the one to be walked over. Poor Denise!

I often wondered what made my father shoot across the hall that night. Couldn't he hear the argument between Denise and my mother? Did he think it was a night visit by a Jehovah's Witness? Did he just want to go ahead and terminate the marriage by confirming my mother's intuition? Was he himself tired of trying to keep peace within the home? In all the commotion, did he think someone was trying to break in? I'm sure in his mind, he had a good reason. I just wish I knew what it was because to everyone else, that was a calculating move, which spoke volumes about what he wanted. Back in the car, we didn't say a word, just observed. We didn't know what was going on really. Maybe Dwayne, Jr. understood it since he was almost a teen-ager. All Keva and I knew was that we had just seen several spectacles: an injured Denise, our belligerent mother, and one or two concerned neighbors.

As one might guess, he didn't come home that night. Apparently, he had gone straight to work the next morning. This was what had prompted my mother to call to try to iron things out. If he were there physically, she may have tried to iron things out literally. Iron straight to the face.

"Let me speak to Dwayne, Sr.!" Mama didn't care who it was who answered the phone at the restaurant.

"May I ask who's speaking?"

"Dis his damn wife, das who!"

I could tell the person on the other line said something like, "Okay, one second. He's dropping hush puppies," because my mother responded, "I don't give a damn what he droppin'." He took pride in the fact that he was a great cook and wasn't about to stop doing anything related to that, even if it were to answer a call from his wife.

During the time it took for him to reach the phone, the cacophony in the air had elevated to pans slinging, water running, cabinet doors crashing, more damns and shits. I realized early on that my mother was somewhat different than the average Jane. A fireball she was. With her, whatever came up really did come out. No filter. She had to talk more with him about last night.

I had finally emerged from the back room, and I just wanted to sit at the kitchen table and finish doing a math puzzle that mama gave me. A nice outlet for a five-year old. I sat at the table and counted on my fingers. There was an occasional look up at her to see what she was going to find in the refrigerator to whip up. I was hangry, angry because of intense hunger.

She decided she would warm up the pinto beans since she remembered in all the drama that we hadn't eaten yet. Maybe she would heat up the collards too. And the cornbread. And the pork chops. Well at least the pintos made it to the stove because he finally reached the phone.

"Hello."

"What you damn mean, 'Hello'?"

"Vicky, I ain't got time to deal wit nunna this right now!"

"Yeah, but you had time to act a damn fool while you was walking around showin' yo' natural ass last night!"

"Yeah, well."

"Yeah, well hell."

"You know what. Just wait right there. This don't make no damn sense. We can finish this right now."

"Well bring yo' ass on then."

She slammed the phone down and started gathering her purse and jacket. I couldn't tell if she was leaving to avoid him or if she was going to meet him halfway. Probably the latter. After she threw the purse over her shoulder, she threw the door open, ran out, and almost carried the door with her. When the door boomeranged back opened, she remembered dinner and called out to my sister, "TaKeva, turn off the beans!"

I glanced over and saw the smoke coming from the pot, but it was nothing compared to the smoke coming from my mother's pot. Hot. Steamy. Pissed. She slammed the door again and locked it. Just like that. She was. Gone.

# my father's construction

djusting to this new living situation was weird. I prayed for peace but didn't want it this way. How would we survive without my mother in the home? So many times in cases of domestic conflict, the father would be the one who would vacate and leave the raising of the children to the mother. After he left, maybe he would pay child support. Maybe he wouldn't. But in this case, we had to learn how to make it day by day with someone we perceived didn't particularly care for family. Mama had gone to try to rebuild her life on broken pieces and would come back to get us. This was what I hoped. And I hoped this was what she hoped. We'd have to wait and see if this is what would transpire. In the meantime, we would have to make the best of the situation.

My father seemed calmer, at least at first. I started to see the old him again. He'd start to joke again sometimes. Deep down, though, I hated him with a passion. It was never really the same. How does one live in the same house with someone whose guts are hated? He was the reason my perfect world had crumbled. Over the next few years, my mother lived with Uncle Q then moved in with her younger sister, Freda. She seemed to be having the hardest time getting back on her own feet. I guess now, I realize that she represented the many women who had placed all of their eggs in one basket. These women hadn't lived on their own before. Right after high school or college, many of them dove head first into marriage and trusted that the relationship would work out. There was no real Plan B because they had been conditioned to stick in there to make the marriage work. Surely, they weren't ones to leave the home, especially with children present. And if things didn't work out, many times, the man would take the high road, find other living quarters, and make sure that she and his seed were provided for. Not in this case, though.

She dropped by the home periodically to make sure we were doing well, but she never moved back in. She started going back to school to get a certificate in technology so that she could find another job. I was crushed at how things had turned. My stuttering problem increased, and it took me some time to wrap my mind around this new normal. Thankfully, many of my friends in the neighborhood provided some sense of relief. Since many were my age and a bit older, I found solace in just hanging with them and being a kid.

I was somewhat stubborn, in that I was determined to have as regular a childhood as everyone else. I wanted to do things like ride a bike like all the other kids. Unfortunately, I couldn't wait to learn this skill from my father like I had imagined and dreamed. The older kids across the street looked out for me. We always raced in the street and learned stuff from each other. This would be the last day that I would not be the only kid who couldn't ride a bike. I had a certain fight in me that said I would not be left behind when it came to things I was supposed to know how to do.

"Erica, I w-wanna l-learn how to r-ride a b-bike." She was like a big sister to me. She was so nice. She was probably seven years older than I, about Dwayne's age. I hung out over there all the time and enjoyed her company as well as her siblings'.

"Okay, you know what. You gone learn today." I can't even remember if the bike was mine or was hers. It was probably hers because I think it dipped in the middle. I can't remember the bar going across. We moved to the edge of the street and stayed out of the major flow of traffic. "Get on the bike, Bernard and don't pedal yet. Just look straight ahead. When I say go, start pedaling. Don't turn around to see where you are, and don't look at me."

"Kay." I sat on the bike, suspended with hands on the bar and feet on both pedals. She held me up with one of her hands on the seat.

"Now start pedaling. I'm right here. Just listen to me and don't turn around." She was behind me holding me up, walking with me, and talking at the same time. "There you go. Just keep going. Just listen to my voice and keep going." We picked up speed. I held on tight and kept my feet moving in their own separate circles. We picked up speed a little, and I noticed she was jogging behind me because I heard her breathing heavier. "Okay. Just keep going in a straight line. Don't turn the handles." We had sped up some more, but I kept up the rhythm and kept the handlebars straight.

"L-Like this?" I thought I was doing fairly well but just needed some more reassurance. I guess she was trying to concentrate too and to make sure I didn't fall because she didn't say anything. "Erica, is th-this how I d-do it?"

"You doin' good, Bernard. Keep going." She was yelling from a distance. I didn't even realize that she had let go. I got nervous and got closer to the grass. I put down one foot and just let the bike fall onto the lawn. She taught me how to ride but didn't mention anything about how to stop. I couldn't believe I had been actually riding by myself. She came running to where I was and congratulated me. "You did good, boy. I told you that you could do it. Next time, just press backward to make the bike stop and then put one foot down on the ground when you almost stop. You won't fall if you do it that way." She picked up the bike and grabbed one of my arms to help me up.

"Th-that was n-nice. I g-gotta do that ag-gain." I would still have to practice to get better, but at least I did it. If I did it once, I would do it twice and then again. That was just my attitude.

Despite this new living arrangement, time kept moving. I guess one could say that was the good part. Days kept coming and going, and we tended to adjust and adapt. Days became weeks and then months and then years. Even though time didn't stop, I still felt in a sense that a part of my development did. I was in hesitation mode, like a part of me just stopped. Maybe it was that the connection between my mother and me seemed to be cut. That link between her and me seemed like it wasn't being nurtured anymore. It just felt weird. She came back every now and then to try to make things work but was constantly met with the usual fighting, scuffling, and abuse. Then she'd flee.

Still trying to get settled herself and find a job, she bounced between Uncle Q's and Freda's. Needless to say, my anger toward her grew. I was indeed upset with my father. That was a given for obvious reasons. But I couldn't shake a deep anger toward her. How could she just up and leave me, Dwayne, and Keva? In my eight-year old mind, she should have just stayed so we could be the Partridge family. Maybe she thought that her absence would have been better for us psychologically. Better to deal with one unpredictable man than one unpredictable man, a strong-willed woman, and a boatload of drama. It was the lesser of the two evils.

We had somehow found a way to get into the general flow of life. School, homework, fights in the neighborhood with peers, knee scrapes, bee stings, cartoons, and the like. Indeed, school was fun for me. It was a place where I knew there would be some sort of consistency. I especially liked lunch and math. After school, the bus seemed like it always carried us miles out of the way before getting to our neighborhood. So we kids were loud and boisterous, trying to enjoy this free ride with friends. But our bus driver, Myra, wasn't having it.

"Y'all too loud. Lower your voices." She knew all of us by name because she always drove the same afternoon route. Like most kids, we got quiet but only for a little while. We found our own comfort in playing jokes and taunting each other during the ride.

"Bernard and Jewel sittin' in a tree, K-I-S-S-I-N-G!" I had a crush on Jewel and everybody knew it. She was dark-skinned and had two ponytails on both sides of her head, tied together somehow at their ends. She was so cute, and she always had the appearance of having Vaseline on her face. She sat in the seat across the aisle from me to the right. Everybody seemed to know when to go in for the kill and tease my feelings for her. They sang the traditional puppy-love anthem while she sat and blushed. "First come love, then come marriage, then come baby in the baby carriage." They kept repeating and repeating and repeating. They were so stupid but funny, but not to Myra.

"I said shut the shit up!" How dare she curse at a bunch of children. Most of us laughed off her anger while others of us took it seriously. The noise just typified our being kids. On one occasion, Myra drove downhill and approached a familiar turn that she normally negotiated. There was no stop sign there, so she only slowed down before making the right turn. "Shut it up!" She glanced through the rear view mirror and stared at Justin, who was up dancing and singing the anthem. When her eyes hit the road again, she was closer to the intersection than she realized. By the time she slammed on the brakes, she was already in the intersection and couldn't stop quickly enough. In front of us was a grassy open field, which continued in a downhill manner and ended with a group of trees. So Myra thought it best to try to make the turn. At least we would be on the road.

Everyone stopped singing and tried to figure out what was going on. When Myra turned, the momentum still wished to carry us forward. As the bus turned, it veered into the lane of oncoming traffic but kept inching toward the field. As most of the weight shifted to the front and back left tire, we all felt ourselves rising toward the left. Jewel's side of the bus rose above ours. I knew the bus would start doing side somersaults as we were sure to end up in the grassy field, but in a moment, we had stopped. My side of the bus was a bit lower than the other side. We were off the road, but the bus was slightly suspended on its side, like it was preparing to tumble. Frantic, we especially listened to Myra now, who was terrified but managed to give us instructions about how to evacuate. "Get in a line and walk to the front and jump off the bus and stand over there!"

Jewel was crying, and so was I. Onlookers congregated and helped out where they could. Apparently, somebody had called 911 because soon cops and ambulances arrived. Somehow, we all eventually made it home without a hitch or any injuries. We had wondered what it was that held us up. It turned out to be some small tree in the grassy area that I'd never seen before. The bus had been slowing down and reached its final resting place against the tree. I wasn't sure how Myra knew how to guide the bus so that it leaned against the tree in the right place. She probably didn't either. I was just glad to be off the bus and home.

Thankfully, no other bus trip home from school was this eventful. We just made the usual rounds, and I'd get dropped off right in front of Mrs. Jefferson's house. The closer I got to home, the less I felt like playing. I'd just get off the bus and head home. Of course, Mrs. Jefferson was always sitting on the porch with her house shoes on, watching cars, buses, walkers, or joggers go by. I couldn't avoid her if I wanted to.

"Hey, Bernie. How was school?" She drank her water with those funny-shaped ice cubes. They were long and in the form of crescent moons.

"Hey, M-Mrs. Jefferson. School was fine." I stood in her yard and observed her legs crossed as her house shoe dangled from her right foot. The shoe looked nasty on the bottom.

"Well, you make sure you get your lesson now. That's the only way you're going to do well in the future. What's your favorite subject?"

"I d-do good in m-math and s-spelling."

"Well." She corrected me.

"M-Ma'am?"

"I do well in math and spelling."

"Okay. Th-thank you." Whatever. I just wanted to get home and pee. I could tell that she wanted to ask about mama but resisted the urge.

"Well gone on home now, and be safe, okay? I got an apple. Do you want it?"

"No th-thank you. We g-got some in th-the house."

"Alright, well be good."

"Kay. B-Bye, Mrs. J-Jefferson." I was walking away and knew she was staring at me every step of the way. I wanted to turn around quickly and say, *Caught you lookin'*, but what good would that do? She would tell me later when I got much older and came back to visit her that she could always read on my face that I really didn't want to go home. She said I looked sad and disgusted. She knew that what was going on was too much for me to handle sometimes. In hindsight, I think she kept telling me to focus on my studies because she knew that would be one of my tickets out and up.

But there I was at eight coming home to an empty house. Grab the mail out the box and go to the door. A latchkey kid in the strictest sense, I'd grab the key from under the mat and head inside. At least I'd have the TV to myself while I ate my Fruit Loops. Two bowls. My father would bring some food home tonight when he got off work around 9:00. Until then, eat whatever.

Later, Keva and Dwayne came home and took their spot on the hierarchical totem pole, and my father would drive in later that night with something for us to eat from the restaurant. Finally. Food. I was starving. After arguing, we three would get ready for bed as normal while daddy had retreated to his room and closed his door. I really wanted to talk to him and tell him about school and the crush I had on Jewel and some other stuff. Guess it would have to wait. Just climb in bed and get ready for the next day.

Sometimes, I would wake up in the middle of the night terrified. I'm not sure why, but I did. Dwayne was in another world. I could hear him breathing, but I wasn't going to lie there and be scared. It was pitch dark, and I just couldn't deal with it. Everybody was asleep, so I got on my knees and prayed that God would make me feel like I was protected. I got up and went knocking on my father's door. I'm sure that being around him would make me feel a little safer. No response. So I pushed the door open. The shag carpet made it difficult to open the door and offered much resistance. But I pushed back and listened to the carpet give way. I approached the bed and watched him sleeping.

"Daddy. D-Daddy." He tossed, turned, and relaxed back into his stupor. "D-daddy!" I got louder.

Thanks to the light from the clock by his bed, I could see his eyes open and take note of me. "Yeah, Bernie."

"C-Can I s-sleep in here?" I didn't want to tell him I was scared because all he would have said was that I didn't have any reason to be scared. I think he knew, though, but just failed to make a big deal about it.

"Come on in, man." He slid over, and I climbed in. So this was where my mother slept. I felt like having a discussion, but before I knew it, he was back off to sleep. And he snored like an ox. I felt a lot safer. All I did was walk across the hall to his room, but I now had a strong sense of protection. Nothing would harm me now. At some point, I'd drift to sleep and get up the next morning to get ready for school again.

When I'd get up the next morning, I'd pretty much get myself ready. My father didn't have to be to work until later that morning after we left for school. So we got ourselves ready before the bus came. Keva would help me pick out my clothes and iron them with an attitude, but at least she did it. Weird. She was only three years older than I and was ironing my stuff. After I got dressed, I'd go back into my father's room so he could finish the final grooming, which is what I secretly looked forward to. He got up out of bed and walked me to his bathroom. I handed him the brush and he went to work.

It seemed like he had magic in his hands. He turned on the piping hot water and ran it across the brush. Then, he brushed the mess atop my head. I wasn't sure how he tamed my kinky afro, but he seemed to do it well. He brushed part of the top to the side and the other top part to the other side. Then, he brushed the rest to the back. His final masterpiece that I couldn't wait for was the thick part that he placed in my head. He'd hold one side and brush the other side until you could see half an inch of my scalp showing. That was my father's construction, my very own part in my head. He'd then put some grease on my face and gave me a light smile. Thinking back, I must have looked hideous, but I wasn't leaving out of that house without his signature creation. I knew I was ready for a great day. And I liked him this way. He was so mild, so approachable, so caring, not like the other man he became sometimes. I didn't know what made Dr. Jekyll become Mr. Hyde, but I tried every morning to enjoy the doctor while he was in.

The nights before my father would craft his construction in my hair, Dwayne and I would get on each other's nerves and eventually retire and just lie in the bed. Dwayne would knock out early, and I would just stare at the wall and the door by my brother's bed, which led to my father's bathroom. On the door, Dwayne had posted pictures and names of a bunch of people whom I had never heard of. Björn Borg, Ivan Lendl, Arthur Ashe, Tracy Austin. I had no idea who these aliens were, but it was his side of the door, and he could decorate it however he wanted. The foreigners in the pictures were all holding tennis rackets, so I guess they were his inspiration since he had taken up the sport and was known to crush most of his competitors. Anyway, I just stared at those pictures and waited. I thought I heard a knock at the door but must have been dreaming. No one ever came to the house this late. I heard it again. There was no mistake. Someone was at the door.

My father answered it. The voice sounded familiar, but I couldn't place it right away. "I am beat. Sleepy and beat. It is freezin' out there."

"Well, just go on to the back." My father locked the door and headed to the back room as well.

I couldn't put my finger on the woman's voice, but I knew it was one I'd heard. "Dwayne, did you get what we needed?" My eyes darted as I tried to focus. "I heard that Fred was selling that good stuff."

"Mm hmm. That shit seem like it's getting higher and higher. That fool gone make a fortune off us hard-working citizens." They laughed. It was Denise. I knew her laugh anywhere. I wasn't sure how she was making out since my mother caught my father over at her house. Frankly, I didn't care how she was doing. *What's that bitch doin' here*, I thought to myself. I didn't like her anymore. I didn't care how many quarters she gave me to play Ms. Pacman.

Since my bed was virtually next to the bathroom, where I got the morning afro parts, I could hear everything that went on in his room, even when the occupants whispered. Plus, I was just a nosy lad. I made it my business to listen to see what I could hear.

After a while, I began to hear some instruments. Not the musical kind but a kind I had never heard before. I focused intently. All I could make out was just a bunch of clangin' and bangin'. The noise came from a bunch of weird-sounding apparatuses. I couldn't really tell, but it didn't really sound right. In fact, the noise tended to bring back the knots in my stomach for some reason. I knew that something was going on in there that wasn't good. There was a bunch of whispering and shifting. Of course, this did nothing but make me listen more quizzically. I never quite figured out why they thought they had to whisper. Maybe it had to do with a guilty conscience. Any other time, my father would talk in his regular voice or yell to the top of his lungs when my mother was around. Now, all of a sudden, he had to whisper.

I never really heard anything else that night. Just the constant clicking of those metal devices and intermittent laughter. But not like a good laughter. It was suspect. At some point, I knew I would become a private investigator to see what all the hoopla was about behind the closed door.

# wait until tomorrow

en seconds left, and the crowd was going absolutely berserk. This game was the most intense each year. The Jordan Falcons were hosting the Northern Patriots, their archrival. It was the battle of battles, and bragging rights came to the victor. Tom palmed the ball and ran the baseline a little until he saw a free man. He bounce passed it to Terrence and ran up the court beside him.

"Falcon!" Terrence shouted the offensive play they would run. He dribbled past center court and took note of where his teammates were as well as the defense. He glanced slightly at the clock, which was at six seconds. He saw out the corner of his eye that Ned had shaken his defender and was wrapping around the left corner.

"Yo, Terrence! Woo-hoo!" Ned gave a high-pitched call that signaled for the ball, and Terrence obliged. But by the time he caught it, one of the opponents ran up to him and started waving frantically in his face to distract his view. Four seconds. It would probably go into overtime.

Just then, Terrence ran back around and all but grabbed the ball from Ned. Three seconds. With a double-team effort to deal with, it was now or never. Two seconds. He got a good look at the rim and nets and just decided on a whim to take a jump shot not too far from the imaginary three-point line. It hadn't been invented yet. One second. He released it, and the buzzer sounded. All eyes followed the ball as it hit the rim, bounced off the backboard, and then fell inside. Jordan had won, and the hometown fans were ecstatic.

The players themselves hugged and gave high-fives. The white players converged onto Terrence, the only African-American player on the court. They grabbed him, rubbed his nappy hair, and gloated in the fact that he was the star of their team. It was undeniable.

51

"Ter-ry! Ter-ry! Ter-ry!" That was their mantra.

"Man, y'all stop. Y'all embarrassing me." He acted like he didn't want the attention, but he knew he'd just earned it. It was good to be accepted by a bunch of white teammates in the heart of the South. That was no ordinary feat.

"We did it man! That was my fault, though." Ned chimed back in and apologized for getting stuck in the play transition.

"Don't sweat it, man. Ya dig it? It worked out cool!" Terrence let him off the hook. He probably wouldn't have done so if they had lost.

They all went into the locker room, showered, got themselves together and headed for home. Right before he left campus, he bumped into his coach, who gave him further affirmation. "Good job, son. Very good job." Terrence knew that he was indeed a rare find, something special.

Even in the classroom, he had excelled. An erudite and articulate young man, his grades were undoubtedly stellar. A's in almost everything were his lot. Many people couldn't fathom how this black kid in the world of white folk in the South could excel and ace his classes the way he did. Success in basketball was expected, but many an eyebrow was raised when the basketball star became the academic star. He ran circles around his classmates and scored exceptionally well on the SAT. His college choices were the best of the best. UNC-Chapel Hill, a local giant, came calling, along with other high-powered universities. But he decided he wanted to go for the gusto. He'd be making the trip to Cambridge, Massachusetts and spend his university years at Harvard.

The short version is that he arrived at Harvard, checked in the dormitory, attended classes for part of the first semester, was unable to handle the stress, experienced a nervous breakdown, moved back to Durham, and struggled to regain a sense of normalcy in life. The long version? Well, nobody really knows the long version because he never has shared it. He generally stayed in his room and suffered alone, leaving the members of his family to speculate what happened and why. A few believed that someone had put something in his drink to drug him. Others thought that he wasn't ready to deal with the culture shock of Cambridge. The big-fish-in-the-little-pond theory. He'd been a star locally but maybe couldn't hang with the big boys.

But then again, Jordan was no little pond. It was a microcosm of talent comparable to the likes of the best universities. Theory after theory abounded as to why Terrence wasn't able to continue to move forward. Irrespective of the whys behind the reality, however, the reality was still real, and the reality was brutal. Uncle Terrence was no longer the same guy.

"Y'all just waited for me to leave so y'all could come in here and watch TV." Terrence came back into the living room where Keva and I sat and minded our business. We were bored and trying to kill time while our clothes were being washed and dried. We didn't have the appliances at home, so each weekend, we had to go to my grandmother's house to make sure we had clean stuff for the week. It was here at this address that Terrence had moved back to, his own house that he grew up in. His mother had decided she'd stick by his side, help to manage his recovery, and let him have his old room back. There was no need to admit him to a halfway house. *Love would conquer all* was the mindset. I disagreed, but it wasn't my house. So he still had his own room, and we had better not think that we were going to change the normal flow of the routine for him. "I was in here first."

He was very irrational sometimes, making absolutely no sense. He couldn't be thinking clearly. Didn't he know we were there just to wash clothes and would be going back home soon? What was the big deal? Then I had to wrap my young mind around the fact that he was sick and that I shouldn't take it personally. "Come on, K-Keva, let's go b-back in the uh-other room." I was always the one who seemed to speak up in asinine situations like this. After we left, he soon left to go back to his own room and shut the door. He didn't even want to watch the television. I'm guessing he just wanted to taunt us and wield what so-called power he had.

So we sat in the meeting room and just glanced at the small television while listening to the added creepiness of what we heard down the hall in his room. The bursts of laughter that emanated from his room would mislead any first-time visitors to the residence, who may have thought he was by nature a jovial person. But we knew better. It was simply a by-product of his nervous condition and was only tamed by medication. It brought back the knots in my stomach and my own anxiety. We knew to stay away and let him do his thing. In fact, when he thought that he was in his own world and nobody was listening, the laughter would ensue for hours straight, interrupted only by periodic water and Kool-aid breaks.

Soon, my grandmother would come from the laundry room slash beauty shop. "Call Dwayne and tell him y'all clothes almost ready. By the time he gets here, y'all should be good to go. And y'all keep it down. Dillard in the back trying to sleep." That's what she called my grandfather.

She had been born and raised in Chatham County and took pride in having a strong, close-knit family. She was a woman who raised her children in a Christian home and prided herself in living by the Golden Rule. A devoted wife and mother, she was also an educator and businesswoman. A licensed cosmetology teacher at one of the local high schools, she also did hair on the side to keep extra change in her pockets. I often tagged alongside her whenever she went to work and got my cheeks pulled by her students, who told her I was so cute. Sometimes, I'd have them unfocused and laughing at me when I turned on the hair dryer and sat under it like I was getting my hair done. She'd upbraid them for joking, but they never informed her that I was the reason they were laughing. The warm air was refreshing. I was always mesmerized at how hot air came out of a chair.

Sometimes, I could tell that she wasn't super-excited to have us there each weekend, but she was a trooper. After all, she had raised her own children. This indeed wasn't her responsibility. I could sense that sometimes she wanted to say, *I sholl wish your mother was here to do these clothes. I'm tired.* And I agreed. I wanted my own mother back. I was starting to hate her more and more for putting us in this situation. Anyway, I was just grateful that Grandma Irma helped us get through a few rough spots that life was doling out. "It's some cake and ice cream in there if y'all want some."

"Ewww! Cake and ice cream!" We echoed her and almost raced each other to the kitchen. We hadn't even seen Brenda come through the door.

"Where in the world y'all going so fast? Slow down. Y'all gone mess around and bump y'all head on something." She had just come in from church. "Hey, ma!" She announced her arrival and noticed grandma in the washroom.

"Hey, Brenda. How was service tonight?"

"It was good. The Lord blessed." She was one of my father's sisters, who loved the Lord and didn't make it a secret. She had finished singing on the praise team at her church that night and finally made it home to rest. Love the Lord she did, but one had not better get her upset because it would be the wrath of God that would be felt. Hell had no fury like her if she was the woman that was scorned, hands down. Her room was not far from Terrence's, and she made a beeline to it, only after she found something to correct Keva and me about, which was customary for her. "Y'all close the freezer door while y'all putting the ice cream in the bowl."

Just as she disappeared into the hallway, Terrence entered. He was going to get his usual glass of whatever was drinkable. He always had to get at least two consecutive glasses full. One wasn't enough. And he always ended his kitchen journey standing in front of the faucet and drinking a full glass of water. Had to even it out. Place the glass on the sink to the left. On his way out, he gave me an affirming stroke on the head, like he was testing out a cantaloupe. I ignored it because I knew that at any moment, he could revert back to his other self, his laughing, irritable self.

We finished our ice cream and soon heard the horn blowing in the driveway. He preferred not to come in. We'd just take the clothes outside, get in the car, and head back home. Grandma came outside and waved at her son.

"Hey, Dwayne. Why don't you come in and get a plate?"

"Naw, I ate already, ma! Thanks, though. We gone head on home."

"Alright, well the clothes should be clean. See y'all next week."

"Bye, grandma." Keva and I said farewell until later. We were going back to where we didn't want to be. Some new events had begun to transpire, and they started when the sun went down.

"W-What you doin'?" I had to hit my foot against the bed to get out my inquiry. I was being nosy as to what Dwayne, Jr. had been up to while we were gone. Many times, he opted out of going to grandma's house while the clothes were being washed so he could have privacy while he did his homework. He was in high school now and was still sharing his room with a pestering nine-year old brother.

"Don't worry about it? Ain't nunna yo' business what I'm doin'."

"F-forget you then. H-Here go yo' s-stupid draws." I'd throw his underwear on his bed. We essentially had gotten back into the groove of our normal brotherly spats.

All three of us had learned an automatic flow of survival in preparation for the coming week at school. It was fall, and for my father, Sundays were primarily dedicated to watching the marathon of NFL games in his room.

After cooking up some smothered pork chops and a host of vegetables for us, he would retreat to his cave and watch the pigskin fly. This was one of the few times he seemed truly happy. He was good at predicting who'd win and who'd lose. This year, he was convinced that Terry Bradshaw would lead the Pittsburgh Steelers to a Super Bowl win. We knew they were playing tonight because of the conversations he had with the boob tube, telling Bradshaw which receiver was open. "Come on Bradshaw, there go Swann right there, wide open. Throw the ball!" Apparently, Bradshaw heard him because we all soon heard him yell in excitement: "Yes, touchdown! Woo-oo-wee!" The "wee" was in a soprano voice.

Keva always managed to get dibs on the living room TV on Sundays when we came home. I didn't worry about fighting her and trying to enforce the ten-second rule if she left. She was caught up anyway in this new show, *The Facts of Life*. I watched it too. It actually taught some pretty good lessons, and I loved to watch Tootie, who was a sassy spitfire who always announced to her classmates when they were in trou-ble.

I had finished most of my homework. Admittedly, I was happy to get homework over the weekend. It helped me keep my mind busy. Even though I would finish most of it on Friday nights, I purposefully saved work to do on Sundays so that I wouldn't be bored.

After we'd all settle down, after the homework, the shows, football, we'd all get ready for another week. All would be quiet until out of nowhere would come a rap on the glass part of the door in the kitchen. Everyone was supposedly asleep, but I always seemed to be the last one who would drift off. My father had obviously dozed off too because the knocking continued, light enough not to awaken the kids if we were sleep but loud enough so that my father would be able to hear it. Since no one answered the door, I decided I would get up, walk through the darkness, use the wall as my seeing-eye dog, and arrive at the door. I lifted the blinds, turned on the outside light, saw a couple of guys, and turned the light back off. I wonder what they wanted. It was around 1:30 AM, and I wasn't stupid enough to unlock the door. I went to my father's room, woke him up, and told him the news. "D-Daddy, somebody at th-the door."

He'd regain consciousness and made sure I got back to bed. "Go on back to sleep, Bernie. You gotta get ready for school in the morning." The nerve of him telling me to prepare for school, and here he was having visitors in the middle of the night.

The guys seemed fine from what I could tell and hear. They were allowed in and chilled in my father's room. My father got a couple of beers from the frig and gave them out. Since my curiosity was piqued, there was no way I was going to sleep any time soon. Dumbo didn't have anything on me because I was all ears. Naturally, I couldn't make out details of the conversations, just a lot of laughing, joking, and the like. Soon, the knots in my stomach returned because I started hearing the sounds of the same instruments that I generally heard every night that there were late-night visitors.

I wasn't sure what time it was when I fell asleep or the time they left. I still didn't know what this strange gadget was, causing all of this clanging noise, almost like cymbals in a marching band clashing but not quite. I made it a point that I would put an end to this mystery. I was always the first one home from school anyway. This was it. I told myself that the next time I ended up at home by myself, I would become a nine-year old version of Shaft, the '70s Blaxploitation icon. This case would be cracked. I couldn't wait until tomorrow.

# lydell's lessons

ll of my teachers the next day may as well have been talking Greek. I paid them no attention because my mind was only focused on the adventure I'd be undertaking when I got home. Mrs. Pollard was talking about long division, a concept I had mastered some time ago. Everybody seemed like they couldn't figure out what to do when there was a zero between some of the numbers in the dividend.

At the end of the day, I ran to the bus and endured the ride. I wasn't even really paying attention to Jewel on today. I didn't really pay attention to Myra's usual rant and rave for us to keep it down either. It was like I was the only one on the bus. Someone had hit me in the head with a balled-up sheet of paper. Still, I didn't care. The bus soon made the left onto McIntosh and, as expected, pulled up beside Mrs. Jefferson's house. She was always sitting in the same place at the same time. Her day wasn't complete until she saw our bus stop by her porch. I couldn't be sidetracked. No time to talk today.

"Hey, Bernie. How was school today?"

"Hey, M-Mrs. J-Jefferson. School w-was fine." I kept walking toward home, hoping she wouldn't make a big deal of it.

"Where you going so fast? Stay here and chat with me."

"I-I gotta p-pee." I thought, *Lord, forgive me for lying.*

"I have to urinate." She corrected me.

"I-I have to ur-urinate."

"Okay. Well, I'll talk to you later. Make sure you do all your homework."

"K-Kay. Bye."

I hurried home and wanted to get a jumpstart on whomever would be home next. Keva was in middle school and had basketball practice, so she wouldn't be home for a while. Dwayne had tennis practice, so he would be detained until later too. And I knew daddy wasn't coming home anytime soon. Things at the restaurant were too demanding. As the head cook, he'd always have to meet the demand for more collard greens, banana pudding, or hush puppies. His hands were tied until closing. Good for me.

I got in the door and realized my prayer earlier was unnecessary. I really did have to pee. I'd gobble up my usual Fruit Loops and start on my mission. I made my way to his room. I wasn't sure why I felt as though I had to tiptoe. Maybe it was because I felt I was in superhero mode. They never seemed to barge into what they were investigating. They appeared discrete and careful, so I followed this example. Right before I stepped into his doorway, there was a knock on the door. Now, who was that? The day I decided I would play Mr. Inquisitive was the day all kind of distractions presented themselves?

I ran back to the front. "Who is it?"

"Bernard, can you come out and play?" It was Franco. He was one year older than I and was a part of the latchkey gang in our neighborhood. He stayed in the cul-de-sac, which we called "the circle," which was right above our street. His parents wouldn't come home until later, and he went around to his friends' houses to kill time and play games. Today, he had chosen me.

I opened the door. "N-nah. I got a l-lot of h-homework. And I'm s-sort of s-sleepy. If you g-gone be a-at home l-later, I c-can come b-by." *Okay. Lord, really forgive me for lying this time*, I thought.

"Okay. Well, I will prolly be ova Rafael house. He got a new Atari, and he said that Galaga was a real good game, so I wanna play it."

"K-Kay. I'll prolly b-be ova there t-too." I really wanted to play Galaga, but it would have to wait. Right now, I wished he would just get out of my yard and leave me alone. He had no way of knowing what I was investigating, but he sure chose the wrong time to want to play. "I'll s-see you l-later." Thankfully, he didn't continue small talk. He made good on his promise to go to Rafael's.

I shut the door and quickly made my way back down the hall. I was finally in the room and commenced my hunt for the unknown. I had no idea what I was searching for but knew I'd be successful once I found it. All I had to do was manipulate it until I heard the familiar sound.

I reached in my father's coat closet and looked up and down. Nothing but coats. A vintage leather jacket. A heavy winter coat. Underneath was his prized collection of LP record albums in a huge milk crate. He was an

R&B aficionado. I scrolled through them and recognized none of the names. The Four Tops, Chuck Brown & The Soul Searchers, The Temptations, The Commodores, Earth, Wind & Fire, Sister Sledge. It must have been hundreds. I must have sat for thirty minutes trying to figure out who these artists were. Parliament, Donna Summer, Funkadelic, The Isley Brothers, Rick James, Gap Band, GQ. The list went on and on. I couldn't believe the costumes a lot of them wore. It was mesmerizing. I had briefly lost focus on my overall mission. I hadn't realized just how much my father was into this kind of music. He never shared with me any predilection he had for any of these aliens. After a second, I did manage to recognize The King of Pop, M.J. Everybody knew about him. But these other artists compared nothing to the ones I listened to and mimicked, like Kurtis Blow and Grandmaster Flash. I had memorized a few of their raps, which kept me cool with the in crowd. But I couldn't focus too much on that right now. I saw nothing in the closet that resembled any kind of machine. So I continued the hunt.

Nothing in the other closet either besides clothes. There was an old-school projector, but it didn't make any of the familiar noise when I rattled it, so I put it back down. I'd go into the half-bath next. I went in and looked around. Nothing but bathroom stuff. I opened the door and stepped foot in my room for a minute, but I knew nothing was in there, so I closed the door. I glanced into the mirror for a sec, only to notice that my hair was a mess. My dad would have to fix it tomorrow morning.

I checked the drawers, especially the ones that opened up like a door. The regular drawers revealed nothing more than his underwear and socks. He folded the sock pairs into balls. That was funny. In the door drawers were nothing but cassette tapes. I was dumbfounded. The room wasn't *that* huge, so maybe it was just that the people who came over just brought it when they came. But I always heard it regardless of who was visiting. I decided to take a break after giving it a shot for about an hour. Since my father wasn't there, I'd watch *Captain Caveman* on his TV today. When I looked out the window, no one was coming into the driveway, so I was free to live wildly. I would watch cartoons while doing what all kids love to do: jump on their parents' bed like a madman.

It started civilly. After about five minutes, I was almost touching the ceiling with every leap. I knew my father would have burst a blood vessel if he would have seen me doing this, which to me made it more fulfilling. I'd simply make up the bed before he got home, and he'd be none the wiser. I would even climb onto the headboard, which was a more standard kind that allowed me to stand atop it and perform a free fall from it onto the bed. As short as I was, it felt like an eternity before I'd hit the mattress from the standing position. Gravity did its job and thrust me face first onto the bed. What was more frightening was convincing myself to fall backward and then with my eyes closed. I had mastered the art of entertaining myself.

Having conquered that portion of the adrenaline-rushing excitement, I'd start again jumping on the bed normally while watching TV. Higher and higher. Until it happened. When I landed on the mattress this time, I heard a clanking. I stopped jumping immediately and thought to myself, *How could I have been so stupid not to check under the bed?* It almost felt like I didn't want to know. Part of the excitement was the hunt. I had better go ahead and satisfy the curiosity, however. For whatever illogical reason, I turned the volume down. I guess I convinced myself that I needed to concentrate, and the noise just acted as a diversion. Sweaty, I lifted up the bottom of the sheet and placed my face toward the carpet. It was dark, so I turned on the light. I still couldn't see it thanks to the shadowy effect from the borders of the sheet. Immediately, I started inching my way under the bed and slowly maneuvered my right arm like a windshield wiper. Nothing. I crawled under the bed more and kept with the arm motion. I finally hit something. I grabbed it, pulled it into the light, and studied it. I had never seen anything like it.

It was some type of scale that resembled the scales used to symbolize justice and equity. It had a gray, silver-like hue and some white powdery residue on one of the faces of the scales. I had never before seen any gadget of the sort and haven't seen one since. After fiddling and playing with it, I figured it probably wasn't a good idea to use it as a toy. Even though I didn't know exactly what its purpose was, I had a feeling that it wasn't a good one. Else, why hide it? Just keep it out in the open where everyone could see it. Why not just put it right on the kitchen table and use it for a centerpiece? The fact that it was hidden raised a red flag for me, and I thought it best to put it back where I found it and fix the bed sheets, which would resume their task of hiding the apparatus and also of hiding the fact that I had used the bed as my makeshift trampoline for the day.

Even though I didn't know exactly what it was for then, I soon found out. This was drug abuse front and center, and we were in the midst of our own war. The visits from strangers increased nightly. They came every night. It only had to be by the grace of God that none of those who came by decided to punish Dwayne, Keva, or me for any dealings gone awry. In hindsight, I realize just how much it is possible for children to have stress that is their own. They become the silent victims in situations that they cannot change. It became increasingly harder to focus in school because, while everyone else was concerned about learning, I was worrying about what would happen that night. Would we eat? Would we be safe? Would anybody go in and do any harm to Keva since she was the only girl in the house? Many times, I'd go in Keva's room so that I could sleep in her bed. After chiding me for disturbing and waking her, she acquiesced often and let me sleep in her space. But part of it for me was that, for some strange reason, I felt like I had to protect her if visitors decided to get crazy. Strange way of thinking for a nine-year-old, huh?

Unfortunately, the situation became unglued at the seams because after some time, my worst fears became realized. My father had gotten to such a point of needing help that he had to go to a recovery facility. The good part was that others in the family finally comprehended how much help he needed and signed him up for rehab at a local center, in which he was required to stay overnight sometimes. The bad part was that we kids were split up. Dwayne would stay in the house since he was in high school. He was responsible enough to keep things straight on the home front. Family would bring him food from the family restaurant. Keva went to Aunt Cammie's, my grandfather's sister. I'd migrate to my Grandma Irma's. I'd gotten pretty close to her. She had started calling me her right-hand man. So I guess that made her my left-hand woman. I just hated being split up. It felt like we weren't normal, like we were like foster kids, not like the rest of the kids in our community. Sure, there was love in the other places we went, but it still wasn't my own regular family. I couldn't express how upset I was with my mother. Couldn't she get an apartment and just let us move in with her? Didn't she know what we were going through? I didn't care anything about the danger she herself faced and endured. In my mind, she was Wonder Woman, and we were her children. I kept thinking that she should do something. Now, here we were split apart.

And it seemed like I was supposed to just take it like a man and express no hurt or sadness about it. Many expected us just to roll with the punches. Plus, I had to stay in that house with Uncle Terrence. There was no telling what to expect on any given day with him. I had to learn how to adjust quickly and walk on egg shells whenever necessary to avoid a bunch of extra drama with him, act like I didn't hear him cackling when I did.

In hindsight, I chuckle at the lack of therapy we as children received during those traumatic moments. As a whole, the African-American community, especially in the South, does not seem to utilize the services of professional psychologists period, let alone to use them to help children process feelings concerning trauma. Maybe it streams from our mindset that, as a deeply religious folk, we'd just lean on Jesus, and He'd make it alright. So that's what I did. My therapy happened each night before I went to bed. At least I knew how to pray and ask Jesus for help. Sometimes, I'd stay on my knees for hours, silent then saying some words then feeling a tear come down. It even got to the point where I had fallen asleep on my knees and woke up, hearing myself asking God to bless this food I was about to receive. *Let me get my crazy self up from here and go to bed*, I thought.

We would each stay at our destinations until the end of my father's rehab. After a few months, our nice family would be back together, and the past would be the past. We could all go back to being kids again and arguing about things that didn't matter. We could hold off a while on being adults and just be kids. No Keva ironing my clothes. No waking ourselves up and getting ourselves ready for school. Finally, we could just be kids again.

I'd gone through the worst of it. Or at least that's what my naïve little mind thought.

Getting back home felt a little weird. I hadn't seen Keva and Dwayne for months. It was good to see them. The arguments we got into signified just how much we missed each other's company. I didn't like the only-child feeling when separated. I needed someone to badger, and coming back home was just what the doctor ordered. I couldn't even really digest why we had to leave in the first place. I was just told that daddy had to go somewhere to get help for a while, so I guess I wasn't surprised that the late-night visitors had started again after about a week that we all returned. I had no idea that the reason he went off for help was to stave off these visits. For me, their reoccurrence was just the old norm that started again, the absent thing whose head was reared once more.

I got back into the regular flow of life. School, friends, and grandma's on weekends. School was fun, I guess you could say. I just sat there so bored because I understood what was taught so quickly that I'd daydream after I finished the worksheets. It was all clockwork. Get to school. Eat lunch. Daydream. Flirt. Dread coming home. Catch the bus. Try to avoid Mrs. Jefferson. Get home. Answer the door if friends come over. Go over friends' house after leaving note about my whereabouts. Be back before 6 PM.

Today, I'd return the favor and go over Franco's house this time. He caught me off guard when he dropped by when I was snooping. I hadn't been there in a while, so I decided to go by his house in the circle. His parents wouldn't be home for a while, so we would kill time by playing Atari, two square, and any other game to pass the time away.

"F-Franco, open the d-door. It's me, B-Bernard."

"Hey." He swung the door open, and we enjoyed our freedom.

"Man, w-what games is th-these? I ain't n-never s-seen these b-before."

"This one right here is called Asteroids, and this one is called Breakout." He had all the new games. While others may have been jealous, I went over his house and played every single new game he got.

"M-Man, this is t-t-tight." I had to kick the chair to get "tight" out. Thankfully, he didn't see me. "W-What you s-supposed to d-do in b-breakout?"

"You have to keep moving the bar at the bottom to hit the ball. Then the ball goes back up and hits the things at the top and then it comes back down. If you miss the ball when it comes down, your turn is over. But the ball gets faster every time it hits the things at the top. See, watch."

Franco had excellent hand-eye coordination. I didn't see how he kept moving the bar so quick to hit the ball. It was as if he knew where the ball would end up before it even got there. It would hit the bar at the top, ricochet off the sides and would go automatically where he had placed the bar at the bottom. "Here, you try it. I'll be back. I'm thirsty."

I tried it but with very little luck. The ball always seemed to escape me. Right before I moved the bar to where I thought the ball would land, I always overestimated. The ball went flying by, and there went my turn. I had two more shots before the game was over. "M-Man, this hard. I gotta k-keep my eyes on th-the ball too m-much. It's making m-my eyes hurt."

Franco came back slurping from a Sprite can and gave me one too. We played game after game and just had fun the ways kids do. In our own way, we made our own fun. After about an hour of wasting time, I decided it was time for me to head back home. "Aight, m-man. I gotta head h-home and d-do my h-homework. Mrs. P-Pollard gave us s-some stupid maf s-stuff." I made my way toward the door.

"Kay. See you later." He closed the door. I heard the lock snap and watched my feet and played my own game of not stepping on the cracks in the street as I made my way home.

"Aye yo, Bernard!" The voice came from somewhere over to the left. I looked up from my game and noticed Lydell as he sat on the stairs by the door of his house, not far from Franco's. "What you doing? Come over here for a minute." He was in high school and was a part of the older group of kids in the neighborhood, in Dwayne's circle. All of us fought each other and teased each other and the like. There was a certain trust the neighborhood kids had with each other. The older ones normally looked after the younger ones because everyone knew that there was a huge number of latchkey kids around. So to stop over Lydell's was no big problem. "Where you get that Sprite from?"

"F-Franco gave it to me. Why? Y-You ain't getting n-none cause it's al-almost gone." While walking over there, I drank the last bit and made that slurping noise to get the last few drops while holding the can totally upright. He would be unsuccessful if he tried to trick me into coming over there so he could steal the rest of my soda. He was crafty like that, always trying to outsmart us younger kids, but I would outsmart him on this one.

"Boy, stop being a damn smart aleck. I don't want none of that soda. I got plenty of soda in the house. You know you ain't supposed to be out your house."

"I c-can be outside m-my house. My d-daddy know I l-leave to go o-over my f-friend's house."

"Anyway, whatever." He shifted the subject. "Y'all know y'all be pla-yin' that hide and go get game wrong." Lydell claimed to be the master at it. He got all the girls, at least in his mind, he did. "I be seein' you tryin' to hump dem girls when you catch 'em."

"Yep." I was proud.

"But you be doin' it wrong. Oh shit, my phone ringing. Wait right there. As a matter of fact, come and wait in the living room." He ran to get the phone, and I opened the screen door and plopped on the couch. It still had the plastic on it. I don't know why black folks did that. The purpose of furniture should be to sit on it and enjoy it, not feel like you're sitting on saran wrap and listen to some stupid crunchy noise every time you move.

I put the Sprite can down and just waited. Outside looked different from this perspective. I could see my house in the distance. The view looked somewhat weird. After waiting for about ten minutes, I was ready to go. When Lydell came back, I picked up the Sprite can. "I g-gotta go home n-now."

"Just hold up! I'm trying to teach you what you be doin' wrong to the girls."

"Oh, okay." I was ready for the lesson. I was all ears.

"One second." He ran to the back and brought back a yellow washcloth. "See, when you get on top of dem, you can't be going fast like a rabbit like you be doin'. You gotta take your time. That way, you can like it and she can like it at the same time. It's all about making sure she feel good. See, lay down right there." He pointed to the sofa.

I was engaged because he was making so much sense. Indeed, I was going super fast when I was on top of girls, in part because I just didn't know what I was doing. This was great. My own lesson about sex. Why didn't Dwayne, Jr. teach me this stuff. So I lay on the sofa. "Now what?"

"So once you see she down, you sort of climb on top of her slow and put your thing right under her stomach. Like this." I wasn't sure why he had to fully demonstrate by unzipping his pants and lowering his underwear, but I thought it was all a part of the lesson. That's what I would do the next time I caught the girl, I guess. "Now you just go real slow, sort of like back and forth." He had placed the washcloth between him and me. I didn't know if he expected to pee on himself or me or what.

"Oh, okay. I th-think I g-got it. I th-think it's s-still gone h-hurt her 'cuz it's h-hurtin' me." The pain was terrible around my pelvic area because of the pressure he was putting on it. "Is it s-supposed to feel l-like this w-with her?"

"Yeah! Just keep going like this when you on top of her." His eyes were closed, and he was looking like he was waiting for some magic moment. I endured because I wanted to learn the whole lesson. I didn't want to miss any part of what he had to teach.

Soon, I got scared because all of a sudden, I saw something white come out of his penis. I never saw anything like that before. I had only seen urine before. I'm glad the washrag happened to be right there to catch it. I didn't know how he knew that he was going to need that. "Ewww. W-What's that? W-Why is it w-white?" I guess he didn't hear me. He was just sort of breathing hard.

He rounded out the lesson with a brief summary. "Alright. That's it. That's all. Just make sure you take your time with her, and don't go fast. Girls don't like that. They like to feel good." He got the rag and made his way to the bathroom. I heard water running and felt a little special. Neither my father nor Dwayne, Jr. taught me quite like this. They were just probably too busy. And even though my private area hurt like hell, this had to be a good thing. My very own private lesson about sex. He came back out and opened the door. "Alright, gone on home. And remember what I told you how to make her feel good."

"K-Kay. Thanks. Bye."

He shut the door, and I walked home. I forgot to get the Sprite can. I guess he would get it and throw it away. As I walked home, I couldn't believe how lucky I was to be singled out and given a personal demonstration. Next time I played that neighborhood game, that girl had better watch out. I now had a new set of skills that she would be sure to enjoy.

Lydell's lessons continued for about a year and a half, off and on. He continued to dress up his instructions as if they were ammunition for me to do it right when I got on top of a girl. But his girl reference seemed to become less and less what he discussed. His focus appeared only to be about pleasing himself. Unfortunately, I kept returning for more lessons. It seemed like every time I left Franco's house, there was Lydell chilling on his porch eager to begin another aspect of the lesson. The lessons had advanced to the point where he didn't need the washcloth anymore. He would grind on me without it, skin to skin, using lotion to lessen the pain and quicken his ejaculation.

He even provided advanced training by having me lie on my stomach while he pleased himself from that perspective. "Now she gone really like it when you do this. She don't always like laying on her back. This is how you switch it up." When he climaxed now, he had become less and less concerned about where his emission went. It would end up wherever. I felt a little weird and embarrassed, but I kept telling myself that he must have thought I was special to be giving me personal lessons of the sort. These were on-the-spot, sex-education lessons at the ripe age of nine.

I hadn't realized I had been duped until it was too late. The advice seemed innocent enough and logical to my young mind, and whenever I played the game with girls, I applied what I learned. I couldn't manage to make the white stuff come out of me, but she was smiling, so that's all that mattered.

One occasion, however, was a little different. I made my way to his porch. "Hey, L-Lydell."

"What you want?" He usually brought up the lessons and asked me if I was ready. There always seemed to be some new tidbit of advice with each lesson, even though nothing really changed that much physically. I was willing to learn as much as I could.

"W-What you m-mean?" I was a bit confused.

"Just what I said. Why you over here?"

I couldn't figure out if it was a joke or not. "W-Well you always t-teach me s-stuff about when I-I get on t-top of g-girls." For some reason, he seemed as if he didn't want to be bothered and was very agitated.

"Yo, just get off my yard, faggot."

"Ya mama." I didn't know what the term meant, but I figured it was something bad since he said it in anger. "Ya m-mama a fagit and your d-dad-dy and your d-dog!" I ain't g-getting off n-nobody yard." In defiance, I stayed on his property and stood my ground. A nine-year old and a high school senior. Arguing back and forth. Both cursing. Both pissed.

"Bernard, if you don't get off my yard, I'm calling your daddy at the restaurant and tell him you won't leave."

"So." Surely, he wouldn't do that, not after he had invested the time and energy into teaching me about how to make girls feel good. So I called his bluff.

He went inside his house, brought out his phone with the rotary dial, and the yellow pages. I stood there staring at him and watched his every move. How did I end up here? Why was I mad? Why was he mad? All I knew was that I was in a situation that I wished I wasn't. Very carefully, he flipped through the restaurant section of the Yellow Pages until he got to the "D" section. He apparently saw "Di" because the pages started flipping slower than before. He then started turning pages with his right hand in small chunks. He found the number to Dillard's Barbecue. "Bernard, I'm not playing. Go home. If you don't, I'm dialing the number."

"S-So." I knew he wasn't calling because if he did, he would have to tell my father that he had been teaching me lessons about having sex with girls for the past year or so. And I know Lydell didn't want to feel his wrath. I knew my father didn't play and that he would have my back when it came down to me and a seventeen-year-old bully. "C-Call him."

He grabbed the old-school rotary phone. He took his right finger, placed it inside the circle with the five, turned the dial until it hit the silver stop, and let go. Then, he dialed the four. He didn't remove his finger because he had to dial the four again. I still stood confident, knowing I hadn't done anything wrong. He finished dialing the number, sat on the porch, and held the receiver to his ear. I still thought he was sort of joking and would press those white disconnecting buttons before the call went through. We stared at each other in the eyes like two tigers.

From where I stood, I could hear the faint sound of the ringing, which Lydell heard loud and clear. Someone on the other end said hello. "Hello. I was calling to speak with Mr. Dillard, please." There was a pause. "Good afternoon, Mr. Dillard, this is Lydell from the neighborhood. How are you today? I'm sorry to bother you this afternoon, but I'm having a slight problem with Bernard. I was trying to get some yard work done after a hard day at school on today, and Bernard won't leave my yard, so I can get it done. I asked him nicely if he would leave, but he's just standing here upset and cursing at me. I didn't want to hit him or physically remove him or anything like that, but I told him that he was going to make me have to call you and disturb you at your job. So I'm calling to see if you could help me remove him from my yard."

I was absolutely floored. He hadn't told him the entire story. Before I realized it, Lydell removed the receiver from his ear and was handing it to me. "Mr. Dillard wants to speak to you." Like a weasel, he was smiling.

"Hello."

"What the hell is your problem?" He was upset that he had been disturbed at work.

"N-Nothing."

"It's obvious you got a problem. You got people in the neighborhood calling me at work. Get your ass out his yard, and take your ass back home. You done lost your damn mind."

"Alright."

"Let me speak back to Lydell." I handed the phone back and started walking home. While walking, I heard Lydell thank my father for taking time out of his schedule to help him with this dilemma. The call was over and he hung up.

"I told you I was gone call."

I didn't respond because I felt tears welling up. I just kept walking. From what I could recall, this was the point that I realized that I had been hoodwinked for well over a year. Lydell wasn't interested at all in teaching me how to sleep with girls. He had seduced an unwitting child and disguised his vile intentions as a deep-seated ploy to satisfy his own lust and curiosity. Now that he was finished with his explorations, he resorted to these means to sever the tie.

My house was coming closer but was still hidden behind a watery veil. I reached the curb and had about fifty yards to go until I heard some maniac speeding through the streets afar off. I heard skids and a revving engine, both of which were noises that came from a constant pressing of the accelerator. I had never heard anything like this in our neighborhood, so I glanced to the right to see what fool was driving in such a manner. I thought I recognized the car, but I was sure my eyes were playing tricks on me. They weren't. I sped up the walking because I didn't want to get embarrassed in public. I made it to the door, unlocked it, walked in and waited for the inevitable. Finally, the car made the right turn at about ten miles an hour and pulled up the slight hill in my yard. My father had decided to make a special trip home to teach me a thing or two. He must have left the restaurant soon after hanging up with Lydell.

He bolted in the door and found me in the living room. "Boy, what the hell is your problem?" He was taking his belt off from around his slacks. His eyes looked like fire.

I would go ahead and start crying out loud so I could convince him not to hit me as hard. It didn't work.

"I'm up there working up to the store and gotta stop because you don't wanna get out somebody damn yard. I ain't got time to keep tabs on you while I ain't here."

70

"B-But, L-Lydell ..."

"But, Lydell nothin'! Keep yo' ass outta people yard." It seemed as though the belt hit me with every word, and then he calmed down some. I was finishing with the crying but couldn't stop the short quick breaths. "You better shut up before I give you something to cry about!" He put his belt back on and disappeared as quickly as he appeared. The car sped off, and I sat in the living room trying to figure out what had just happened. Needless to say, Lydell's lessons would be no more.

# the family vineyard

One of the reasons I had done pretty well in school, especially in math, was because of skills learned at our family restaurant, Dillard's Barbecue. The brainchild of my grandfather, the restaurant taught me some rich lessons about a sense of numbers and helped to teach me discipline. The restaurant would eventually be one of the few BBQ eateries featured in the Special Features section of the DVD version of the movie *Friday After Next*, featuring Ice Cube and Mike Epps as Craig and Day-Day. You could actually see Dwayne, Jr. in the background of the clip as he helped to wait on a customer.

My grandfather was born in Rosedale, Mississippi, later went on to attend and graduate from Tuskegee Institute, and moved to Durham to start a family. He was quite a stoic man but had a heart of gold. He had nine fingers and a stub. One of his fingers had gotten cut off while he was using a machine to cut meat at the restaurant. His finger got in the way and paid the ultimate price.

Regarding his going to Tuskegee, he always sat down with me and told me the same story over and again about how he managed to succeed there. He left Mississippi for Alabama with little money in his pocket, a dream, and determination. Booker T. Washington was one of his heroes because of the pull-yourself-up-by-your-own-bootstraps work ethic that he espoused. The conversations we had dated back to when I was a lad. He always spoke to me like I was an adult. No baby talk from him. So I had to listen and act like I knew what he was talking about.

"I left home and I didn't really have that much support." We sat in the living room at my grandparents' home as he told me the story. My grandmother was asleep, and Terrence was on his usual back-and-forth Kool-aid journey to the kitchen. My grandfather always seemed to look past him and his nervous laughter. This time was no different. He just went on with his story. "My mother couldn't help me as much as she wanted so I just had to stay focused and make money the best way I could. So I started selling O'Henry candy bars on campus and loved the feeling of making money to survive." That's where his business acumen developed and thrived.

"O'Henry c-candy bars? I didn't even n-know they h-had those back th-then." I was contributing to the conversation as best I knew. I couldn't have been any more than thirteen at the time.

"Yeah, man. I learned how to work hard. Learned a lot from Booker T. See, a lot of people misunderstand him. He was a hard-working man who opened the door for a lot of colored folk and even white folk."

"Really?" As if I even knew who Booker T. Washington was. I sipped from the hot tea and pastry my grandfather had made for us.

"And when you go to college and major in business, you'll learn how to be a good business-thinker and run the business well."

College? Major in business? Run the business? I just wanted to enjoy my life and be a child. I wanted none of this grown-up talk. But I dared not move. He was one of the few who spoke to me about my future, even if I had little clue about what I wanted to do. And I learned to appreciate these conversations, even if he talked about much of the same things: his sacrifice, his perseverance. All of that focus had culminated in this, his baby, Dillard's Barbecue. Honestly, I wasn't thinking about college. In the meantime, I would just work at the restaurant on Saturdays, take orders, make change, and the like. I'd needed money for the week in case I had to buy my own dinner from Domino's Pizza.

I would find myself readying for work on those Saturdays, no longer expected to be watching cartoons. Keva was preparing to hang out with Karl, her boyfriend at the time. Dwayne, Jr. was getting ready to hang out with his friends. He worked at the restaurant all week long. This was his chance for a break. My father was up and out, bright and early, to start his shift at the restaurant. He was the head cook and had to get the food ready. Our phone bill hadn't been paid, so I had to do the next best thing. I would get dressed and make my way across the street to use the phone so I could call my grandmother. She'd pick me up and drop me off at the restaurant and keep my clothes in the car for the next day. I'd ride with my grandfather home after work and would be ready for church. I had to get in contact with her first, though.

There I was, headed across the street, knocking on the door. Mrs. Carter always came to the door with her usual smile. "Hey, Mrs. Carter. JoanTasha there?" I was verbally lazy. I was asking if Joan or Tasha was home. Mrs. Carter knew what I meant. She hollered toward the back of their house.

"Joan? Tasha? Bernard here to see y'all." I think they took to me really well because they had a brother who shared the same name as I.

"Th-thank you, M-Mrs. Carter."

Tasha came to the door. "Hey, B."

"Hey. W-What y'all d-doin'?"

"Nothin'. Just watching TV. You can come in."

I grabbed a seat, and we all just chilled. "What y'all eatin'?" I was quick to notice food cooking.

"Mama cookin' some beans."

"I'm h-hongry too. What else y-yall got?" The nerve of me to ask for food at a neighbor's. In hindsight, I'm quite embarrassed about it. As a youngster, though, I guess I was in survival mode all the time.

"We'n got nothing but some oodles o' noodles."

"Oh okay. Th-That sounds good."

She boiled some water and dropped the noodles in. Just then, Joan came from the back. "Hey, Bernard."

"Hey."

We all watched TV and talked about nothing. Tasha had put the noodles in a bowl and gave it to me. I often wonder in hindsight if they knew sometimes I didn't have food at home to eat. I didn't make a big deal about it. I knew I wouldn't starve. But I will always remember how they let me in and treated me as a younger brother.

I'd eventually get around to asking to use their phone to call my grandmother.

"Hey g-grandma. Can you come pick me up?"

"Where are you? I thought y'all phone was off."

"It is. I-I'm across the s-street."

"Okay. I'll be there in about an hour to take you up to the sto'."

"Kay."

After hanging up, I'd chat a little bit more with Joan and Tasha and would laugh with their brother if he came in. Their mother would eventually pass away, but I will never forget how that family made me feel welcomed in its home and how they never hesitated to share what they had with me.

Grandma would come by in her light blue Buick. "You here by yourself? Where everybody at?"

I had gotten used to it. I learned how to entertain myself or go across the street and hang out. "They g-gone."

"You got your stuff?" She wanted to be sure I had my clothes for the next morning.

"Y-Yes." I threw them in the back seat and got in.

"When I passed, the restaurant looked pretty busy. You ready to go to work?" She had to drive past the restaurant to get to my home and was commenting about it.

"Yeah, I'm r-ready." Sometimes, I didn't want to go, but I guess it beat just sitting around the house with nothing to do.

"Well, just learn as much as you can while you working there. You won't be there forever. You gone get a good job and make a lot of money one day. Just make sure you learn how to take care of your money. Spend a li'l. Save a li'l." She seemed like she had the inside scoop about where I'd end up. Unlike my grandfather, she didn't necessarily think I'd end up working in and for the business all of my life. "Get out here and make somethin' of yourself. You can't worry about what you got and what you don't got. You just gotta keep at it and do good in school. You want some gum?"

I never really responded. Most of the time, I just rode and listened to her monologue. I didn't even know how she decided what she'd say next. None of the topics seemed to relate to the other, but she seemed to be saying the right stuff. "Y-Yeah." She broke a piece of Doublemint in half and gave it to me. In no time, we were at the restaurant.

"Thanks g-grandma."

"Alright. I'll see you tonight."

"Bye." I shut the door and walked in.

Like clockwork, the place was packed. I had little time to get myself together. I assumed my position at the cash register and started taking orders.

"May I help who's n-next?"

Mr. Bradley stepped up. He always ordered the same thing. I could have ordered for him. "Lemme get a trout dinner with collards and potato salad. And a medium sweet tea." I had already written his order on my pad.

"Anything else?"

"That's it."

And off his order went to the back. Denise picked up the paper with the order and started fixing it. I really didn't like her because she had started spending more and more time at our house and spending the night. To me, she was a home-wrecker. As I got older, I started to appreciate when my mother had slapped her in the face when she caught my father at her house.

I took the next order. It was a new customer.

"I think I'll take a chicken dinner."

"White or dark?" I had to get clarity.

"Umm, let me get the breast and the wing."

"What two sides would you like?"

"What y'all got?"

"Collards, pintos, potato salad, cole slaw, French fries, fried okra, lettuce and tomatoes." I had memorized the items and it just rolled off my tongue. After she told me her choice, I placed it with the others and kept working to keep the Dillard machine running. "Order up, Tam."

"Got it, babe." And off she went to the races to start getting that order ready. Tam was short and a bit pudgy, with freckles and short hair. She was very upbeat and happy-go-lucky.

When orders were ready, I punched in amounts on the cash register without hesitation. I told Mr. Bradley that his order had come to $9.27. When he gave me a twenty, I just opened the cash drawer and knew in my head that his change was $10.73. I had developed a good sense of numbers over time. I was only thirteen and could figure out the change without a calculator. This would prove to be good training ground for strengthening my love for math. Beyond working in the store, I seemed to continue to do really well in math classes at school, especially on one occasion when I was in the seventh grade.

"Come on, everybody. On the bus. Let's go!" Mrs. Everett was rallying us together because our departure time was 9:00 AM, and it was 9:20. "Peter, let's go. Come on, Bernard."

I was a little late getting on because I had misplaced the permission slip my father had signed to allow me to go on the trip. I had finally found it and was rushing to get on. We were on our way to participate in a state-wide meeting of middle schools for a club called Career Exploration Clubs of North Carolina. It was just a time we could get away and have a good time with teachers and parent chaperones. There would be food, fun, and a lot of learning about possible careers that existed. There were also mini-competitions in which we could participate. Mrs. Cochran took the liberty to enter me into the math competition and told me at the last minute. "Just go in there and do the best you can do."

I really didn't feel like it, but I obeyed. I couldn't find the room at first, so by the time I walked in, everybody was quiet and working. I saw nothing but a sea of white. I hadn't seen so many white kids in one place at one time ever. I sat down and began working. Many of the calculations resembled many of the situations I faced weekly at the restaurant. There were several items listed with prices given, and following were questions about that scenario. For example, one question asked, "How much change does the person receive back if they give you $20?" Just like Mr. Bradley did. I finished the exam but must have done something wrong because all of the white kids were still working. I turned in my exam and left. I was the last one to show up and the first one to leave. It was no telling what the proctors of the exam were thinking about me. To be honest, I didn't care. I just wanted to go and get back with my friends.

During the awards ceremony for the math challenge, they called some of the white kids to the stage for getting second and third and called me to the stage as being the overall winner. Mrs. Cochran looked at the other teachers in awe as I walked past her on my way to the stage. "Well, I entered him, but I didn't think he was going to win." She was talking to Mr. Flowers, one of the home economics teachers.

I was somewhat numb because I felt all eyes on me as I walked up. *Just stay focused, walk up the stairs, don't trip, get the certificate, and go back and sit down. Great, now they want to take a picture on stage with all three of us. Yeah, great, put the black kid in the middle. Why are they taking forever? Smile. Act happy. Get the hell outta here.*

I never really thought how much working at the restaurant had prepared me for success.  On one level, it was just something I was supposed to do on Saturdays as a youth.  On another level, it helped develop in me a good work ethic and appreciation of the value of a dollar.  Further, it helped me to realize that I could compete with others, despite the color of my skin or of anyone else's.  Thankfully, math was colorless.  This would be one of the greatest lessons that I would cherish throughout my life.

As positive as the family restaurant was in terms of its ability to keep me from going hungry and teaching intangible life's lessons, there was another set of lessons it brought with it.  I have grown to understand that owners of a family business must consider the maturity levels of those who are to assume leadership, those of the next generation.  If the successors are not responsible, even if they are of your own flesh and blood, it may not be advisable to release the business into their hands.  It becomes similar to casting pearls before swine, to cite a biblical reference.  For all of the hard work and energy expended to get the business to a certain level, it becomes disheartening when new leaders fail to have the same passion and drive as the owners.

In my own observation, I noticed how my grandfather's sons were given a thriving business to manage and take it to the next level of success, perhaps to establish chains so that growth and expansion could occur.  For many of them, however, the end result of the leadership they assumed culminated in limitless access to money, women, and drugs.  A great sense of sobriety and clear thinking must accompany anyone who leads a business, especially one that is family-owned.  Decisions made in this special situation do so much more at impacting one and his or her family.  The family name will either thrive or suffer in the community based on individual choices.  The legacy of the family name becomes much more at stake.  And maybe deep down, this was not a career that my father or uncles really wanted, which is an idea that has to be explored when it comes to a family business and its upkeep.

Family business owners must address the possibility that the children may not be as passionate about the business as the parent owner.  While parents have the innate desire to provide for the family and put systems in place to solidify a future for their children and grandchildren, they also have to respect their children's decision to choose another career path. This becomes a sensitive topic because it is possible for parents to take offense to their children's decision not to carry on with a business that has done well over the years. The owner could view their children's decision as a selfish decision not to keep the family legacy alive. But what parents must realize is that, at the end of the day, it is the son's or daughter's right to pursue the path of life that he or she believes is appropriate. If this is a path that does not include working at the family business, parents must not just respect this decision but encourage it, however painful. Doing so could very well translate into a happier son or daughter, as they would not feel like they were only existing to carry the dream of someone else, not their own.

I often wonder how my father's life would have been different if he had pursued something different in life. In my younger years, I noticed how angry he was as a person. I wonder how much of this anger was based on feelings he may have had concerning expectations placed on him to run the business. For it was at the height of his taking the leadership of the business that the spousal abuse transpired. It was at the pinnacle of his reign that the infidelity increased. What should have been the happiest moment of his life was turning out to be the most irritable. The people he chose to keep around him weren't those who were focused on excelling or soaring. The eagle was hanging out with the turkeys. His choice was to run with those who had a reputation in Durham for running in drug circles. Maybe he had finally decided to rebel against others' wishes. Sadly, it was a type of rebellion that didn't just affect him. It affected those close to him, those who loved him.

I guess the positive side of his experience is that he never tried to convince Keva, Dwayne, or me to do anything. He just let us choose our own path. In part, he was a bit distracted with his own set of challenges. But he never really told us outright of any of his expectations concerning us, good or bad. At least we'd be following our own dreams, even if they were as simple as being a professional basket weaver. It would have been our dream, and we would have probably been the most content and successful basket weavers around.

In all, the tightrope of running a family business has to be walked carefully and wisely. Owners have to put their all into making sure the company lives beyond them while being supportive of the decisions and choices of their offspring, which may or may not include toiling in the family vineyard.

# ghetto-fied toni

**B**ernard, hurry up! Gary gone be here in a minute to pick us up." Keva specialized in giving orders, of course. This time was no different. We had to be ready for track practice. It was the summer, and we were all excited about having something to do to pass the time away.

"Okay. I heard you the first three times! I can't even use the bathroom in peace!" At some point, I hadn't struggled as much with my speech. Here recently, the stuttering was off and on. Most of the time, I managed to get my thoughts out without hesitation. But not all the time. "J-Just wait!"

"You know Gary don't like to wait for us." Gary was another of my dad's brothers. A Vietnam vet, like Uncle Q, Gary was dependable with picking us up and taking us to the track to practice with the community kids. But he didn't just pick us up. He was also one of the track coaches himself. He was pretty athletic and had a well-built frame from lifting weights over the years. I guess Vietnam had him trained to think like a soldier in all aspects of his life because he was a stickler for time. When he drove up, he wanted us to be standing outside, waiting on him. It was either that or we'd have to walk to Shepard Middle School and be late. So we would rush outside and wait at the end of our driveway. As we headed outside, Keva told me to lock the door.

"Why can't you l-lock it?" I always snapped back. We were oil and water.

"Boy, just lock it."

I had my bags and my Gatorade. I always liked how Gatorade tasted after track practice. It tasted so sweet, unlike when we were just drinking it around the house. It tasted bland and boring when we drank it then. As I went back to lock the door, we heard the revving of Gary's car as he hugged the curves on the road en route to our house. He had a killer car, a small gray sports car that rivaled a Porsche, if you asked us.

"Hurry up, Bernard. You hear Gary coming."

"I'm going as fast as I can." I heard the lock click, pulled the key out, and started running toward the end of the driveway. Gary had appeared almost magically. Keva had gotten in the car and was talking with Ashley, Gary's daughter, who ran too. The door rested open, inviting me in.

"Bernard, let's go!" Gary barked out his orders. Didn't he see me running already to get to the car? And didn't he see all the stuff I was carrying? "Let's go! Let's go!"

As I ran down the slight hill, I was almost at the car. And then there was the dreaded crash. I couldn't believe it. The Gatorade had slipped out of my hands right as I got to the car. Sadly, engineers hadn't mastered the art of making the plastic bottle yet. The glass bottle had slithered its way to freedom outside of my grip. I just stared. I could almost taste the orange flavor as it ran toward the street. He, Keva, and Ashley were all laughing. It was as if time stood still until the general snapped me out of it. "Bernard, just move the glass out the driveway and put it on the grass. It's gone. You'll have to get another one later. Let's go! We runnin' late!"

I finally got in the car, and we were off. For the length of the trip, we were all relegated to the fetal position. I didn't know how anybody was supposed to ride in a car like that and enjoy the journey. It looked sleek from the outside, but once you got in, it was the epitome of discomfort. And then we had to endure the so-called singing from Gary. It was torturous. With no radio, Gary started belting out long chords from some imaginary song that only he could obviously hear and make sense of. As he shifted the car's gears, a long deep tone emanated from his voice box for about two seconds. And then another low note for two more seconds. Then higher, three seconds. No words, no hook, no bridge, just noise.

*Please, Gary, just shut up and drive!* It almost came out of my mouth on many occasions, but I guess I had better appreciate the ride and block him out as much as possible. It was common knowledge that you shouldn't drink and drive, but in Gary's case, to make this noise and drive should have been a hard-core offense on so many levels. Thankfully, we would arrive at the track and be freed from this prison of space and sound.

Outside of simply having something to do during the summer, I decided to run track for a couple of reasons. First, I had to outdo Keva. She started running and was dusting all of the girls on the team, and she did it so effortlessly. I couldn't figure out how she had gotten so fast. Maybe she got it from my father, who was a great high-jumper, as mentioned earlier. It was probably in the DNA. Keva ran circles around the girls and boys alike. Even Dwayne, Jr. was one of the star tennis players at Hillside at the time. So I figured the athletic gene wouldn't skip over me.

Subconsciously, though, I think the reason I started running during the summers was to help me deal with the drama in the home. It was a healthy outlet I could look forward to in order to develop an extended family of kids my age and other adults who would be role models for me. The friendships I would develop would be long-lasting and quite meaningful. We didn't just run locally. Because of many corporate sponsors, like IBM and the like, the team traveled to different cities in North Carolina and crossed state lines to Georgia, Florida, and Maryland. Parents would volunteer to be chaperones for overnight trips, and we were able to do just what we knew how to do best: be kids. We didn't have to worry about what we were going to eat or who would be visiting late in the night or hearing drug paraphernalia in the back room. We could just be kids.

Running for the Durham Striders was more than being involved with just another sports group. We learned responsibility, leadership, discipline, and camaraderie. We learned how to win and lose gracefully. Many of these life's lessons have followed many former athletes into adulthood as they moved on and raised their own families. The leaders of the track club weren't without their own set of challenges because part of the club's mission was to reach out to many at-risk kids, which meant canvassing for kids in sup-posedly dangerous neighborhoods, like McDougald Terrace, Cornwallis, Few Gardens, and Braggtown. You just didn't go into these areas without living there or having an arrest warrant. When many of the kids from those areas joined the team, coaches had to deal with attitudes galore, but the rewards ended up outweighing any initial difficulties experienced at the outset. To be honest, kids from these neighborhoods were the best athletes, and when you got to know them, they were the most loyal friends.

So every summer from six years old to seventeen, the Durham Striders served as a surrogate family. There was a certain bond shared with most of us on the team. We were all enduring grueling practices, sometimes running until what we ate for lunch came back up again and nourished the grass. But it was just something that came with the territory of being a runner. We felt each other's pain and grew to respect everyone's ability to stick it out year after year. College became a reality for many of the runners who may not have been able to get there without the structure and network of that track program. Over the years, I grew pretty close to some of my new brothers and sisters along the way, in particular with Toni. She was from McDougald Terrace and was straight up hood, full of drama. Although I went at it with Keva regularly, I was pretty reserved with those outside of her and Dwayne, Jr. But it was a little different with Toni and me. No one would have pictured that she and I would become hanging buddies. And as one might guess, our initial meeting would have its own share of theatrics involved.

"Let's go, Janice!" We were pumping her up as she stood at the starting line for the 200-meter dash. We were in middle school, and Janice was the bomb. She had gone undefeated this year and was looking to round out her perfect season at this, the middle school championship. "Don't worry 'bout none of these other g-girls. They ain't got nothin' on you. It's just a m-matter of time! You gone win, and erbody else gone be l-looking stupid!" I had taken up the art of talking junk on behalf of my teammates. It was a strategy that seemed to work in my mind. The other runners would become psyched out and lose focus mentally, which was half the battle when it came to the sport. "You got it, Janice! You got it, Janice! It's all y-yours!"

"She *think* it's all hers!" Somebody decided she would respond to our taunts. We looked on the sidelines, away from the track, to see who else was encouraging their own teammates. We kept looking and couldn't see anybody and heard the response again. "Yeah, that's right. She *think* this race all hers! We'll see at the end who gone take it." Even Janice herself looked around to see who it was threatening her sure victory. Admittedly, she was used to hearing us trash-talk on her behalf and never heard any rebuttal. But the rebuttal indeed was in full force. And it came from a source that caught us all off guard.

"N-No she ain't t-talking junk, y'all." I was trying to egg on my partners in crime, my teammates, to dwarf the comments made by this unheard-of runner. She was actually one of Janice's competitors, who was awaiting the start of the race as we were. Janice was in lane four, while this girl was in lane two. Since it was the 200 meters, they were staggered, so this loud mouth would be able to see Janice throughout the entire race, especially into the curve.

"You heard exactly what I said! I ain't over here stuttering like you!" She kept jumping up and down to keep her muscles ready for the race.

"Oh snap, Bernard, she got you on that one." She really had. She hit the jugular. My teammates acknowledged her successful remark. I tried to act like it didn't hurt and tried to laugh it off, but this girl was ruthless. She was serious.

"If she win, she gone earn it 'cause I'm comin' for her." She kept up with the comments.

Janice was never one to brag. She let us do it. We only did it because she was able to back it up and let her feet do the talking. She was much more humble than we. We used her talent to support our inadequacy. "Yeah, well we'll s-see. You b-better be saving y-your breath f-for this r-race you getting r-ready to lose." I couldn't resist.

"Aight, check wit me after the race." She just had to have the last word.

The starter approached his mark and began his chant. "Runners, take your mark!" All of them started stretching and assuming their initial positions. After about thirty seconds of getting themselves together, all the runners rested in their starting blocks in the universal crouched position, waiting for the next command. All except the loud mouth who was in lane two.

"Look, y'all. She d-don't even know h-how to get in the s-start position. Erbody and th-they mama know how t-to do that." The peanut gallery started laughing, as we watched this amateur stand at the starting line in a motionless running position. She ignored us and focused on her race.

Even the starter himself chastised us so that the girls would be able to concentrate. "Quiet at the start!" He turned his head toward us, and we got the message. He donned a pair of black and red headphones, whose purpose was to deaden the pop from the fake gun. There was finally silence. The starter continued. "Set!" He yelled this command and held the word for a good two seconds. Most of the girls raised and held their behinds in the air in expectation of the sound of the gun. I have to admit that I glanced a few looks at Janice's butt while it was in the air. She was cute, and that was the only time I could do it without getting in trouble. The amateur stood still, no movement, still in that wack, motionless position. Nobody wanted to look at her butt anyway. She was too hood-looking for me, and it was no telling what the back of her would reveal.

All of a sudden, the gun went off. That fool in lane two was the first one to take off, almost like she was used to the sound of gunshots in her own neighborhood. After all, she was running for Holton Middle School, which was situated in a questionable part of Durham.

"Run, Janice!" We were all screaming. By the time she was coming out of the curve, she had passed all the girls who were to the outside of her. Coming into the straightaway, she was in the lead. We could see that the girl in lane two had passed everyone too as she came off the curve. As fate would have it, this had become a race between Janice and Ms. Loud Mouth. We were still standing by the starting line, so we could only see the race progress from a distance. As we watched, we saw how the gap between Janice and her continued to shrink. We were trying to figure if the gap were really closing or if it was just because of the perspective from which we were viewing the race. It looked like they were running neck and neck. Athletes from both teams were rooting for their teammate to win. Those in blue and white uniforms were cheering for Janice, while those in red and white ones shouted for the other girl.

We couldn't believe our eyes. Nobody had come close to defeating Janice, and here was some no-named, ghetto girl about to do the honors. We could only tell who won by the uniforms that would remain in celebratory mode after the race. As we watched, we only saw a patch of red and white continue to jump up and down while the clump of blue and white stood still and seemed to look on in disbelief. As did we. We hovered around the starting area and watched the runners come back to get their sweat pants and other garments. Janice seemed very content in getting second. We were obviously more embarrassed than she was. The issue of her getting beat was ours. We had pumped up her abilities to a degree beyond our ability to deliver. "Nice run, Janice!" That's all we had the strength to muster.

"Thanks!" Janice was fine and started putting on her sweat pants. She had taken off her spikes and carried them in her hands. She tossed them to the ground and started putting on her regular sneakers.

"Go, Toni! Go, Toni! Go, Toni!" That girl was making her way back to get her stuff, and she had her own moving red-and-white entourage. Her teammates were singing her praises incessantly. She was just smiling and taking it all in. All I could see were her white teeth shining through her super dark-skinned tone.

On her way back to her belongings, she caught my eye and started in on me. "Yeah, talk that shit now!" She wasn't concerned with Janice. To her, Janice was never the adversary. I was. "What?! I can't hear you. What was that you was sayin'?"

I really couldn't say anything. I knew about how to save face quickly, and this time was no different. The solution was to ignore her. "That's alright, Janice. You'll g-get her next time. It w-was just luck. Sh-She got you this t-time 'cuz o' luck." Janice had already gotten dressed and was leaving and was surely paying me no attention as the instigator. I yelled again so that both she and Toni could hear me. "You'll g-get her next time."

"You ain't got to talk to me through her. I'm standin' right here. You ain't got to talk in codes." Toni wasn't backing down.

"And you ain't g-got to tell m-me w-what I got to do and w-what I don't got to do." I just decided to address her directly now as I had before. There was no buffer between us. Virtually, everyone had walked away other than us.

"Yeah, well we see who won the race. All that talkin' you was doin' didn't do nothin'. We see who won, and it won't no luck." I sort of liked how she stood her ground and didn't back down. Sort of reminded me of me.

"Yeah, well w-whateva!" I started walking away to join my teammates, leaving her there to get dressed. "We'll see n-next time."

After the school year ended and the summer track season started, I would meet up with familiar classmates at the track to talk about how fun the summer season was going to be with all the traveling and all. I had no clue that Toni's ghetto self was going to be a part of our in crowd now. As a bunch of friends and I sat in our own comfortable circle, she came strolling up to where we were since she was in our age group. The coaches had found out who she was and put forth a special effort to recruit her to be a part of the team. Their aim was to try to make an impact in the lives of those who had the talent but might not have had the exposure or opportunity to show it. Just my luck that she just happened to be one of the ones they hoped to change.

"What y'all looking at?" She was never one to bite her tongue or mince her words. To us, she was an outsider and had to earn our friendship.

"You!" I was the ringleader.

She barked back. "Well, y'all better hurry up and figure out what you trying to figure out 'cause I ain't the one!"

Coach Teddy made a formal introduction. "All the old heads, I need y'all to meet Toni Scott. Make her feel welcome. She gone be a great part of the team this summer. Ain't nobody with *no* school during the summer. We all a part of the same team."

*Whatever*, I thought.

"So y'all get to know her, and treat her just the same as everybody else on the team." Coach probably sensed a little bad blood and thought he'd put out any fires before they started.

We eventually let our guards down and started to get along. Over time, we couldn't believe just how stupid we felt that we were at each other's throats. It was probably that we were just young and immature, typical middle-schoolers. Ironically enough, Toni and I would become the closest of friends. Throughout high school, we would get pretty close. Of course, we ran track together, marched in the band together, won dancing contests together, the whole nine. If you saw one, you saw the other.

I never would have guessed, though, that our camaraderie would have a unique and special twist, which would be revealed a little later in my high school years.

Never.

# nerd

S trangely, I found solace in doing things academic. While most children were steeped in other distractions, I was able to find some sense of satisfaction with reading and learning. Of course, I enjoyed video games too, but it was something about reading and doing math that kept my mind sharp. Plus, I could read and temporarily enter a new, non-judgmental world. As a family, we didn't travel a lot, but reading helped me to go places I had never been. It kept my horizons expanded. At least I could imagine what those places would be like, be they fictitious or actual.

By the time I got to middle school, I fit right in. I had ended up in the gifted and talented program, otherwise known as the GT program. Keva had just finished middle school and warned me that it was going to be hard for me. I often wondered if she just said those things because she was just being Keva. After all, she and Dwayne, Jr. had conspired to scare me in my earlier years, telling me I was adopted. They looked more like each other and resembled my father. I, on the other hand, didn't look like them but looked like my mother. Such a cruel joke until I understood how biology and genes worked.

Even though I didn't remember taking any tests to be labeled as gifted, I was glad that I was placed in such classes. They kept me challenged and stifled my boredom most of the time. My teachers were great. I didn't know how they were able to stimulate our minds, but it seemed like things clicked pretty quickly with me. I still ended up bored in many classes because I would finish assignments and just sit, daydream, and wait for the next assignment. In my language class, I had just finished a worksheet on some topic like active and passive voice and sat with my cheek resting in my hand.

"Bernard, are you finished?" Ms. Rivers was circulating throughout the class, monitoring our progress. She was the GT language arts teacher for

Rogers-Herr Middle School as well as for Shepard. She taught us and then drove to the other school and taught there. She was very motherly and was sharp as a tack. I'd later discover that she was a Spelman graduate, did more study at NCCU, Duke, Oxford in London, and would finish her PhD at New York University in English Education. She'd also eventually go on to become the Interim Dean at University of Maryland Eastern Shore after a short stint at Bennett College. And she was a single mother. But right now, these were her pre-PhD days. Right now, she was just Ms. Rivers, and she wanted to be sure we were staying focused.

"Yes, I f-finished."

"Okay. Great. We'll move on in just a minute. Just look over your answers. We'll grade them together soon. That's a nice outfit, by the way. Who bought that for you?"

"My g-grandma." My face lit up.

"Well, she has some great taste."

"Th-Thanks." While daydreaming, I'd find myself laughing to myself at her googly eyes and wide smile. The glasses didn't help either. The frames were huge, and the lenses made her eyes appear even larger. To me, she looked like a dark-skinned version of the Cheshire Cat. She always seemed so happy-go-lucky too. How could anybody always be that happy? She spoke softly but with a certain command that was undeniable. There was no mistaking. She knew her stuff and knew how to convey it. But she seemed not just to be concerned about our grades. She appeared really interested in us as growing people, as young adults finding our way in life.

She'd remain my language arts teacher for my three years at Rogers-Herr. We read novels like it was nothing. *Ivanhoe*. *The Spook Who Sat by the Door*. *Great Expectations*. I couldn't believe I was in my early teens and reading so voraciously. I was saddened a little because I had grown attached to her teaching style and had to get ready to enter high school to start a new experience. She seemed to make learning interesting and helped us to think outside the box. She expected students in her class to soar and not use anything as an excuse to underachieve.

I had taken much of her advice to heart, as I had become president of the seventh and eighth grade classes, which amounted to nothing more than popularity contests. Whoever made the best-looking buttons for students to wear normally won the competition. Honestly, though, I was mostly a figurehead, having no real responsibilities. I hadn't really thought that winning would make me have to stand in front of my peers and give speeches at certain points during the year. This was a nightmare for me. Hadn't I remembered that I had this nervous stuttering problem? Why would I put myself in this position? Strangely, however, it seemed like whenever I had to speak publicly, God would always help me get through it. The stuttering would always seem to subside while in the moment of speaking from the podium. I never could understand how I was able to deliver a speech with no stuttering and then struggle to talk in normal circumstances. One of life's greatest mysteries to me.

About two weeks before my middle-school career came to an end, students would have to sit through an awards ceremony. Since I had served as the class president, I was awaiting that award and then I'd be gone. There was no way I was sitting through that drawn-out episode. They never got around to giving rewards for service to the class, so I was bummed about that. Ms. Fletcher, the school guidance counselor, walked onto the stage and made an announcement: "Good afternoon, everyone."

"Good afternoon, Ms. Fletcher." We all sang back in chorus.

"Now, we are going to give awards to the eighth graders with the top overall grades. We are giving trophies to students who have the top ten grade point averages all the way from sixth grade through the eighth grade. When we call your name, please walk up the steps to the stage and stand in order."

"Oh Lord, not this," I whispered to Vanessa, a fellow eighth-grader. We had forgotten that they did this every year. They called the nerds up on stage in this free-for-all spectacle. I wasn't the smartest, but I wasn't the dumbest either. I knew I'd wind up somewhere in the top ten because most people in the GT classes normally did.

She began reading, starting with number ten. "The tenth highest grade point average goes to Travis Hightower." There was applause from the crowd. Students were really getting with it. Most of them were in the younger grades. They thought we were giants and knew everything. Travis made his way to the stage.

"Number nine. Dwight Daye. Number eight. Justeen Young." Applause. By the time she got to number four, I realized that I was not in the nerd league. "Number four. Peter Sewell. Number three. Vanessa Owens." Vanessa scooted past me and rolled her eyes to suggest that she really didn't want to go on stage.

"Number two.  Vladimir McGloin."  He was a cool kid.  Half Filipino.
Half Caucasian.  But he acted just like all the African-American students.
We had broken him in to our social norms.  He was very smart, almost a
genius in most of our estimation.  We just assumed he'd be first since he was
the only non-African American kid in our class.  We just figured that's what
was supposed to happen.

"And the eighth grader with the highest academic average in the entire
class for all three years here at Rogers-Herr Middle School is . . . Bernard
Dillard.  Please come forward and stand in the front."

I sat for a minute, trying to process that she called my name.  Then in
shock, I wasted no time in going forward.  I couldn't express to anybody that
I thought there had been a mistake.  This couldn't be happening.  Were my
grades really that good?  I had gotten a lot of A's over the years, but I didn't
realize that it had placed me at the head of the class.  I looked at Vanessa on
stage.  It looked like she was mouthing something like, *Alright now*, and
looking at me up and down.  I guess it was her way of saying congratulations.

I just stood and sort of glanced over the audience.  The students and
teachers were still clapping.  I felt a little strange and puzzled.  How in God's
name did I get here?

However it happened, I had to deal with the obvious and grim reality
that I had now officially achieved my new and bona fide title of nerd.

---th-thirteen---

# night in, night out

---

fter summers of running, traveling, and enjoying the company of extended family, it was back to the humdrum reality of living in that boring home. By the time I reached high school, I had pretty much gotten used to not having my mother around. She had moved into her own government-assisted apartment and had found odd jobs to keep herself afloat, a sure deviation from the path she had imagined she'd follow as some man's wife. I must admit that she wasn't prideful about some of the jobs she held down. From a sandwich artist at Burger King to part of the maid staff at the local motel, she always seemed to find a way to make it. I was still disappointed that we couldn't move in with her, but I had discovered how much she was really struggling to make it. I had resolved that she couldn't really give what she didn't have. My emotions concerning her fluctuated between sympathy to anger to pride back to sympathy. She didn't let life beat her down and drag her into an abyss of depression, but I still wished she could have found a way to fight for us and get us out of that hellhole.

I knew she still struggled with the effects of my father's actions of abuse, but she rarely let the air out to reveal her deep feelings to us. I have always had a feeling that she wrestled with low self-esteem, loneliness, and mild depression. As we would chat at different points in life as I got older, she would always refer to the drama and abuse she suffered over the years of the marriage as "what happened" or "the thing that happened." But she seemed to find her rhythm with life and somehow managed to keep moving.

Meanwhile, my father's home provided little by way of nurturing and strength. I'd have to find that elsewhere. And since I was in high school, I'd have to just suck it up and be responsible for my own transition into young adulthood and manhood. On the way, I'd have some successes, some stumbles. All in all, I just sort of felt my way into what I thought being a man entailed. I was glad I had at least figured out that being a man-in-the-making meant realizing that my destiny would be shaped by a power higher than myself. This was very reassuring for me. Although I could never really put my finger on how I would make it through, I always had some deep sense that I was being led and would continue to be led to a place of purpose and meaning. Strangely, this strong sense of direction helped me to weather any and all situations in the home that always seemed to suggest defeat and weakness. In hindsight, I still shudder at how I was able to maintain a certain focus amid what successfully destroyed others who underwent similar pressures. Statistics suggest that most youngsters, especially in the African-American community, tend to drift toward the vortex of that which surrounds them, good or bad. A part of me, though, always seemed to embody a salmon swimming upstream, against the tide. The supernatural focus and direction I felt were forever palpable. *It won't happen to me* was the constant mentality I possessed when it came to whether I'd end up in life's pitfalls. And maybe it was a certain decision I had made in my pre-teens that helped to keep me fueled and focused.

I had ridden home with my grandfather the night before. Business at the restaurant was booming, and both of us were tired. Thankfully, we didn't have too far to travel, just a couple of miles straight up Fayetteville Street and we'd be there. I'm not sure what granddaddy was talking about. I'm sure it was important. I was dozing off and hoping he'd stay awake for the short drive. I forgot to tell grandma I'd be coming over. I just brought my Sunday bag with me to be prepared. By the time we got home, grandma and Uncle Terrence had turned in. I guess I'd take a bath in the morning. No reason to start rustling and making a stir on tonight. I determined just to go to bed, smelling like barbecue and pigs' feet.

We walked in and dragged ourselves to our final resting spots. The gas fireplace was aglow with the pilot light, and all the greeting cards and candles lined themselves on the coffee table and mantle, the typical grandparent home setup.

"Well, here we are. Grandma will be up in the morning." I could tell he was dog-tired. He worked himself hard, especially on Saturdays.

"Kay. G'night. S-See you in the morning." My thirteen-year-old body was feeling the strain. I knew this wasn't something I would do the rest of my life. How could people handle the physical and mental strain of being on their feet all day preparing food for customers? I only did it once a week and was drained. I couldn't imagine going through this every day.

I heard him shuffle his feet back to his room in his semi-pimp walk. It wasn't intentional. One leg of his seemed to be longer than the other one. As he went off into the blackness toward his room, he sort of hobbled up and down, humming some spiritual song.

I made my way to what was understood to be my room whenever I stayed over. It was actually Aunt Raquel's room. But she was no longer there. After going away to college at Bennett, she had gotten married and moved to the Midwest. Her room was now mine to enjoy. I threw my bags down and forced myself at least to wash my face. I fell to my knees by the bed, said a prayer, and climbed the mountain to reach the covers. It appeared unusually high, almost as if I had to scale a mountain to get into it. I hoped that I would never twist, turn, and fall out of it while sleeping because it would have been about a mile's journey downward. Its legs almost touched the ceiling. It almost felt like a bed of a king. And right about now, the king needed some serious R&R. I didn't know when I drifted off, but all I knew was that I felt like Rip Van Winkle. After what seemed to be a quick moment, the sun shone through the window and awoke me. A new day had cycled in and made its presence known.

I didn't realize how thirsty I was when I woke up, so I decided to do something about it. As I left the room, I heard the TV on in the kitchen area and knew my grandma had gotten a jumpstart on the day. I didn't know how she did it, but she got up early enough to wake up roosters. She put the Army and its famous we-do-more-before-9-o'clock slogan to shame. It was early Sunday morning, and she had already fixed breakfast, cleaned the living room, and had almost finished dinner. She was looking at the television, but the volume was down. She didn't yet know I had made it in with granddad on last night, so I thought I'd surprise her. I'd sit quietly behind her on the green, wool sofa and wait for her to get up to do something. She'd be startled once she saw me, and we'd both laugh it up. I moved sneakily to my position and waited. I glanced at her and noticed that she had a huge pot on the floor between her feet and was mumbling. She was snapping green beans and throwing them in the pot. This was the last part of the dinner that she was cooking. She'd have the entire dinner prepared before we left for church. I quietly waited and just listened to the snaps. I got bored and wished she would just turn around. And without notice, it came out of nowhere.

*Help, Lord! Help my family, Lord!*
*Bless Dwayne, Lord! Bless Gary, Lord!*
*Bless Dillard, Lord! Help him at the store!*
*Give him strength to make it!*
*Bless Brenda, Lord! Bless Raquel, Lord!*
*Help my children, Lord! Help my grandchildren, Lord!*
*Bless me, Lord! Bless my sisters, Lord!*
*Bless that boy, Lord!*

Honestly, I wasn't sure what to think. I wasn't prepared for that. I just wanted to surprise her, and now I had ended up listening to my grandmother cry out in prayer for her family. And she literally was crying. I had never witnessed her like this and had no idea how to respond. So I just kept sitting. No way was I going to get any water while this was going on. And she was loud. How did nobody else in the house hear her?

*And help Gary, Lord! Bless them at the store, Lord!*
*Bless Terrence, Lord!*
*Yes, Lord! Help, Lord!*
*Touch my family, Lord! Help my family, Lord!*
*Please, Lord! Touch that boy, Lord!*

I figured that the Lord knew whom she was referring to. With all the instability going on with my uncles, it could have been any of them. Or it could have been me or any of my boy cousins. I was thankful that I wasn't God and didn't have to decode cryptic requests and interpret tears. In fact, I started tearing up myself. I didn't know why, but I did. I had prayed since I was a little boy, but I hadn't heard any kind of prayer like this. She was praying just like she expected something was going to happen. She had so much conviction. What was inspiring her must have released its hold because after about five minutes or so, she calmed down and stared sniffling. I decided not to say a word and snuck out as stealthily as I had snuck in. I made my way back to my room and got back in bed without her knowing that I was there.

Apparently, my grandfather had made a run back to the store that morning because I heard him come through the door by the kitchen. By that time, grandma had finished with the morning's prayer service. I left my door cracked, so I slightly overheard their conversation.

"Morning, dear." She had enough time to pull herself together before he walked in and to him probably only appeared to just be watching TV and snapping beans. He had no idea of the warfare she was recently engaged in.

"Hey, baby." He responded. "Had to take care of some payroll stuff at the store this morning. Had to make sure the checks were ready for Tuesday. I tell you, it's something keeping up with this business. Oh, did you see Bernard? He came home with me last night."

"Naw, I didn't know he was here?" She sounded a bit doubtful. "You sure he here? I ain't heard a peep outta nobody this morning." She asked almost as if she hoped he was wrong or joking.

"Mm hmm. Go look in the room."

I heard her drop the plastic bag with the beans in it and start shuffling toward my way. I sank in the covers and turned toward the window and acted like I was sleeping. She opened the door and apparently glanced in to see if he was telling the truth. I stared at the wall and feigned sleep, changing breathing patterns and moving as if the opening of the door awakened me. The door shut.

"Lord, I didn't know he was in there, Dillard." I still didn't know why she called him by his last name.

I eventually got up and made my way to the kitchen and acknowledged both of them. Granddad was eating breakfast. "Morning." They both turned and looked at me and spoke.

"Hey, Bernard." He looked up and quickly went back to inhaling his grits and sausage.

"Hey, man! I didn't know you were in the room." Grandma made her confession. She was trying to gauge whether she thought I heard her earlier, but I kept her guessing.

"Yeah, I w-was in there. J-just sleepin' and th-then I heard y-y'all in here." I was lying.

"Alright, well go ahead and wash up. Then you can come over here and get some breakfast." She was relieved.

I washed up and went back to the kitchen. After I got my grits, toast, sausage, and juice, she scurried over to the stove and turned the eye on high.

She wanted my eggs to be hot when I ate them, so she always timed it such that as I sat down, she would walk that hot, black, cast-iron skillet over to the table with the egg still frying in it. "Grandma, you gone b-burn me."

"No, I ain't. Just move your face over." Craftily, she slid the fried arrangement to my plate to round out the breakfast course.

After I ate, I put my dishes in the sink and saw that afternoon's dinner. The pressure cooker was smothering the green beans she had snapped earlier. It had started whistling somewhat like a kettle until my grandmother put the small top on it. Then, it just began to hiss like a snake. I was always fascinated by how that pot did its job.

Terrence had been marching to and from the kitchen all morning. I never knew why he was up so early. It wasn't like he was going to church. And he somehow always knew how to get on my grandmother's last nerve on a Sunday morning. We all knew he was mentally unstable, but sometimes, I think he did stuff out of spite.

He had his own car that was operable and functional, but he specialized in asking to drive my grandmother's car wherever he thought he had to go in the hours leading up to church time. To this day, I never figured that one out. His car sat in the driveway, while we sat stranded, waiting for him to return so we could head out. When he finally returned, my grandmother and I would dash out to the car and zoom to church. My granddad had already left. He drove separately. In fact, Terrence didn't start these shenanigans until after he left.

"Terrence, you know we got to go to church. I don't know why you do this every Sunday." She was like a broken record. He said nothing. He just plopped her keys in the drawer. I shook my head, and we headed out.

Since I had started hanging out more at my grandfolks' house, I had gotten into the rhythm of going to church. For me, it was fun. To me, a lot of people who came seemed to start the countdown to when the service would be done. I couldn't understand that. Why come if the only thing on the mind was not being there? But again, maybe I was just a kid and hadn't learned quite yet how to do things I didn't really feel like doing. I'm sure the adults had the inside scoop on this one.

I was slightly depressed because of how things were still going at home at my father's, wanting a change but not being able to do anything about it. To this day, I never discount the realities and challenges that young people face. They are dealing with situations nowadays that dwarf what I faced as a youngster. I try to be sensitive to young people who have that smile on the outside but are bleeding inwardly, especially if they are products of a broken home or survivors of sexual abuse. I have discovered that they just don't have words to express the brokenness or violation. They do what they know to do. Somehow, they just keep going.

It was good for me to find comfort in the church. People there were pretty down-to-earth. Occasionally, it was a place for a good comedy show, but all in all, it was effective in helping me deal with life. Overall, people were genuinely nice. There were a few bad apples, but I was learning early how to separate the questionable acts of people with the love of Jesus. If I wasn't careful, I would categorize some people's shady attitudes as what it meant to be a Christian. I'm glad I was smart enough to realize that my focus was on the Lord and not on people. He was the One who looked out for me and gave me my direction.

The service started out well with its tradition and songs. After the choir sang, Pastor Thomas got up and commenced with his message. The truths were ringing strong for me, even at such a young age. I guess a lot of the heartache and struggles I faced took away much of the desire to play and fall asleep. I actually listened to what he was saying and felt a deep sense of connection with his words.

"And the Lord can give you strength to make it. He answers prayer. If you pray to move the mountain, He just might not move the mountain. But He'll give you the strength and tenacity to climb it." He knew how to say it to keep you encouraged. It seems as if he were a fly on the wall of my own life. There were definitely some mountains in my life that wouldn't budge, no matter how hard I prayed. I took his words to heart. He kept going. "And He'll put his nail-scarred hands in yours and lead you in the way of life. You may not have all the fine clothes and nice cars, but when it's all said and done, Jesus will give you peace in the midst of confusion."

Everybody was giving amens in confirmation. By the end of the message, Pastor Thomas asked everyone to stand and made an appeal. "Is there one?" He was asking if anyone wanted to come up and accept Jesus as a personal Savior. I didn't know exactly what it meant, but I knew it was nice to be able to get help with life. I had already been praying as a kid to help myself get through a bunch of family drama. What more was this than just an outward sign of something I already thought I was doing anyway? I was only thirteen but felt like I'd lived a couple of lives already. I believed I was

ready. I wasn't sitting with my grandmother. She was in charge of commu-
nion and sat with the other church mothers, who were all donned in white
with their doilies on. "Is there one?" I wasn't sure what song the choir was
singing to assist the pastor with his plea, but it must have worked.

Soon, I felt myself walking to the front. Some looked at me as if to say,
*You're too young to be making a decision like this.* But I kept walking down the
center aisle toward where Pastor Thomas was standing. He was sweating and
carrying on. "Come on up here, Li'l Dillard." Everybody started smiling and
clapping. I was the only one who came down. "I want y'all to know that
God ain't concerned about no age. If he think he ready to give his life to the
Lord, then he ready. And look at him. He standing up here just as bold as
any adult. God used plenty of people in the Bible who were just teenagers.
The three Hebrew boys, Daniel, and He even called David when he was a
young child. So don't tell me that God can't use young people." As I stood,
I wasn't sure why he felt the need to justify my choice. I had made my decision whether he could find justification for it or not. Everyone else seemed to
get on board, though, as he kept finding scriptural references as to why my
decision was valid. He came over to me and put his hand on my shoulder and
told me he was proud of my decision. I couldn't get past how much sweat
I saw on his face, almost like he had just run five miles. I smiled. I didn't
think to look over at my grandmother. It all went so fast. I'm sure she was
proud. She hadn't forced me to do this. I made the decision alone. "Sister
Williams, can you come over here and take his information?"

She came waltzing over and started asking me a barrage of questions, including my full name, address, and the like. I couldn't figure out for the life
of me why she needed my full name, even my jacked-up middle name. Sadly,
the only thing I could remember about her questions was that her breath
was putrid. It was indeed a case of halitosis. But there was nothing *simple*
about it, and it was without question very *chronic*. It made poop smell like
magnolias. I guess 7-11 had run out of Tic Tacs or Big Red, and somebody
was scared to tell her the obvious. This was just my luck. I had heard that
giving your life to the Lord wouldn't solve all of your problems. In fact, I'd
heard that, when you gave your heart to the Lord, this was the point where
things in life could get worse. But this was ridiculous! This was wrong on
so many levels. I didn't expect it to get this worse. This soon.

Her breath had put on karate shoes and was truly kicking. I was hoping
this wasn't a foreshadowing of things to come concerning what more I had to

endure in life, an introduction to the rest of my life, as it were. I hoped this wouldn't be a metaphor for more hurdles I'd have to leap, more storms I'd have to brave. I'd endured enough already, and I just wanted some relief and a break from any modicum of stinkiness, figuratively and literally. And this wasn't helping. She stood there smiling and talking as everyone kept clapping. My eyes were watering, not because I was in a deep, emotional space. But I needed oxygen, and I needed it fast. I just stared at her and tried my best not to collapse under the assault. I'm sure people would have thought I'd been slain by the Spirit of God, but I would have known differently.

So as I stood there answering her questions, I learned the rhythm of holding my breath while she asked the questions and breathing again when answering. A pretty sly move for a kid. As I walked back to my seat, I was waiting for some strange thing to happen, maybe a wind gust to confirm what I did was right, an angel to come by and give me a nice fist bump, a halo to start warming the top of my head. Nothing. I sat down and felt sort of stupid. The other kids were looking at me like I was crazy. How dare I interrupt the service by actually responding to a public call for commitment to Jesus. I just acted like I didn't see them. I somehow knew that what I did was right for me and that God would continue to help me on my journey.

"Will you *please* get out my way?" Keva was trying to get past me in the kitchen. I was staring in the frig, trying to determine what I wanted. Grapes? Kool-aid? Cake? "I 'on't see why you standing in front of the 'frigerator with the door open. You know what's in there and what ain't in there. Standing there looking stupid wit the door open ain't gone change nothing."

"Don't w-worry 'bout it. You ain't p-paying the bill." I got smart back.

"I ain't got to ta know what you doin' is stupid." She brushed past me and nudged me on purpose to get me out of the way.

"Keva, stop playin'."

"Well, get out o' the way."

We were both now in high school. I was a freshman, Keva a senior. But one would have thought we were still kids. Both of us had to be the one who was right. We had managed to fend for ourselves pretty well, though, given the reality. It had just become second nature for us to get into survival mode, even if it meant striking out at each other. Both of us were always at each other's throat. Dwayne, Jr., now pushing twenty-one, had tried college, NCCU, but had to stop mostly because of a lack of financial support. He seemed to process instability a little different. Whereas Keva and I kept fighting to make our situations better, he seemed to just let chips fall where they did. He already had a laid-back personality. And if things presented too much of a challenge, he just went with the flow of life. He would work several jobs and eventually end up at the family restaurant as a key employee.

High school was a little more of a challenge and required more dedication to get through. Keva always tried to terrorize me whenever I made a transition from one level of education to another. She would tell me something like, "Wait 'til you get to high school. It's gone be way harder than middle school." I never could tell if this was her way of trying to scare me or her strange way of trying to be a mother and keep me focused. Either way, I took heed and studied my behind off. I was pretty focused, but it would be a little difficult to do so at night while trying to finish writing papers or doing math problems because of the obvious.

After daddy would come in from working, he'd see me sitting at the kitchen table with a lamp on as I attempted to solve some problems. It must have been 11:00, and he'd seem as if this was the end of a hard day's night for him. "Hey, Bernie. What you working on?"

"Just some math stuff."

"Okay, good. Don't stay up too late, though." Interesting advice since I knew that, according to history, he'd be staying up pretty late with his own distractions.

"Kay."

Pretty soon, I knew the inevitable would happen. Like clockwork, somebody would come knock on the door around midnight. My father would never hear it, so I would look out of the kitchen door window and just stare. "Dwayne there?" I wouldn't respond. I'd close the window blinds, walk back to his room, and tell him that someone was at the door.

He'd let them in, and they would start their late-night funfest. There was no masking or cover-up. By this age, I knew very well what was transpiring. When the door opened, I didn't even look up to acknowledge the people entering. Maybe there were two, no more than three. I would just stay preoccupied with figuring out some triviality, like applying the logarithmic properties to some equation.

"Wassup, Li'l Dillard?" They saw me working and thought it rude not to speak.

I didn't respond. I acted so engrossed in what I was doing, but my heart was really hurting.

"Bernie, don't stay up too late." My father repeated his earlier advice. I guess he wanted them to catch a glimpse of how much control he had and how great of a fatherly job he was doing. All smoke and mirrors. I wanted to tell him he already told me that, but "Kay" only managed to come out. They'd all go back to his room and close the door. By this time, I was normally tired, so I strained to hear the fun that was going on. All I could manage to hear was the clanging of the instruments used to weigh what I assumed was cocaine. I never really knew for sure. Night in, night out. This was the pattern I just buckled down and dealt with. *This can't last forever* was often what I'd tell myself. *Just try to keep going and keep praying* was the stale advice with which I'd counsel myself. I'd retire around 1:00 in the morning, climb into the bed, and just try as much as possible to zone out whatever happiness was going on the next room over.

To this day, I remain amazed that nothing happened to Dwayne, Keva, or me during these late-night visits. Someone could have easily taken advantage of us to get back at my father for any transactions that may have gone awry or for any other vendetta that others may have had against him. With Keva being a female, his so-called friends could have violated her in a fit of rage toward my father. Seeking revenge on children happens more frequently than most people want to admit as it relates to drug involvement and settling scores with users. I remain grateful, however, that God kept His eye on us in that respect and protected us. Maybe He knew we were fighting to survive already and that this probably would have been too much to bear.

# stay focused and move forward

T ypically in the mornings, it was the same ole same ole. Keva would get up before the crack of dawn and start preparing herself. She had grown up to be a beautiful girl, although I would have never told her that. I would often hear her stirring about, being her own parent and preparing herself for school. Her goings-about would awaken me, so I guess I'd better get up too. My father was knocked out from the revelry the night before. If we depended on him to get us ready, we'd be out of luck. I questioned Keva as to why she had to get up and start getting ready so early. With the sun still asleep, there was nothing but pitch darkness outside. Why did she have to leave so early?

"Because I can. I got to go meet Karl." He was her boyfriend.

"Keva, you can see Karl w-when you get to school when the school bus comes." I tried the best I could to rationalize with her to wait. "Why you just can't wait 'til it get l-light outside?"

"Because I feel like leaving now." She had a stubborn sense like my mother. Once she made up her mind to do something, she did it. Case closed.

And this was all complicated by the fact that the city bus she had to catch was the next neighborhood over. The shortest route there from where we stayed was scary. She had to walk all the way down our street and make a right through a thick set of woods. I couldn't believe she could be so stupid to make this decision every morning. This fueled my anger toward my father even more. Why couldn't he get up and tell her she couldn't do this? He had no clue she was making this decision. In her mind, it was okay, so that's all that mattered.

What made the situation even worse was that it was known that Crazy Ed hung out in the wooded area. He had a well-known mental problem and just made his dwelling among those trees and branches. I had even walked by that same area one afternoon on my way home and saw him chilling there, laughing with himself at some apparent inside joke. He was too creepy for me. How could Keva keep putting herself in such a potentially dangerous situation? And since it was so early in the morning, hardly anybody would hear her if Crazy Ed lived up to his name and confronted her and did something egregious. This was the argument I posed to her, very well thought-out and delivered, so as to dissuade her from continuing the insane pattern. But Keva was Keva. I could have hauled in three wheelbarrows' worth of evidence as to why this was a bad decision, but it was always met with the same response from her.

"So!" It was a statement and not a question to be answered. That was that. She would grab her book bag and head into oblivion.

Almost always, I did what I only knew to do. I'd walk back to my room while Dwayne slept, fall to my knees, and have at it. *Lord, please protect her. I don't know why she decides to do this, but protect her. Don't let that man do anything to her while she going through the woods. In Jesus' name.* I had heard from somebody that God protected fools and babies, and Keva was definitely no baby.

After she left, I got myself together. Showered. Dressed. Got my homework papers together. Needed lunch money, so time to wake up daddy.

"Daddy." I leaned against the door and pushed it against the shaggy carpet until it cracked open. I heard all snores. "Daddy." I got louder. My yellow ride would be here soon, so I had better step up and get what I needed to get. "Daddy!" This time, I almost shouted.

"What, Bernie?" He asked like he didn't know what I needed.

"I need lunch money." We went through this every morning. I didn't know why he just didn't give me money for the week. That would have been too much like the right thing to do.

"Hand me my pants." He said it as if I knew which pair he was referring to and where they were. I just fiddled around until I picked up something that had what I thought was a wallet in it. Finally, I had struck gold and would be able to buy my pizza for another day. What should have been a simple act seemed to always turn into a main event. Now I could catch the bus in peace and leave him to get his rest before he left for work.

Strangely, I always would think the worst when I arrived at school. I just knew there was always a possibility of getting to school and finding out that Keva hadn't made it. I tried not to let these thoughts dominate me, but I had learned how to be a realist and was just wired to consider all options, whether good or bad. I guess my experiences thus far had taught me to stay on guard, expect the best, but not to be surprised if things went southward. Whenever I got to school and saw her during the day, I was thankful that God had protected the fool one more day.

I had decided to keep up with the running in high school. Keva had stopped running and switched her interest to basketball. She had taken up the forward position on the team, much to the disappointment of Coach Rumsfeld. He was an octogenarian and had the respect of everyone in the Durham community when it came to shaping and molding the lives of the young people. He was the oldest high school track coach in the country and received several awards for this distinction and had several track meets named in honor of him. He was the no-nonsense track coach, who had a known reputation for dragging his athletes through the mud to get them in shape to win championships. On a deeper level, though, his commitment was really in helping us deal with life and the challenges it presented. At almost every practice, he never ceased to use my sister as the standard for baton-passing for relay work.

"Hell, the best person I've ever seen receive the baton from someone is Bernard's sister, TaKeva Dillard. There's no one else I know who can pass that baton better than she can." Coach Rumsfeld was bragging, and I'd just stand and roll my eyes in my head because she wasn't even there at the practice. Mostly everyone would look at me and wonder why she wasn't out there running. "But no, she decides she wants to be Ms. Michael Jordan and play basketball. She needs to be out here running with you guys." I had to listen to this every time we did relay work.

"Bernard, why your sister ain't out here running?" Toni was inquiring about Keva's choice. Toni and I had remained close and were running at the same high school now. The drama we went through when we first met was water under the bridge. We ran together during the summer, and now we ran together at Hillside.

"I guess because she wants to play basketball." I was tired of coming to her defense for making her own choices.

Coach Rumsfeld specialized in breaking us down and then building us back up. He had that old-school mentality. He was a torturous stalwart whose way it was. With him, there were no shortcuts to success. He trained us like we were getting ready to go off to Afghanistan or Iran. Practices were gruesome to the point that it wasn't uncommon for us to be on the side of the track regurgitating whatever it was we ate earlier that day. His slight smirk seemed to be just the approval he needed as a sign that we were giving our all. And he never hesitated to show that his aged lungs were just fine.

"What are you doing, Dillard?!" We were running 400 meters and were clear on the other side of the track, but I could hear his ticked-off voice like he was running beside me. "Get up there, Dillard. Ain't no way that Meechie should be in front of you. Get up there. Right now!" We were running on a dirt track, but this was no excuse for him. We had better be ready to compete with the other schools once we got on the real one.

When we finished, he chastised me again. "Look, son, you not giving all you got. If you don't wanna work, don't come out here wasting time." I walked off pouting and catching my breath from just running the lap in blazing speed. There was no satisfying him. I was only a freshman, but he kept hounding me like I was a senior. I partially blamed Keva for setting the bar in his mind too high for what he perceived was the talent level for all Dillards. After practice, though, he turned back to normal and became more of a father figure. It was like night and day. He'd always shoot the breeze with other coaches while the athletes filed in their cars and drove home and while others climbed in the cars of those who were picking them up. Naturally, I was always the last one left, waiting to be picked up by someone I knew wasn't coming. Somehow, I felt like Coach knew about my situation at home, but he never confronted me about it. Maybe this is why he demanded so much of me so early. Maybe he called himself teaching me how to be tough and not to succumb mentally to external pressures. Whatever his strategy, it always ended on a mild note.

He even found the time to make us laugh and to joke with us. We had just finished practice one day and, out of nowhere, he asked us, "So what was the fruit that Adam ate in the garden that made him get in so much trouble?" All the girls had left for the day, and he was going to school the fellows with a joke he learned earlier in his life. He and Coach Miles, who was his assistant and my Latin teacher, were smiling cunningly at each other, wondering if we'd crack the code.

We guys looked at each other and wondered what this inside scoop was. I decided I'd go for it. "Everybody knows it was an apple, Coach." I'd go ahead and state the obvious but was obviously wrong.

"Nope." Coach Rumsfeld quickly shot my answer down. "What was it, Ricky?"

Ricky had no earthly idea what was being discussed. "Man, Coach, I 'on't know."

"Y'all guys don't know nothin'. Hell, y'all so smart but ya don't know nothin' about Adam in the garden. All this book knowledge and ya don't know nothin'." He and Coach Miles started laughing again. This recent comment was to provoke Wes, who was a year ahead of me, first in his class academically, and a fast runner.

Wes took the bait. "Well, it doesn't say in particular, Coach Rumsfeld. We're not really allowed to assume the kind of fruit that it was. That would be a type of literary fallacy, to impose our own ideas, which the story is silent about." We all looked at him and burst out laughing, including both coaches.

"Nope," answered Coach. "Ah, hell, Wes, you're too smart for your own good. Call me up when you pass the bar. I'll need a good lawyer when I turn ninety." He always prefaced his response with *Ah, hell*. "C'mon, Meechie. What was the fruit that Adam ate that got him in so much trouble?" Oh Lord, why did Coach single out Meechie? This was a guy who could have pursued a career as a stand-up comedian. It wasn't necessarily what he said. It was how he said it. Many a day, we'd get in trouble with Coach because Meechie was so busy cracking jokes that we lost our focus during the workout. And this was just what Meechie wanted. His own stage. While he smiled a wide smile, Coach asked him again, "Ah, hell, son, what was the fruit Adam ate while he was in the garden that got God so upset? Was it an orange? An apricot? Grapes? Kiwi? What was it, Meechie?" The chuckles continued because we all knew Meechie had something up his sleeve.

Knowing he had a rapt audience, he stepped away from the crowd to single out this, his moment. He looked at me, looked at the other guys, looked at Coach Miles and then back at Coach Rumsfeld, lifted both arms and hands to declare himself on the level of a god and belted out, "IT WAS A CHERRY, COACH!!!"

We all ended up on the ground laughing uncontrollably because we couldn't contain ourselves. As soon as he said it, we got it. Meechie had solved the riddle. He gave Coach Rumsfeld the precise answer that he wanted. Coach Rumsfeld was laughing so hard that he was tearing up, wondering how it was that this boy was able to figure out the solution. He took out his hankie and wiped his eyes and wiped under his nose, next to his signature mole. Coach Miles' white visage started turning redder than . . . well, a cherry. Even Wes understood the undercurrents of the response. We couldn't believe that Meechie had caught on to the coaches' sneaky test of what we knew about the birds-and-the-bees component of our manhood. And he made it worst by jumping up and down in 360s with his arms still raised, like he had won a boxing match with Muhammad Ali. "It was a cherry! It was a cherry, Coach!" He kept voicing the victor's chant.

Such was the personality of Coach Rumsfeld. Sure, he knew when to be tough, but he also knew when to laugh and how to inch us closer to the manhood arena. Out of all the guys, though, he seemed to take a liking to me, maybe because I was often the last one waiting for a ride that wasn't coming. After he drove up beside me as I was walking home one day, he just agreed to drop me off at the restaurant after practices.

"C'mon, Dillard, let's go." It was a little out of his way but not too much. Plus, he could play father for another ten minutes. He only had daughters, so he relished the time that he could shift into father mode for his athletes. The restaurant was only a five-minute drive but not the way he drove. I'd climb into the front seat of his bluish car and know I'd be in for my daily dose of grandfatherly advice. I would just stare out of the passenger's window while he dropped the knowledge on me. "It's a whole lotta kids out here, son, who waste the opportunities they have. They get caught up in a lot of stuff that they shouldn't."

I tried to rationalize the reason for this. *Why is he talking to me about this? He acts like I'm a hoodlum or something. Didn't he see how hard I worked at practice today? He had to see me over there throwing up. It's just no satisfying him.*

"You gotta realize that you gotta have your own goals and work toward 'em. It's all about focus in life. You can do whatever you put your mind to.

You just can't be wishy-washy and think you gone achieve some'm. Are you listening to what I'm sayin', son?"

*Why is he driving so slow? He must be going eighteen miles per hour. I can probably get there quicker if I walked. Just sit back and watch all the other cars zoom by.*

"Yessir."

After what seemed like an eternity, we finally pulled into the restaurant parking lot. He had given his daily advice and was ready to release me.

"Here we go, Mr. Bernard."

"Thanks for the r-ride, Coach. I really ap-ap-preciate it."

"I know, son. Just stay focus and make something of yourself."

"'Kay." I didn't know what that second part meant, but I was just ready to get out of there. "See you t-tomorrow."

"Alright, son."

I'd enter the restaurant and head to the back and start on my homework. I had gotten used to not hinting to my father that he was supposed to pick me up. I guess he figured I'd keep making things work as I had been doing. After eating some chittlins, potato salad, and collard greens, I'd finish up with my school work and just wait until closing time, hop in the car with him, and head home.

Later in life, I'd write Coach Rumsfeld a heartfelt letter of thanks for all the time he invested to keep me aiming high and looking forward. In it, I'd reveal the details of what I had endured and intimate my feelings of gratitude toward him. Even during college breaks, I'd go visit him, sit in his living room, eat a slice of sweet potato pie that he offered, and provide him updates with how challenging college life was. We'd laugh and reminisce and move on. He eventually passed away, but the lessons that he imparted to me live on in decisions and choices I make day to day. Whenever I feel like slacking, I can always hear his authoritative and distinct voice, that voice in the car, the voice yelling across the track, prodding me along and encouraging me to stay focused and move forward.

# looking into a mirror

L
ife in high school was rather eventful. I had managed to keep myself fairly busy in spite of how I thought things should be. Nowadays, it seems like the dysfunctional family is the new normal. The aberration seems to be the regular two-parent model. Hence, I discovered that being successful coming from environs like mine was not necessarily anomalous. Strangely enough, I had found fulfillment in taking on leadership roles in school. Somehow, I convinced myself that participating in school politics was a good way to help me stay focused and give back to my school and community. Over the years, I had been voted in as president of my freshman and sophomore classes. I wasn't running unopposed, so I didn't win by default. I had managed to connect with my classmates to the point that they trusted me to be their voice. I wasn't quite sure what I was thinking by getting involved in these capacities. Maybe in my mind, it was just something else to do to fill up the time and space in my world. I lost the run for junior class president. Harmon won that one. His father would eventually become mayor of Durham, so I concluded he had a predisposition to win. It wasn't too bad losing to someone who probably had leadership in the blood. Even though I lost that race, my junior year still proved to be eventful in its own way, especially as it related to Toni.

That spring school day started out as it normally did. The normal pizza and fries for lunch had hit the spot. A group of friends and I ate in Ms. Pratt's class while she graded papers and prepared for her class on next period. I had to hurry up and finish my homework because it was due in trig class, which was right after lunch.

"Y'all, w-what's the cosecant of theta in number four?" I was asking a few of the other students who were also in the same class and who ate lunch in the same room.

"I sort of got stuck on that one too when I was doing it." Peter was talking in between pizza bites. "You just gotta draw the right triangle, find the missing side, and then use the definition of cosecant. Like opposite over adjacent or hypotenuse over adjacent. Something like that."

"Oh, aight." I took his advice and just looked up the definition of the term. "Okay, I see. It's j-just one over the sine, so you flip the f-fraction for opposite over hypotenuse. I hate those weird trig functions."

We finished eating, and I finished my homework. The bell rang to signify the end of the lunch period, and we headed out. "Bye, Ms. Pratt." We'd be back after trig for her English class. "I left my English book on the desk. You know how they get with us going to our lockers in between classes."

"That's fine, Bernard. Just go ahead to math before you get marked late."

We all made our way through the cramped halls. People had their Walkman radios and their cassette tapes, pressing rewind to get it queued before class started. I got to Ms. Robinson's class, grabbed my seat, and changed one final answer before turning in the homework. Toni came bursting through the door and made her announcement.

"I'm here, y'all!"

"So?" Nona made everyone in the class laugh by trivializing Toni's presence.

"So this!" Toni slyly shot her the bird and plopped in her seat right in front of me.

"Girl, you stupid." I couldn't resist.

Our friendship had mushroomed into something great, far past our initial encounter when I thought she was ghetto. Honestly, I still thought she was ghetto, but you just had to get to know her. Her mode was set to survival, too. She had come a long way. She herself was finding a way to rise above her own challenges. She was a year ahead of me, had won the race for vice president of the student government, and was applying to colleges. She said she'd probably go to Pitt on a track scholarship, but she hadn't made her final decision yet. Of course, she was making her mark on the track team in high school. Coach Rumsfeld loved him some Toni. He made her the poster child for conquering competition. Admittedly, McDougald Terrace was the projects that made her tough. She really had no other choice.

Ms. Robinson had started in on the lesson. She had decided to review the properties of the right triangle and was saying something about one of the homework problems. She had drawn a right triangle and drew theta. As I was following what she was saying, Toni quickly turned her head around, stared at me, and started shaking her head left to right, like she couldn't believe something that she knew.

"What?" I whispered so as not to disturb the flow of the lesson.

"Boy, you ain't gone believe what I got to tell you."

"Toni, what?"

"I'll tell you after class."

"Toni, why you g-gone sit up and do that? You know I ain't gone be d-doing nothing but thinking about it all p-period. You shoulda just w-waited to just tell me after class."

"I know. I just wanted you to know that I got something to tell you. You ain't gone believe it."

"And so, Toni, what did we say was the definition of tangent?" Ms. Robinson was trying to regain management of her class as a whole, and she wasn't about to let Toni or me disrupt her lesson.

"Umm. Let's see." Toni was trying to remember.

"Bernard?" Ms. Robinson was trying to focus me, too.

"It's sine over cosine." I knew that one already. Glad she didn't ask me about secant.

"Okay, good." Ms. Robinson continued the lesson, knowing she had accomplished her task of regaining our focus.

Toni kept looking straight but slipped me a note from a torn sheet of notebook paper. I opened it and read it. *I'll let you know after class.*

I had tuned Ms. Robinson out for the rest of the class. What was so important that Toni looked the way she did? I'd just have to wait until the class was over, which seemed to be forever. Soon, Ms. Robinson wrote the homework problems on the board, which were due in a few days. Once the bell rang, we packed up and started walking into the hallway.

"Boy, you ain't gone believe this. I was just chillin' and sittin' at my house on yesterday with my boyfriend. We was just talkin' and talkin' and I mentioned how you and me were real close and on the track team together."

"That's the news you been m-making me wait for?" I felt like a balloon that had been deflated.

"Just wait. I'ma tell you. You so impatient." She resumed the story. "And we kept on talkin', and you ain't gone guess what he told me."

"What, Toni?" I was irritated, and she knew it, so she decided to drop the bomb.

"He said y'all got the same father."

I leaned back on one of the lockers, resting my right foot on it for balance. I was gauging whether or not this was a joke. "Toni, whatever. Stop playin'. This ain't April Fool's Day."

"Bernard, I swear, I ain't playin'. He said y'all got the same father."

I saw in her face that she was serious. I knew her and her joking face, and this one wasn't it. This face with which she stared at me was stone cold and showed no trace of humor. "His name is Marko, and he stay with his mama over in McDougald Terrace."

"You *is* serious!" It was a statement, admitting a type of defeat. Toni was a year older than I, so I wondered how old he was. "Is he older than you?"

"Yep, he a few years older than me." On the timeline for my own family, this placed him in between Dwayne, Jr. and Keva. I never really looked for information like hidden secrets in my family. They always seemed to search for and find me, though. "You can come over my house tonight and meet him if you want. He's cool."

I didn't really know how to respond. How do you respond to someone who says, "Oh yeah, by the way, my boyfriend is your brother?" I agreed to meet him, just to satisfy my own curiosity.

Much of what happened the rest of the day seemed blurry. I didn't really know what to expect. I decided not to tell Dwayne, Jr. or Keva until after I really met him. I never knew with Toni. She still could have been trying to throw me for a loop. I just didn't know.

Later that night, Toni called and said she was on her way to come and pick me up. I had a driver's license but no car, so she offered to swing by and take me to his home. As we rode over, I still kept thinking she was going to finally admit to this cunning ploy and head to McDonald's or someplace to get something to eat. She pulled up to some house close to the projects and turned off the car. We both stepped out, and I followed her to the door. I wasn't sure why, but I was shaking a little. The truth of the matter was that she was not lying. I was entering a home full of strangers who probably knew more about me and my beginnings more than even I did.

Toni walked in just like she lived there and stood at the door, beckoning for me to come in. I tried to lighten the mood by joking with her as I walked in. "How you gone invite m-me inside a h-house that ain't even y-yours?"

The humor was overshadowed by the returning stuttering issue, a sure sign confirming my nervousness.

A lady sat on the couch with her legs crossed. She kept moving the leg that did the crossing back and forth, making it appear to bounce. She sat and pulled on a cigarette. The living room was a little dark, and no real effort was put into making it brighter. I only saw her faintly but saw the hot orange color at the end of the cigarette, which illumined in the darkness when she pulled on it. I even managed to make out the smoke she exhaled.

"Hey, Bernard."

"Hello." I didn't know how to address her because I didn't know who she was.

"How's your daddy?"

"He d-doin' good."

"Tell him Pam said 'Hello.'"

"Okay."

We kept walking toward the back. Toni filled me in. "Das Marko mama."

That was a fine time to tell me. I just spoke with another other woman. We kept walking toward the back. "Marko!" Toni just yelled for him out of nowhere. We approached the door toward the end of the hall, and suddenly he came out into the hallway and startled me.

"Wassup, yo."

I stared at him and couldn't really say anything at first. I just stared at him somewhat, trying to quickly see my father. I had heard about these types of situations in families but never thought it would hit mine. Hoping it wouldn't come off as rude, I just simply stared at him. Even though I couldn't necessarily see my father, I strangely saw me. It seemed as though I was staring into a mirror. I realized the power of genes. "H-Hey, man. H-How's it going?" At the outset, he appeared to have somewhat of a tougher exterior than I and rightfully so. He had to learn to make it on the streets of the projects. But even though I didn't have to work my way around the projects, I had my own daily battles with living in my own unpleasantries, so honestly we weren't that different. And let's face it, both of us were lacking a father, him physically and me emotionally.

"Marko, this Bernard. Bernard, this Marko." Toni tried to ease the tensions.

"Yeah, I th-think I figured that out by now, Toni." We three sort of laughed.

We went back into his room and just sat. What do you really say to someone in this situation? *Nice to meet you? How's it going?* I had no clue. We chitchatted about something that was unimportant in the grand scheme of things. So after about an hour of talking about nothing, I decided that I should head home. After saying our goodbyes, Toni and I walked out, and she drove me back home. I'm sure I said goodbye to Pam, but I don't remember doing so.

During that time, I only thought about how it related to me directly and how this was yet another secret swept under my own family rug. On a larger scale, though, I can't help but think about the number of children who have to deal with the realities of not knowing who their fathers are or not having a relationship with their father. I believe strongly that a great deal of the anger that young males and young women display is a direct off-shoot of their lack of feeling valued by their fathers. It's a quiet demonstration of disapproval for how they as children have been disregarded by their own male flesh and blood. Finding acceptance through promiscuity, the drug scene, gang families, and other avenues can be attributable to a sense of fatherlessness or shunning from fathers, both directly and indirectly.

And by "fatherless," we expand the definition to include situations not just where the father is physically missing from the home, but situations in which the father is physically present but emotionally detached. It becomes comparable to dangling the carrot in front of the horse's mouth. The rider sits atop the horse and holds the stick with the carrot attached only a short distance from the horse. The rider then makes the horse chase the juicy, tempting carrot. Of course, the horse sees it and goes after it only to realize that the distance between horse and carrot will forever remain the same. Arguably, this becomes more torturous for the horse because the carrot is so close but yet so far. And all the horse can show for its carrot-chasing effort are heavy panting and aching muscles. It almost seems better if the carrot was not a goal to reach for than for the horse to see it and not be able to attain it. Over the years, the physical presence of the father but emotional void of his nurturing has been the all-elusive carrot that many a child has struggled to capture, often to no avail. It is this hazardous game of chase, of cat and mouse, that has contributed to much rage and frustration in the lives of so many young adults.

A few statistics caught my attention as they relate to the absence or presence of this man we call the father. Most of these findings are not shocking but still demand consideration:

- Fatherless children are at a dramatically greater risk of drug and alcohol abuse, mental illness, suicide, poor educational performance, teen pregnancy, and criminality (*Survey on Child Health*).
- There is an interesting correlation between male and female gang involvement and the absence of a father in the home. In El Paso, which has a large Hispanic base, some of the gangs have colorful names like Folk Nation and Los Fatherless (*TELEMASP Bulletin*).
- Children who have an involved father who displays affection are more likely to be emotionally secure, confident to explore their surroundings, and have better social connections with peers. They are less likely to get in trouble at home, school, or in the neighborhood (*Fatherhood: Research, Interventions and Policies*).
- It is when fathers work full time or overtime and children perceive that they do not spend enough time with their fathers that their bullying behavior toward other children at school increases (*Science Daily*).
- Numerous studies find that an active and nurturing style of fathering is associated with better verbal skills, intellectual functioning, and academic achievement among adolescents (*Psychological Reports*).
- 80% of rapists motivated with displaced anger come from fatherless homes (*Criminal Justice & Behavior*).
- Even in high crime neighborhoods, 90% of children from stable two-parent homes, where the father is involved, do not become delinquents (*Development and Psychopathology*).
- Boys who grow up in father-absent homes are more likely than those in father-present homes to have trouble establishing appropriate sex roles and gender identity (*Fatherless Children*).
- Fathers wield a priceless effect against bullying. For a would-be bully, knowing that there is a dad and that he is often seen in the school, is a strong deterrent (*Our Family World*).

Of course, there are always those who defy either of these statistics. Indeed, there is no strict sense of causality with regard to any of the data, good or bad. In other words, the lack of a father does not *cause* teen pregnancy, for example. However, one cannot deny that there is a strong correlation with these statistics and whether the father is present or not. The ultimate punchline underlying these statistics is that we need our fathers.

The effects of a father's absence transcend gender, race, sexual orientation, socio-economic status, and the like. We have got to come to a point where we agree that a father's wallet is no substitute for his physical and emotional presence. This omen is probably the only beast left, which does not discriminate. Its effects are sure and long-lasting, unless intervention happens. This is why we as men have to step up and become role models to those who have no fathers and not prey on their vulnerabilities and their need for love. We as uncles, teachers, actors, athletes, cousins, coaches, and basic concerned males must reach out and serve as role models. Even though we may not have had the best examples of fatherhood, we have to pay it forward by garnering strength to break the cycle of neglect and pour into the lives of the next generation of youth so they can reach their full potential.

Needless to say, Marko, my brother, managed to do the best in life that he could. After my initial meeting with him, I only ran into him once more in Durham. My grandmother and I were in the grocery store, and we three all ended up in the same checkout line. She sensed something peculiar because as he and I spoke, she realized how similar we looked. When we got outside, I broke the news to her, after which she confessed, "You know, I looked at him and then looked at you and then back at him again. I was sholl just getting ready to say that y'all look mighty much alike."

As was her nature to try to make the best of awkward situations, she approached him before he drove off and did her best to make him feel welcomed. "You know, I want you to always feel like you a part of this family. Things in life don't always go the way we want them, but just know that even though I don't know you that well, I still want to say that I love you."

"Thank you, ma'am" was all he could muster in response. His loss for words was understandable. He was finishing up his teen years and probably didn't miss much what he never had. He never really saw the carrot anyway.

I didn't bother trying to cultivate a sense of bonding with him either since he had entered his own adult world and sense of autonomy. To be honest, I was trying myself to survive the best way I could. At this point, it was every son for himself. He managed to survive the best way he could, given the resources in life that he had. He moved to Kansas for a while with another one of his girlfriends, who also happened to be another friend with whom I ran track. He moved back to Durham and, as far as I know, grew to become a functional part of society. I can't fathom, however, how hard it has been for him and others like him to stay afloat emotionally and fight through the silent pain of figuring out how to make the transition from boy to man without fatherly guidance. Somehow, I have a feeling that he has navigated his way through life to the best of his ability and has turned out pretty well.

# she was the only one

"Hi, Raquel, I just wanted to bring these muffins over here to you all this morning. I was outside clipping some bushes, and I heard your boys through the window just laughing away. It really brightened my day!" Peggy had come over this Saturday morning and was bringing some goodies for us. We had no knowledge that our laughter spilled outside. We were just acting foolishly by default.

"Thank you, Peggy. I didn't even know they were that loud in there."

"Oh, they are no problem at all. It was actually refreshing. *Their* laughter made *me* start laughing. Anyway, let me get back over here and finish clipping these bushes. They talking 'bout rain tomorrow, and I need to get this done."

"Alright, well thanks again, girl. Have a good one." Raquel closed the door and headed upstairs. She startled us a little when she opened the door to where we slept. We were busy talking about nothing and laughing about it. "Ms. Butler just came over and brought some muffins for you guys. She said she heard y'all laughing through the window. What in the world is so funny this early in the morning?"

We couldn't explain because we honestly didn't know, but we just kept on laughing.

"You know what? Y'all need help." She closed the door and went back downstairs.

What Peggy hadn't realized was that only one of the guilty parties was one of Raquel's boys. I was the other culprit. I was visiting for a few days. Enzo and I were lying in our beds and acting our age, simply joking about anything from some family members to the music on Scooby-Doo. Enzo, my cousin, was the oldest of three and slightly younger than I was. His mom, Raquel, was my father's sister and was the only one of them who had

119

managed to move away from the Durham area. I hadn't understood what possessed her to move to some place as otherworldly as Michigan, but she seemed to like what it offered, including the cold temperature and frequent snow. Maybe she just decided to stay after getting her master's from Western Michigan. But whatever floated her boat was her business.

Their family came back to Durham to visit on occasion. Even though they weren't my immediate family, there was a sense of sadness I'd experience when they visited. I'd frequently compare their bliss and happiness with the turmoil I was enduring and would become withdrawn and a bit angry. I was happy for them but always felt like I didn't quite measure up. But whenever I made it up north to visit them, Enzo and I made it a point to act as foolish as we could.

"Oom-pepe-oom-pe-oom-pe-oom-pepe-oom-pe-oom-pe-oom . . ." We were mimicking the music on certain parts of Scooby-Doo and would make our own adaptation of it. It was a language and code that only we understood, which made it that much funnier. It was a great experience. I always managed to force my way into what I thought was a stable family structure, even if it were only for a weekend or so. I was determined to have some sense of normalcy in life. And this weekend would be spent in the Midwest, enjoying this newness of experience.

Our only preoccupation was with laughing and having fun. I could take a break from having to act like an adult. I could be a kid again, and I simply reveled in it. They had a ping-pong table downstairs, where Calvin, one of Enzo's brothers, and I would spend a lot of time facing off against each other. I also spent a lot of time in Uncle Devyn's homemade studio. He was a lover of music and had his own music studio cave downstairs, where he could get away from the humdrum daily goings-on. I spent a lot of time there, not because I was such a lover of music but because it was such a different space. I had never seen anything like it and was rather enamored of the simple but interesting setup.

We had loosely planned the day. We'd eat, relax, and have fun somewhere in the city. At some point during the day, Aunt Raquel and I ended up in the car to go pick some things up in the city. Enzo and his brothers were with their father taking care of whatever business they had to tend to at the moment. I just sat in the passenger's seat, taking in the beauty of the city and admiring some of the historic sights. It was refreshing to see something different, something other than the banalities of Durham.

"So, how you liking it up here?" Aunt Raquel broke the silence.

"It's real nice. It's way different than Durham." I was admiring the city overall.

"Are you okay? You don't seem as happy as you used to. I know you always had to deal with the stuff at home, but it seems like something else is bothering you." She was probing.

I hadn't realized she had been studying and reading me. "Well, yeah sort of, but it's okay. It's not a big deal." I was hoping she'd drop it.

"Well, how long have you been bothered by it?"

"I think ever since one of Dwayne's friends touched me the wrong way. I've been thinking about it a lot but didn't want to worry anybody about it."

"Really? When did this happen?"

"Um, a while back. When I was about nine or around that time."

"How long did it happen?"

"Off and on for about a year. He acted like he was trying to teach me how to sleep with girls, but now I see that's not what he really wanted to do."

"Oh, my God! Bernard, I am so sorry." She had begun crying quietly. I glanced over to her and saw a tear roll down her right cheek.

"It's okay. I just deal with it and try not to worry about it." In a sense, I was comforting her. Over time, I had learned how to compartmentalize it, keep it in its place, and move forward the best I could.

"Well, just know that you don't have to commit suicide or anything like that." I guess she wanted to make sure she addressed the most extreme case of options I'd possibly consider.

"Suicide? I like living too much." Interesting statement coming from a sixteen-year old. I really did like life. I couldn't quite understand those who wanted to end their life. I guess my reliance on Christ was helping to give me some sense of peace and perspective. "Naw, I ain't killing myself. To be honest, I don't even think I'd know how to. I'd probably mess up trying it." We both laughed. "I just hate mama." I said the statement in a matter-of-fact manner, out of the blue. It seemed to come out of nowhere, and it struck her by surprise.

"Why do you say that?"

"It don't seem like she care about us. Seems like she just left and don't really care about us and all those people daddy bringing in the house." I thought Aunt Raquel would come to her brother's defense, but she remained quiet and let me speak. "She know h-how mean daddy is. I d-don't see why sh-she don't come and get us and t-take us outta there." The stuttering had started back. I was obviously upset by it. "I w-want to leave from there."

"I see." This was all she said.

"I really j-just don't understand it."

We continued to talk about things on a smaller scale, but it felt pretty good to finally be able to talk to somebody about those things that were tucked away in the dark recesses of my heart and mind. I have always remained grateful for Aunt Raquel and her ability to see something wrong and initiate conversation about it. If nothing else, I felt as if I mattered in some way and that my life was worth inquiring about. A burden had been lifted, and I realized that she was the only one who helped me to open up about something so tragic. We finished with our errands and got back home and blended back in with everyone else. Soon, we went to bed. Enzo and I started acting silly again, laughing well into the night about nothing.

"Y'all, that's enough! Please keep it down." Aunt Raquel yelled from her room. So we kept joking but quieter. We were laughing until we were crying. Eventually, I said something to him, and he didn't respond. That was my cue that he finally went to sleep, so I had better follow suit. I stared at the ceiling and tried to count the weird things that stuck out through it. Pretty soon, they vanished.

*I had been running block to block, but the guy chasing me with the gun was gaining ground. I decided to keep running, bobbing and weaving between trees to secure some type of protection. I got to some abandoned building that had a ladder and decided to climb it. He kept shouting my name, saying he was going to finally take me out. I climbed like it was no tomorrow. By the time I knew it, I had climbed to the ninth floor. He was climbing too and shooting, but he kept missing. By the time I got to the top of the building, I didn't think to throw something down to kill him. Just run! The building must have been about a mile long and ran out. By the time I turned around, he was only five feet from me. "Let's see you get out of this one," he exclaimed. I looked over the edge of the building and realized my only option. "You not that stupid," he reminded me. But I was. I looked back one final time at the gun pointed at me. I turned around and jumped into the air. I fell swiftly and saw the ground approaching. This was it. It was over. I only waited to feel the hardness of*

*the concrete and the breaking of the bones. I accelerated fast, and a split second before I hit the ground, it happened.*

"Bernard. Bernard." Aunt Raquel had appeared into the room and was gently poking my shoulder.

I was gathering myself, trying to figure out what was real and what wasn't. She had awakened me right before I hit the ground. I didn't know how she happened to appear at such a timely crossroads.

"Yeah, Raquel."

"Meet me downstairs for a second. I need to speak with you about something." She was whispering so as not to awaken Enzo. He was knocked out anyway. Why did she want to talk now? I was dead tired. It must have been about 2:30 AM, and there was no movement in the house other than ours. She secured her robe and headed out the room to proceed downstairs. I grabbed my shorts so I wouldn't be walking around in my Fruit of the Looms.

By the time I got downstairs, she was sitting and had turned on one of the lamps in the living room. We both sat, and I still was in a quandary as to what this was about and why it couldn't wait until later. She was yawning and wiping her eyes and let me in on the secret.

"I was sleeping, and the Lord woke me up and told me to talk to you."

"About w-what?" I didn't inquire about the Lord waking her up. I assumed that part was true. I just was not clear about what was so top-secret.

"One thing you should realize is that your mother has tried the best that she could to deal with the situation with your dad. For some reason, a lot of women were having abortions around the time your mom was pregnant with you. And your mom was going through a lot with Dwayne, even when she was pregnant with you. So she really did well to carry you the entire time while she was going through what she was. So I don't want you to hate her. You may not realize it, but she has had to deal with a lot of unfortunate things because of some choices that my brother has made. So I know you may not understand all of it right now, but just know that she is doing the best she can in order to survive. It may seem like she isn't concerned about you guys, but it's probably more healthy for you guys that they aren't both there fussing, fighting, and carrying on. Just know that she's doing the best she can do right now."

This was it? This was the reason she woke me out of my sleep? To tell me not to be angry at my mother? What did she have to gain by telling me this? After all, my father was her brother. She was not biologically related to my mother, but she had become an advocate for what was right, irrespective of blood relationship. She chose to go out on a limb and call a spade a spade. No one else in my family, especially those not on my father's side, had taken the time to attempt to help me make sense out of something that seemed so out of control. Aunt Raquel was the only one who helped me understand this part of my life from a different perspective. While I was still somewhat confused about the situation as a whole, I at least could think about it outside of my sixteen-year-old box for once. Maybe she was right. Maybe it would have been worse if mom had stayed. Maybe this was a hard truth that would make sense for me later. "Alright. Thanks." That was all I could muster. I was still sleepy.

"So let's go back to bed. I know you tired, but I just thought you should know that more is involved than maybe you can understand right now."

"Okay."

We hugged and went back upstairs. I climbed back in bed and heard her close the door to her and her husband's room. I continued to process what she said, wondering if the dream I was having would pick up where it left off.

# the trash bag

I had begun spending more and more time at my grandma's. I was virtually there every weekend now. We had developed a pretty strong bond and just enjoyed each other's company a lot. We had come a long way from her washing my back during my bath when I was a kid. I actually remember covering my privates with the washcloth, trying to hide what she had seen since my birth. Neither did it help that the cloth was wet and revealed every inch of what I tried to hide.

"I got it, grandma." I was six then and wanted to show her I could handle washing my own self now.

"Okay. You sure you got it? How you gone wash your back?"

"I can get it."

She let me be me.

And now I was older. It was toward the end of the summer of my junior year. I was back from participating in the LEAD Program in Business at UCLA. I'd been chosen from a nationwide pool and was now preparing for my final year of high school. The first day was on tomorrow, and, as was our custom on Sundays after church, my grandmother and I just lay on her bed, watched TV, and talked about whatever. We'd generally take a nap after dinner. Then, she would take me back home so I could get myself together for another week.

"So you all ready for tomorrow?" She was doing something to her robe.

"Yeah, I guess so. It's gone be here whether I'm ready or not."

"Hmpf. I guess you right about that. Time don't wait for nobody."

"Mm hmm."

"Let me turn on this news to see what they talkin' 'bout. Seem like every time you turn on the news, somebody gettin' shot or shot at. They act like it's a crime to put positive stuff on there. It's plenty of folk out here doin' good stuff. I bet ain't nobody knocked your doors down to find out about that program in California you were in this summer, did they?"

"Naw. But, grandma, they ain't *making* you watch it. You can turn the channel and watch some'm else."

"Well, you gotta know what's goin' on in the world." She had a way of still justifying why she was a faithful viewer.

We heard a jumping noise. We both realized it was Uncle Terrence in his room, in his own world. We knew just to leave him alone and let him deal with his own sense of reality. As long as he took his medication, he would be fine. So we continued our discussion.

"Well, I hope you enjoy watching who house got broken into and everything else they show." I laughed. "You know, grandma, I'm sort of tired of stayin' with daddy. You should let me move in here since it's my last year before college. I have a lot of stuff I gotta focus on, and it still be too many distractions in that house."

I could tell she really didn't want to talk about it. "Really?" She tried to find something to say. "It's only one more year. I'm hoping he'll step up and be the father you need. I don't want to take the responsibility away from him." She always hoped for the best for her son. As for me, I was past hoping. I needed change. I had been hoping all of my life that he'd do the right thing more consistently. I needed to move on and let him get himself together on his own, and I let her know it.

"Yeah, but he had all my life to get himself together. I don't want to stay there anymore. People still be coming in and out all night. I'm sick of it."

"Yeah, I know. Just try to deal with it one more year, and you'll be in college and won't have to worry about it. Plus, I don't have any room for you to put your clothes and stuff."

I jumped off the bed, ran to her closet, and pushed back her dresses to reveal some empty space. "My clothes can go right here."

She glanced at the space I created and chuckled. "Boy, you would make a good lawyer. You sholl know how to plead your case." She laughed again.

But I wasn't joking. I was serious as a heart attack. I had been praying for a way out of that living situation for years, but nobody seemed to take me seriously. The truth of the matter was that I was living it. They weren't. The only ones who really understood where I was coming from were Dwayne, Jr. and Keva. I didn't know how Keva was managing to do well in her studies at NCCU and living home at the same time, but I took my hat off to her for struggling through it. "I just don't want to be there anymore."

She kept my hopes up somewhat. "Well, let's give it another month. If things just don't go right, then we'll see what we can do."

"But I don't know why you think he would change in one month when he ain't changed over the years." I still argued my case but then relented when I saw it was getting me nowhere. I pushed her dresses back to their original places. I was slightly disappointed, but that wasn't a new feeling.

As the night progressed, she drove me back home and said she'd see me later. I entered and encouraged myself. *Just one more year and that's that.* I'd just have to try to keep a cool head, ignore what I saw, and march toward a better day. School was starting tomorrow, and I was pretty psyched.

The new school year was upon me. It was exciting to be a senior but still a little hard to focus. Last night was no different. My father's late-night company was annoying and still making things quite difficult. I'd get home after track practice and try to do some homework before the usual madness.

Keva came home about 6 PM and did her normal best to get on my nerves. "Will you please move?" She was trying to get by my chair to get to her room.

"Ain't like you that big, Keva. Just go by." So she pushed her way through, bumping me. "Keva, why 'on't you stop playing so much. I'm trying to do my work." I'd decide to take a break for a couple of hours and let Keva have the house to herself. I didn't feel like putting up with any friction right now. "Keva, I'll be back."

"So what you want, a cookie?" She couldn't resist.

I had decided to go chill at Ray's, another friend. He was a senior too and understood where I came from when I told him I needed some time to get away for a second. All we did was talk about what schools we were going to apply to for college. His mom practically lived in the kitchen. She was always cooking something when I came over.

"Baby, you hungry?" She shouted from the kitchen.

"Yep." Ray answered quickly.

"I ain't talkin' to you, boy. I'm asking Bernard." She clarified.

"No ma'am." I was lying. We laughed it off.

"Ma, how you gone ask him if he hungry and not me?"

"Boy, be quiet. If you hungry, you get yo' butt up and fix yourself some-thin' to eat. You ain't crippled, at least not yet." We laughed at her mild threat while she continued slinging pots and pans.

After a while, I decided to head home so that they would have some time to eat their dinner. I was hoping daddy had cooked something because I was starving. "Aight man, I'ma head out and get home. I'll catch you tomorrow."

We walked toward the door while he bounced the basketball.

"Ray, don't be bouncing that ball in my house. I 'on't know how many times I gotta tell you that." He couldn't get anything past her.

"Alright, Miss Bunson. See you next time. Have a good night."

"Okay, sweetie. You have a good night too. Keep those grades up. I want to see you walk across that stage for graduation."

"Yes, ma'am. I'm definitely going to be there. I can't wait." She really didn't know why I couldn't wait, but that was all she needed to know.

"Aight, man, I'll get up wichu." He closed the door and bounced the ball by habit, and I heard them going at it again through the closed door. Both of them were too hilarious to me. But they were good people.

I walked home in about ten minutes. I didn't realize how dark and how late it had gotten. It was pushing 8:00, and I hadn't eaten anything since lunch. I noticed Denise's car in the driveway. I still remembered the slap my mother gave her when I was a little boy and laughed about it to myself often. She and my father eventually had a child. So I guess she saw our house as hers in a way. I didn't care to speak with her. She stayed in my father's room, so I didn't have to worry about bumping into her.

When I walked through the door, it was good to notice some food wait-ing to be devoured. On my way over to the stove, Keva yelled some weird news to me. "Bernard, Ms. Rivers called you while you were gone."

"Huh?" I thought I misheard her.

"Ms. Rivers called."

"For what?"

"I 'on't know. I ain't no psychic. Her number on the table."

I hadn't seen or heard from Ms. Rivers since I was in her sixth-grade class in middle school. It had been a while since I had seen those googly eyes and huge glasses. Teachers normally didn't call your house unless you were in trouble, and surely they didn't call if you were six years removed from their class. I didn't worry about eating at the moment. I just wanted to satisfy the curiosity that her call had raised and dialed the number.

"Hello," she sang.

"Hey, Ms. Rivers. It's Bernard. K-Keva told me you called." I tried to masquerade my confusion with excitement.

"Hi, Bernard!" She was ecstatic that I called back. "Do you need some shoes for school?"

That was weird. Even if I didn't, who would say no to an offer for shoes? "Sure. I think I do need some." Expecting her to say she'd be over tomorrow, I waited for her to set the shopping schedule.

"Okay, great. I'm on my way right now."

I was thrown for a loop. "Really? As in right now?" I didn't know what to say.

"Yep. The mall closes at 9:00, so I need to leave now since it'll take me about fifteen minutes to get there. Tell me where you stay."

After giving her the directions, I hung up still in a daze, trying to figure out what prompted this. I just got myself together, tried to eat something, and kept looking out of the window to watch for her lights. It seemed as though she got there in only ten minutes, instead of the usual fifteen. I told Keva that I'd be back. It was no use in telling my father. His door was closed, and he could have cared less anyway.

I ran outside, saw the lights shining off Ms. Rivers' glasses, and hopped in the car.

"Hey, Ms. Rivers!" She had another pair of glasses, more up-to-date and less bulky. She looked great.

"Hey, sugar. How are you?" We hugged while both sitting in the front seats. "Well, let us go. The mall closes at 9:00." So we made our way out of the driveway.

We engaged in small talk and caught up with how things were going. I never spoke with her concerning matters of my household, but I had a feeling that she probably knew.

"So how is school going?" She'd start with the obvious question since she was a teacher.

"Things are going pretty well. My grades are good. I'm still running track. And this year, I'm the president of the student government. My classmates elected me."

"Wow! You are just doing it up. By the way, would you believe that as I was on my way to your house, every traffic light I got to was green? Even if it was red, by the time I got to it, it turned green."

"Really? That's sort of crazy, huh?" I didn't know how to respond.

"Well, Vic and Larry are doing well." Those were her two sons that she was raising alone. She had presumably left them at home and told them she would be back.

"Yeah, I see Vic all the time at school." We were both in the marching band. I didn't see Larry that much because he was a few years behind us. I was getting ready to ask her how she remembered my number, but she started again.

"It's just so good to see you. You're growing on up, aren't you?" It was rhetorical. "Just look at you."

Before I knew it, we were pulling into the parking lot of the mall and had to hurry. It was 8:35, and we'd have to figure which store was our destination.

"Alright. Let's go." She led the way.

I still wasn't quite sure what was going on. An hour ago, I was chilling with Ray and his mom. Now, I was walking in a mall. Everything felt like a blur. Before I had a chance to ask her why she called and had to do this on today, we reached the shoe store. We looked at some sneakers and semi-dress shoes. I tried a few on and walked around.

"How do they feel? Are they comfortable?" Ms. Rivers glanced at the shoes as I stood in front of the mirror on the floor.

"They feel pretty good." They really did, so I settled on the hush puppies. They'd go well with my Levi's.

"Ma'am, we'll be closing in about five minutes." The clerk was reminding Ms. Rivers of the time.

"Okay. Thank you, ma'am. I think we're about ready to buy these."

I took them off and handed them to the clerk. Ms. Rivers walked up to the front and took out the wallet from her purse. I sat on the store bench and put my own shoes back on. I'd have to throw away my socks when I got home. There was a hole in the left one. Ms. Rivers handed the clerk a credit card as I sat staring out of the store. The store gate was partially down. We were the last customers, so it would be shut closed once we left.

"Alrighty. I think that does it. Here you go." Ms. Rivers handed me the bag of shoes, and we both ducked a little as we walked out to clear the gate.

"Thanks, Ms. Rivers. I really appreciate it."

"I know you do, baby. You've always been a grateful child. Even when you were in my class, it was 'thank you, this' and 'thank you, that.' That's going to carry you far."

We made it back to the car and headed back to my house. It was refreshing to have been thought of. Granted, in my mind it could have waited until tomorrow. I was exhausted and had to prepare myself mentally for the stream of traffic that would probably be flowing through the house on tonight. Ms. Rivers was driving much slower since we had accomplished our mission. As we approached my neighborhood, we continued small talk. I told her that I was taking some pretty tough courses. Calculus. Physics. English comp.

"Wow, calculus? That sounds pretty tough." She was chiming in.

"Yeah, it seems like it'll be pretty hard. But I'm glad I ended up with Ms. Kipling. She has a good reputation for explaining those concepts well."

"Have you started thinking about your colleges yet?"

"Sort of. I know I'm going. I just haven't figured out where yet. I have to take the SAT again so I can bring my verbal score up. I did really well on the math part, but those reading comprehension passages are hard to understand. I got around a 1200." This was when the SAT maximum score was 1600. "And I got to start asking teachers for letters of recommendation and stuff like that."

"Well, stay on top of it. You have it in you to do it."

"Thanks." Just then, we pulled into my driveway and drove up the small hill. She put the car in park as I grabbed my bag. "It's not really that easy with my daddy doing the stuff he doing, though. I'll be glad when I leave. I can sort of start fresh and let him keep doing what he been doing all these years. All these people be coming in and out while I'm trying to do my school work. It's crazy." She just sat and listened. "I don't know how Keva can do her studies at Central and live here at the same time. College is hard. Maybe that's why she sort of tough on the outside, 'cause that's the way she handle what's going on in her own way. Anyway, let me go in. Thanks again for the shoes. Gotta get ready for tomorrow." I reached for the door and opened it. I let my right foot rest on the ground outside while my left foot remained planted inside the car. It was back to the drawing board.

I uttered one last parting statement. "By the way, Ms. Rivers, maybe you should let me come stay with you sometime."

To this day, I still struggle with wrapping my mind around what happened next.

With a solid and serious face, she responded, "I know you're going to think this is weird, but the Lord told me in church this morning to buy you some shoes on tonight. He also said that if you asked to stay with me sometime, it would be a sign for me to take you in right on the spot. So would you like to come stay with me right now?"

Right then and there, I couldn't believe my ears. I literally started screaming really loud and crying because I had prayed countless days to be in a better environment and saw no signs of it happening. I could barely respond because I still thought this was too good to be true. This was the whole reason she had re-initiated contact in the first place. "Thank you, Jesus! Thank you, Jesus!" He had heard my prayer. "Yes! Yes! I want to come stay. I want to leave from here. Thank you, Jesus!"

I looked over at Ms. Rivers and saw that she was crying too. Here was a single woman who was already raising two boys and who had stepped outside of her comfort zone. She herself was also in school writing her dissertation for her PhD and didn't need any further distractions. She could have easily used the excuse that she didn't have a man to help her, but she obviously relied on God to get her where she needed to go.

And she was such a cut above many teachers nowadays. Today, we have to be concerned with teachers and their motives for wanting to get close to students. A glance at many a news station reveals that more and more teachers are getting caught in the web of having sex with students and muddying what should be a professional relationship of molding minds for the next generation. While it is true that teachers are not expected to follow the exact actions of Ms. Rivers, per se, we as a society should continue to hold educators' feet to the fire when it comes to setting high expectations for students and providing a sense of role modelship to those who are trying their best to navigate life's journey. And at this pivotal juncture, Ms. Rivers was helping me navigate mine.

My high was briefly tempered by a reality I hadn't considered.

"What do I say to my father? I'm not sure what he'll think about it." I posed the issue.

"Don't worry about it. I'll come in and speak with him. You just grab as many of your things as you can carry."

We walked in, and I was pretty frightened. I wasn't sure how he'd respond. So as Ms. Rivers waited in the kitchen, I went to his door and knocked. "Da." No response. "Da," I called again.

"Yeah, Bernie." He heard me this time.

"Ms. R-Rivers in the kitchen. She w-wanna know if she c-can talk to you." The stuttering was back.

"Okay. Just one second."

That was all I was going to do. I quickly went into my room. Dwayne, Jr. was lying on the bed and saw me scrambling. "Boy, what you doing?"

"I'm leavin'," I replied without looking up. I was trying to figure out how I was going to somehow arrange all of my stuff in a moment's notice. My things were everywhere, and I didn't have a real suitcase. After glancing around, I just decided to empty some clothes out of a trash bag in my closet and started stuffing whatever I could into it. I grabbed some underwear, some socks, some pants, a few shirts. I started moving quicker when I heard my father walking down the hall toward the kitchen. *Lord, don't let him say I can't go.* I kept stuffing the trash bag frantically with whatever I could find. Shoes. Coats. Nothing else could fit. I couldn't even close it all the way.

Soon, my father stuck his head in the room and spoke to me. "Bernie. That's fine. You can go."

It was music to my ears. "Okay. Th-Thanks." I bear-hugged the trash bag and headed out of my room.

As I walked, Denise came out of my father's room and made a surprising statement. "Bernie, you don't have to leave. I'll leave." Apparently, my father told her I was on my way out.

"No, th-that's okay. It's probably b-better if I leave." I didn't even tell Keva goodbye. Ms. Rivers was already back into the car, and I beelined straight for the door. I got outside, locked the door, and made my way somehow to the car. The back car door was opened so I just plopped the bag in the back seat. Some of the clothes came out, but that was fine by me.

I got in the car, still on Cloud nine, and inquired to Ms. Rivers, "What in the world did you say to him? I didn't hear him put up a fight about it or anything."

We started driving off. "I just said, 'Mr. Dillard, I think it would be a good idea if Bernard came to stay with me for a little while. He's a senior and is taking some really tough courses. I could help him prepare his college applications and give him a lot of support that he'll need at this time in his life.'"

"Wow, really?" I could barely believe it.

"Yep. And he said, 'Ms. Rivers, I think that would be a great idea. I really want him to have all the support he needs to make it. I appreciate you taking the time out to help him. He a good kid.' I told him that I'd take good care of you and that was that."

Needless to say, I was in a dazed state for the entire drive home. She was talking about something, but all I could do was stare out of the window. I had prayed ever since I was a young guy to have my father "fixed." After that, my focus had shifted to my being removed from the situation. Although I endured those living conditions for most of my young life, it was interesting that the prayer was answered when the timing was right, not before, not after. It was right when the new school year had started.

We pulled into her driveway. I managed to lug in the trash bag full of my belongings, while Ms. Rivers carried my new shoes. I came in and saw Vic and Larry.

"Hey, Vic. Wassup, Larry."

"Hey, wassup Bernard." Vic was pretty calm, cool, and collected.

"Yo, Bernard, my main man! He gone be staying wit us, mama?" Larry was younger, more energetic, more opinionated and outspoken.

"Yes, he's going to be staying with us for a while." Ms. Rivers placed the shoes downstairs next to the sofa.

It was pretty late, and everyone was tired, especially Ms. Rivers and me. So she started providing instructions regarding my transition. "So Bernard, you can just put your stuff over there for the time being. Vic will have to clear out part of his dresser on tomorrow for you to place your things in. You can use Vic's bathroom and shower. We don't have another bedroom, so you'll have to sleep on the sofa here. I'll bring you some sheets and a pillow."

"Alright. Thanks." I placed everything down and just unwound, still in a bit of confusion.

By the time everyone retired, it must have been around 11 o'clock in the evening. I lay on the white couch just looking around, taking in the surroundings of someone who had been my teacher in middle school. I have come to discover that there really is no chance meeting in life. Purpose and destiny work hand in hand to bring the people into your life at the appropriate time.

Regarding the living conditions, I didn't mind sleeping on the couch at all. In fact, I actually liked it. I had rather sleep on a couch that was in a house of peace than sleep in a gigantic bedroom in a house full of mayhem and uncertainty. As I look back, though, I had no inkling that the night before this one would go down in history as the final night that I would ever spend under the roof of my father.

eighteen

# it ain't goin' nowhere

I woke up the next morning and still couldn't believe the reality of the new place I was in. I remember that I woke up smiling. I didn't worry about the trash bag. I wasn't concerned about the white sofa. I'd just wear whatever I wore on yesterday on today. Vic had finished in the bathroom and told me it was all mine. Getting ready felt so weird. I wasn't solely responsible for making sure everything was a go when it came to getting ready. I heard Ms. Rivers project her voice, "Everybody needs to be up now. We're leaving in forty-five minutes."

Wow, that was such a difference from what I normally experienced. My father was normally knocked out as I was getting ready for school. I had to wake him up every morning to make sure I had lunch money before I left. And that would take about four or five tries. That wasn't the case at Ms. Rivers'.

"Vic, you up? Larry, you up? Bernard, you up?" She was checking.

"Yes, ma'am." I was the only one who responded. The others apparently were used to it and didn't feel obliged to answer."

"It's some cereal in the kitchen. Make sure you eat some of it, okay?" She was giving me some more morning instructions.

"Okay, thanks."

Pretty soon, we were heading out the door, all except Larry. We sat in the car waiting for him. He finally came out, wrestling with his belt and lugging his knapsack. He locked the door and came running.

As we drove to school, Ms. Rivers started praying out loud. "Father, we thank you for a good day on today! Guide us and help us. Let these guys do well in school and get high marks. Let them be excellent examples and make right decisions. Don't let the enemy sidetrack them, and don't let them get with the wrong crowd. Help Vic with his wrestling. Help Larry with his

138

studies. Help Bernard as he runs. Help all of them with their grades." She spoke with quite a bit of passion and then got silent.

Then Vic started. Apparently, he knew it was his turn. "And Lord, be with us on today. Protect us from danger and harm. Help mama teach to-day, and let us come back home safely." After saying some other things, the silence prevailed again.

Larry started next. "Lord, help us with our school work and help our friends. And Lord, please . . . let the lunch be good." He started giggling.

Ms. Rivers stared at him through the mirror. "You know what, Larry? You're going to learn how not to joke when we pray. This is serious." Vic chuckled to himself, and so did Larry. Admittedly, I couldn't resist the urge either. I turned my head toward the window and laughed a little. Larry had finished.

"Bernard, you can pray if you'd like as well." I was caught somewhat off guard. Never had I prayed out loud. Most of my prayers were done quietly at night by my old bedside. It felt more comfortable to me that way. I didn't have to worry about anybody else hearing what I said. I was normally in my own comfort zone, just talking with and by myself. I never actually really thought about praying in such a setting, in such a round-robin fashion. So I declined. "No, thank you."

She didn't make a big deal out of it. "Okay, no problem. So Vic and Bernard, I'll be by to pick you up after wrestling and cross-country practice. You all should be finishing up around the same time. Larry, you'll just have to wait for me to pick them up, but you can go by the school library and get your homework done before I come by. Don't just waste time after school and lollygag and get nothing accomplished. Time is of the essence. So don't waste it."

"Ma, you know I'm not a time waster. I'm always on the mark." Larry countered.

"I guess that's why you're always the last one outside every morning when we leave, because you have your time management all figured out, huh?" Touché.

"Mama, you always gotta analyze everything and be one up on me." Larry admitted defeat.

"That's my job, baby."

This raillery was actually pretty refreshing. An actual conversation. Actual discourse. A family. I got this sometimes with some family members.

But this type of banter was few and far between. Most of the time, it was just Keva and I, bickering back and forth about nothing. It was good to have some sense of interaction to start the day. We pulled up at Hillside and all three of us boys got out. "See y'all this afternoon. Love ya."

We headed toward the school.

"Bye, ma." Vic started.

"See ya later, alligator." Larry said his goodbyes in his usual humorous way and held up the peace sign, without turning around.

Ms. Rivers got in one last shot as she yelled from the car, "Larry, tuck your shirt in and fix your belt. Stop looking like you don't have any home training." He obeyed as we and some other students who heard it started laughing.

"Bye, Ms. Rivers." I ended the goodbyes.

"See you later, Bernard. Do well on today."

We all walked inside the school and went our separate ways. I wasn't sure what today would hold. I had on my same old clothes from yesterday, but I went in with a new sense of beginning and a fresh start, and that was alright with me.

After cross-country practice, I hung around Coach Rumsfeld's car, waiting to go home. I had become a creature of habit and waited for my daily ride up to the restaurant. When I remembered I had a new ride home, I started walking toward where I was supposed to meet Ms. Rivers.

"Hey, Dillard, where you going?" Coach Rumsfeld noticed my walking away.

"Oh, I have a ride today, Coach. I'll see you on tomorrow."

He looked half-shocked, half-disappointed. I guess he was loving the father-son thing we had going on. But things had changed. I didn't worry about getting into the details with him. I just kept walking.

Living with Ms. Rivers wasn't boot camp, but she always had specific instructions for us. It was largely due, in part, to the fact that she was a single woman, raising a group of possible statistics under her roof. The plight of the black man was bleak, but she was going to make sure she did what she could to make sure her sons survived.

I observed a lot and spoke very little. I noticed the postcards on her refrigerator of all the places she had traveled and gotten degrees from. I saw
the picture where she was the only African-American in the group during
her studies at Oxford in England. I decided that someday I would study
there. I had heard of the Rhodes Scholarship and knew that study under
that scholarship would allow for a great scholarly and cultural experience.
I couldn't help but wonder how she could do all of this as a single lady.
Ms. Rivers seemed to set the standard for those women who had been dealt
a hard blow but who rose from the ashes and took life by storm. Many of
them relegated themselves to opinions and whims of others, instead of taking life by the horns. She seemed to represent all of the women who refused
to succumb under life's pressure and feel like they had to sacrifice their
worth and their value to do things out of character to make ends meet.
Rape victims, divorcees, and other women who have had to overcome similar obstacles could look on Ms. Rivers as an example of rolling with the
punches and remaining in the fight of life. She refused to take down and
to adopt the victim's mentality. Instead, she made waves, fought back, and
kept her integrity in the process.

For me, at the time, I was just interested in dinner. We all sat down for
dinner on one occasion and just engaged in small talk. I enjoyed this time.
It was really great to be able to talk about how things went at school and at
practice. Before I realized it, I looked up and saw all three of them staring
at me.

"Dang, Bernard, slow down. It ain't goin' nowhere." Larry belted out.
I was embarrassed because I honestly didn't realize I was eating so fast.

"Larry, zip it." Ms. Rivers always seemed to say the right thing at the
right time. In a calm voice, she reminded me. "Bernard, you don't have
to eat so fast. There's more over on the counter. It's also not good for your
health when you rush and eat like that." Larry was still laughing at me,
and Vic was laughing at Larry. Ms. Rivers stared back and forth at them,
achieving none of her intended results to get them to knock it off. In fact,
they laughed louder.

Ms. Rivers continued, "Bernard, this fork here is the salad fork, and
this one is the dinner fork. And then this one here is the one you use for
dessert. This spoon is to be used if you have soup. Normally, this glass
would be used for water, and this one would be used for tea or some other
drink."

Dumbfounded and without seeming disrespectful, I inquired, "This is too confusing. Why does it even matter which one of these I eat with? The food is all going to the same place."

Without being offended, she answered, "That's true for eating here. But some of the places that God is going to take you will require that you know and be accustomed to using the proper dinner etiquette." Her sons were still laughing.

Still confused, I just gave in. "Oh, okay."

It was quite good to learn small lessons like this along the way as I stayed there. What seemed insignificant and irrelevant at the time proved to be quite needful for me as my life progressed. It was good to have a sense of brotherhood with Vic and Larry too. Even though we were all relatively the same age, I learned much from them in many ways. In particular, I learned how to have more fun, loosen up a little, and not take life too seriously.

When we finished, we got ready to do our homework. Ms. Rivers tackled the dishes. "Larry, take this trash out, please. And Bernard, would you sweep in the kitchen, please?" Vic had excused himself.

As we did our requested assignments, the phone rang. Ms. Rivers answered with her low, calm tone, almost in a singsong fashion, "Hello."

I swept and eavesdropped a bit on Ms. Rivers' side of the conversation.

"Hi, Mrs. Dillard. How are you?" Silence.

"Good evening to you too. We just finished eating dinner."
Silence.

"Mm hmm. He's doing well. He's such a fine young man."
Silence.

"Yes, he was very agreeable and gave me his permission to take him."
Silence. I figured they were talking about my father.

"Yes, ma'am, he's in here sweeping right now."

There was a long pause as Ms. Rivers held the phone up to her ear with her shoulder as she washed one of the pots.

"Right." Ms. Rivers interjected this word periodically during my grandmother's apparent monologue.

I kept sweeping, even though I had really gotten up everything on the floor.

"Yes, ma'am. I know you've been a wonderful grandmother to Bernard. I remember his coming into my sixth-grade class and mentioning how you had bought him so many great things. I don't want you to think I'm taking him from anyone, but I felt that he could really benefit by being in this environment, especially since he'll be graduating this year. I can offer whatever assistance he needs in getting his college applications together and things of the sort. I think it's great that he has so much support."

Silence.

"Well, here he is. I think he's almost finished sweeping." She turned to me. "Bernard, your grandmother would like to speak with you, darling."

I stopped sweeping and held the broom as I answered the phone. "Hey, grandma."

"Hey, man. How you doin'?"

"I'm doin' good."

"I talked to Keva, and she told me you had moved in with Ms. Rivers."

"Yep."

"Well, you know you can come here. I don't want you thinking you had to go outside the family to get help."

"No, I didn't think that, and I never thought that. All this just happened so fast. I'm glad that it did, though." Ms. Rivers sensed the flow of the conversation and gave me some privacy by removing herself from the kitchen. "It's not like I called her or anything to come get me. It just happened."

"Well, that's fine, but I want you to come on over and stay here." She was making an offer for me to move in.

"No, that's okay. I'm fine here. Plus, I even asked you to let me move in when we were both lying on the bed. Remember when I pushed your clothes back? I just figured you had good reasons for not wanting to do it."

"Yeah, well, I just wanted your father to have an opportunity to step up and do the right thing. I guess I never thought that things had gotten *that* bad."

"Well, I don't complain about stuff that much. I just deal with it. But when it gets to be too much, I try to talk about it, and that's when I asked you if I could move in. Plus, you would have to get up and take me to school every day because the school bus doesn't come out there. And Ms. Rivers gotta take Vic and Larry to the same school anyway, so it's not a big deal for her." I couldn't believe how I was lining up my argument for wanting to stay put. Maybe I *would* make a good attorney. "This may be the best thing for right now, so I'm staying here with Ms. Rivers."

She didn't want to hear that but realized I had made up my mind and how stubborn I could be once I did so. "Well, just know that I love you and that you can come here anytime."

"Yeah, I know. Thanks a lot. Love you, too. Lemme get to finishing my homework. Talk to you later." I hung up and started on a paper I had to write.

Staying at Ms. Rivers' was indeed a breath of fresh air. I remained focused and got used to my place on the couch. I knew it would only be temporary, as I'd be in college the next year. I spoke with my grandmother off and on while I stayed. I guess she wanted to be sure that I didn't forget that she loved me too. Of course, there was no way possibly I'd think that, especially after all that she had done in my life since I was a lad. But I guess she wanted to keep it in the forefront of my mind.

One time when we spoke, she convinced my grandfather to call and speak with me to no avail. Why was all this effort being placed into removing me where I now felt comfortable? I wasn't sure if it were a pride thing or reflective of a kind of thinking in which dirty laundry was not exposed to those on the outside, but it irked me to no end. When I spoke with her again, she convinced me to come pick up some things from her home. While Ms. Rivers waited outside in the driveway, I went in my grandmother's laundry room and got the items. Before I left out, my grandmother was blocking my exit and instructed me to sit in the salon chair.

"Now I want you to know that it is your family's responsibility to raise you. I was speaking to Madge at the church, and she chewed me out and told me to go get you from that other lady's house and to stop being selfish. She told me that you really needed some help and she was surprised that I didn't listen to you when you said you wanted to stay here. It was like a bell went off."

I wasn't sure where this was coming from, but I stood my ground. "No, that's okay. I'm fine where I am. I think the Lord set it up so that this is the best situation right now."

"Yeah, well, 'Thus saith the Lord' to me too." She surprised me with that one.

I didn't feel like arguing, so I got my stuff and headed out. "Well, I'll see. Maybe I'll move in after this quarter is over. I don't want to keep moving and moving and moving."

Sure enough, after that quarter ended, I held true to my word and decided to move in with my grandparents. A part of me always wondered if I would have moved there if Ms. Rivers hadn't taken that bold step to remove me from my previous living condition. It was such an admirable step to move me in with no extra financial assistance and no promise that I would or could do anything for her in return. It had to be a pure gesture of love.

Since then, I learned that she had taken in another young lady before me until she finished high school. She had also taken in three young blood cousins of hers a few years after I left. Their mother lived in East Harlem but was distracted by substance abuse. She moved them to North Carolina and raised them as her own for a while. She was a real trooper and put actions behind mere words. She truly made a difference in the lives of those who needed a little extra push to make it. It was probably at this pivotal point that I realized that it doesn't take someone in the immediate family to make a difference in the lives of others. All it takes is someone who cares. She was proof positive that everyone in the church was not a hypocrite but that some people actually lived what they professed.

Greater still, this was a lesson to me that God indeed listens to and answers a heart that is sincere in prayer. I hadn't put on a big show to be heard or pleaded my case with tons of family members, but I prayed in my own way with no set script and no set preconceived way of how He would answer. But God in His own way and in His own time rearranged circumstances in my world with lightning speed and without warning to assist me and bring me one step closer to fulfilling His aim in my life.

# may this wind be

A fter the quarter ended, I decided to move in with my grandmother. My room was Aunt Raquel's old room. It seems as though change was the only thing that was constant in my life. I was trying to keep my grades up, but it was tough, having to juggle living in one place and then another and then another. We had gotten into a pretty stable routine. My grandmother would get up in the mornings and drive me to school. I'd start riding again with Coach Rumsfeld, a decision he welcomed with open arms. I could become his son again and listen to all the advice he was so happy to give me. Once I finished my homework and got something to eat at our restaurant, I'd generally ride with granddaddy home.

Of course, now that I lived there 24/7, I had the privilege of dealing with Terrence on a more consistent basis, something I would not have chosen. I had dealt with drama in my father's house and just basically wanted peace and quiet like I had at Ms. Rivers' place. Sadly, I would soon discover that that peace was short-lived. As much as I tried to fit in with no drama, everything seemed to push his buttons. I really just wanted to be left alone so I could stay in my corner and do my work. I would generally sit in the living room and try to focus. He'd purposefully come into the vicinity where I was every ten minutes to drink some of the juice he bought. He was hiding it in the far corner of the living room. That was just the way he did and thought. What was everyone else's was his, but what was his was only his. And he hid it to make sure no one else would drink what he had purchased. I had gotten used to his heavy footsteps and the slight shuffling sound of the same pair of jeans he wore every day. The back-and-forth motion of one leg's meeting and separation from the other caused the noise as he made his rounds. Such a consistent and annoying chorus. When he had entered the living room for the umpteenth time and the chorus had stopped, I knew something was brewing in his mind.

I continued ignoring him, hoping he'd just go back into his own world. I had gotten myself into a rather comfortable study position, sitting on the floor with my legs underneath the coffee table and trying to find the integral of some mathematical function. Although I didn't hear him anymore, I knew he was still in the room. I then allowed my eyes to glance from the notebook paper to the carpet to my right and noticed his worn sneakers as he towered over me, seeming to observe on my paper what had my undivided attention. Hoping he was spying on my mathematical explorations to offer me a way to solve the problem, I alternated between jotting down some unsuccessful path to the answer and watching his shoes. Unfortunately, solving some dumb math problem was not on his agenda, for he made the most off-the-wall inquiry.

"You got a dollar?" He started his antics whenever my grandfather wasn't around. He seemed to respect the patriarch's presence a lot more than his mother's and mine.

My gut instinct just said to ignore him because he wasn't all there. So I did.

"Bernard, you got a dollar?" He asked again. And I ignored him again.

"Bernard, you got a dollar?" He was unrelenting. Or just bored.

And I was fed up. I remained seated and stared up at him, noticing how disheveled he really looked up close and barked, "No, Terrence, I ain't got no dollar!"

Before I knew it, he had drawn his hand back and hit me across the head with an open palm. I pushed the table back and stood up and charged at him and we fought. "What's your damn problem, fool!" I lashed out.

"When you tell a grown man you ain't got no dollar, that's the problem." He responded in the best logical way he thought possible.

I knew deep down, he was lashing out against me, in part, because I reminded him of his prior motivated, directed, driven self. Now, he was sick and on medication, and whenever he skipped his dosage, anything could and usually did happen. This was just one of those days that made me wish that I had stayed at Ms. Rivers'. Clearly, my grandparents had their hands full in looking out for Terrence, and I didn't feel like walking on eggshells to appease him.

My grandmother had come in and tried to defuse the situation but failed. "Terrence, you just stop and act like you got some sense." But both of us drowned her out and kept with the scuffling. I didn't get into many fights, but it didn't mean that I wouldn't if backed into a corner, even with my uncle. In the hallway, he pushed me into picture frames on the wall, and they'd come crashing down. My grandmother would often physically force herself into the middle of us. Then, his anger would turn toward her.

"And you ain't nothing but a damn bitch and a whore!" He exploded, and I pushed him again. But he stayed focused on her. "I can't believe how much of a whore you are. Having six damn children. That's just being a whore."

I couldn't believe my ears. This is when I realized that his problem would need more than just some surface treatment. There was a void in him spiritually that only the Holy Spirit would be able to fill. Much like the demoniac in the scripture, who cried and gashed himself with sharp stones, Terrence would only receive real and substantive help from the Lord. No medication, no shock treatment, no one-on-one with Dr. Phil, or no efforts on his own part would provide the remedy he needed to overcome the challenges for the station of life he was in.

My grandmother calmly started walking back toward her room while he followed and continued with the insults. "Terrence, you need to take your medication. That's not you talking."

He knew she was right but didn't care. "Just a whore! You just a whore!" He followed behind her, and I followed behind him to continue the fight.

At some point, he must have calmed down because I stopped hearing the insults. But what would keep him in the future from doing something terribly outlandish that he thought he couldn't control? I could tell he faced a constant tug-of-war within his soul because almost invariably, after our physical confrontations, he'd always come and knock on my door while I was still fuming from our encounter. "Bernard, I just wanted to apologize and say 'I'm sorry.'" So I knew he had a heart. Still, after a while, he'd manage to regress back to the ogre and continue to cause quite a stir.

I'm not sure if my grandparents thought they would be viewed as failures or if they thought it was just the nice thing to do to allow him to remain in the home. But I always felt like his progress was hindered more than it was helped by this decision. At this point, I was just in the crossroads of a bunch of bickering and commotion. Even my father's house wasn't this animated. I had jumped from the frying pan into the fire. Why hadn't I just stay at Ms. Rivers'?

Terrence thankfully retired for the night. Grandma had apparently turned in, and granddad returned and retreated too. I decided I'd intake the serenity of it all, sit by the gas fireplace, curl up with a blanket, and just kick back. Moments like these were rare, so I learned how to make the most of them. Leaning back in the La-Z-Boy, I frequently stared into the gas fireplace, becoming mesmerized by the blue flames that danced from its base. The heat was a sleeper's dream too. Before I knew it, I had drifted into a world of bliss and peace. Almost forever blissful.

Before I realized it, I was awakened by aggressive body convulsions that I could not control. Every inch of my body gave way to involuntary tremors. How stupid of me! I had fallen asleep in front of the fireplace and had apparently inhaled above-normal levels of dangerous gases. Or at least this was my thinking after having a chance to think about it over the years. At the moment, though, I didn't care what was the cause. I needed help. Strangely, I didn't run through the house, shouting for help. I got up from the chair and tried my best to walk to the kitchen. Maybe drinking a little something would calm me down and help the shaking subside. I ran the tap water into the unstable glass in my hand. As I drank, more water streamed down the side of my mouth than went in. I was having no success. Convinced this was it, I decided just go to my room. I was walking as if I were on an invisible tightrope, trying to keep my balance. I felt as though I would tip over any minute. Once I got to my room, the convulsions seemed to get worse. Was this really the effect of being zapped with such a gas? The pain was unbearable, and my breathing got more and more shallow. I decided that I'd kneel by the bed and just ask God for help. Besides, in my mind, this was the only way I had really learned to deal with difficult matters. It had helped before. Perhaps it would help now.

*Lord, help me*, I whispered. My body continued shaking. I was trying to figure out how it was able to shake like this. The only thing remotely similar that I'd experienced was my body's reaction to cold weather, a mild shivering. This was that magnified about a hundred times, and it just kept going. *Lord, help me*, I would whisper again. Nothing. After staying put on my knees for about another minute, I decided I'd just climb into the bed and deal with whatever would follow. I was at peace. Once I got under the covers, I just closed my eyes and let my body do its thing. So this was what it was like to make The Transition. I was wondering when the proverbial white light would appear. And so I waited and shook, shook and waited.

In an instant and much to my surprise, an invisible hand touched some-where around my chest area. When it did, I was forced to exhale one major breath, and the convulsions ceased immediately. I opened my eyes and saw the same darkness that prevailed when my eyes were closed, so I closed them quickly again. I was trying to see if I was still alive. The shaking had actu-ally stopped, and I was breathing normally. *Thank you, Lord*, I whispered. I felt a tear glide down the side of my face as I lay in the bed. *Thank you, Lord*, I whispered again. To date, I hadn't told anyone of this occurrence. In part, I am still trying to make sense of it myself. All I know is that I had been teetering on the borders of life and death and lived to see another morning.

As one might guess, though, I never fell asleep in that La-Z-Boy again.

As slow and painstaking as my life seemed to be going, here I was, all of a sudden having to make a decision concerning the next phase of my life. The truth of the matter was that I was tired. Sixteen and tired. Inside, I felt like an old man. Just really wanting to go somewhere and not come back. I had re-solved in my mind that suicide for me was not an option, but if for some strange reason I disappeared, it would have been okay for nobody to try to find me. Tired of hoping. Tired of believing. Tired of acting happy. Tired of fighting and hold-ing on. If you would have seen my grades, they wouldn't have signaled that I was a tired kid. But I was tired of keeping up my grades. Tired of succeeding against the odds. Tired of praying. Just tired. Mentally drained. I was a Maybach on the outside but felt like I had been driven 300,000 miles, but I had to focus on the next phase of my life, irrespective of who I thought was onboard with mak-ing my life work. Which college would be graced with my presence? I guess that was even a milestone, to be even thinking about going to college.

This was something exciting for me during this time. Yes, I was tired. Yes, I had to overcome a few things. But this was about to be a new chapter in my life. The more I thought about it, the more I felt up to the challenge. A certain sense of direction and purpose overshadowed me during this time, and eventually I honestly got happy about it.

I just didn't know where I would go. I knew that I wanted to leave Durham. I had to leave the familiar and learn how to spread my own wings. I didn't want my parents or grandparents or anybody else shielding me from making any mistakes in life. I had to learn how to be responsible and learn to make right choices and respectable decisions on my own with no safety net. But I would still apply to Duke. If I had to stay home, I wanted to go to one of the best universities in the country. And why not consider the school in whose hospital I was born?

As crazy as it sounds, even though at this time I had moved in with my grandmother, I always placed my father's address as my permanent address. Something in me wanted a sense of success to be attached to that home. A part of me still wanted to belong there and make that residence have some semblance of honor. So I thought if I applied to a prestigious school and mail the information there, my father would see it and be impressed at my consideration of top-tiered schools. Whenever I told my grandmother that I had to go by daddy's house to pick up a college application, she would always inquire why I just didn't have it sent to her house. Didn't she understand my reasoning? This would get him to straighten up. Silly me. By the time I got to his house, the applications would just be sitting on the deep freezer with all the rest of the other junk mail.

I ran in while grandma stayed in the car. "Tell your daddy I said 'Hello.' I'm not coming in 'cause it's gone take me too long to get in and out." I hopped out and went toward the door. The house looked much smaller than it did when I was younger. The door was unlocked so I went in. He was in his usual lair in the back. I grabbed the mail from the freezer. I couldn't believe this was the same kitchen where all that arguing and fighting and slapping went down. I'd just grab the mail and keep walking to the back.

"Hey, dad. Just came to get my mail." I had to shout it a little because his bedroom door was closed, and he didn't make any move to open it, so I didn't either.

"Hey, Bernie. What's up?" I could tell he was just lying on his bed, probably eating dinner.

"Nothing. Just stopped by to pick up my mail. Grandma said 'Hey.'" Would he say anything about the Harvard or Yale application? Or the one from Dartmouth?

"Okay. Tell momma I said I'll probably be down there this weekend to get a haircut." Guess not. Nothing about if I was even contemplating college. Nothing.

"Alright. See ya later."

"Okay, Bernie."

Leaving out, I shut the door and headed back to the car. I could feel tears welling up in me a little. I wasn't sure why, but they were. I remembered the parts he used to place in my hair and the fact that he did teach me how to tie a necktie. But why was I still trying to invest energy into having a so-called relationship with him? Apparently, he didn't want one, given that he never really tried. I just needed to man up and move on. I got back to the car and had to gather myself. My grandmother wouldn't understand. Times before where I said something about her son, she would always rush to his defense. In her mind, he could do no wrong. So there was no reason to try to explain my feelings to her. I would just make small talk and deal with my own sense of loss.

"Daddy said 'Hey.' He said he'll probably come this weekend to get his hair cut."

"Oh, okay. That'll be good. Maybe I can cook something so he can have a nice meal."

I could never really understand how she was so concerned about him, a grown man, having a freshly cooked meal. Maybe it was a southern thing. I like food, but I don't think that I would be so overly concerned about whether a grown man, especially my son, had a home-cooked meal once he reached a certain age. If anything, he should have been concerned about whether or not his mother had a decent meal in her old age. I guess I will never understand what society calls a mother's love. No matter how old a mother gets, it's rumored that she will always cater to her male child and will always treat him like her baby, even if he just robbed a bank or killed somebody. It's something about that mother-to-son connection, as weird as it may be, that will cause her to fight a literal army for her male seed. Even if he steals money from her to support his drug habit or steals her jewelry, a mother tends to constantly see the good in her "little boy," while everyone else wants to throw him under the bus. Strangely, this same connection doesn't translate to her daughters. She and her daughters can go at it tooth and nail, and whatever lessons the daughters need to learn, the mother makes sure she learns it through the school of hard knocks. There is virtually no coddling effect from mother to daughter in comparison to the over-nurturing effect that exists from mother to son.

I have not yet determined if this is a truth that is prevalent mostly in African-American communities or if it is one that transcends race. But it is one that surely needs to be addressed if society as a whole will move forward and progress. I have learned that we men have to step up, be accountable, and take responsibility for our own destiny. Our mothers, if we were fortunate, have done fairly decent jobs in raising us, but at some point, we have to break the "little boy" attachment and refuse to allow her to keep us in breast-sucking mode. Although this is her natural inclination, we must become men and learn to keep the cord cut and begin to sow back into her life by making sober life decisions without the heat of her watchful stare.

Applying for college was exhausting but refreshing. This was going to be my gateway for a new start, a new me. It was good to be around a group of positive classmates who were all focused on furthering their education too. I felt privileged to be in the midst of so many talented peers. I remember on occasion, for example, visiting Renee, who was a few years older than I and a powerhouse of a student leader at our high school. She was such a leader, and I was always drawn to people who overcame odds and showed quality leadership, irrespective of gender or age. Somehow, during my junior year, I found out where she lived and just started showing up to talk with her about life and reaching goals. In hindsight, the conversations she and her mother must have had after I left had to border on hilarious. The nerve of my just showing up unannounced, talking about, "Hey Ms. Porter, is Renee here?" Here I was, just appearing at her doorstep to glean whatever tidbits of wisdom I could concerning becoming successful and how to make it in the real world. At the time, Renee had hung around the city to study at Duke and was doing well there. She had come through the same high school as I and was making a mark in the world. This success thing was possible. Who knew she'd go on to finish Harvard's Law School and become Special Assistant to the President for Justice and Regulatory Affairs? As in President Obama.

And then there was my classmate Syd, who we couldn't wait to see play during basketball season. He was a one-man show, who wound up at Wake Forest and went on to the NBA. He played with the big boys, hooping with several teams, including the Nuggets, Celtics, and 76ers. Unfortunately, he would endure a freak accident involving an all-terrain vehicle in 2008 and have to deal with paralysis. His spirit would become so intent and focused, though, as he gave back to the community through his foundation. He was ' essentially outshining many of us who retained bodily movement and helped us realize and appreciate the fleeting nature of life.

It just felt good to be at a school where so many students weren't afraid to aim and shoot high, even though ours was an inner-city, predominantly black training ground. Many students could have easily succumbed to many of the negative perceptions held by so many in the community at large. Even though they lived within the school district limits, several parents chose to send their children to private schools so as to avoid the supposed ghettoness of our school. Obvious at Hillside, though, was a strong sense of family and caring. Teachers there were the cream of the crop but also had a strong commitment to helping you navigate your way into young adulthood. They recognized you were human, had problems, and offered strong guidance when necessary. Not to mention that the school had a band that was second to none. The band was known to bust a move or two during game half-times and parades. It even had a featured cameo in the movie *The Ink Well*. Hillside indeed was a unique place that nurtured its citizens and strengthened them for academic excellence beyond the school walls.

We classmates had written essays, typed forms, gotten teacher recommendations, and the like in preparation for the college experience. There were application fees, but we who were adept at using our financial background to our advantage always included a woe-is-me letter, which explained how paying that fee would be such a burden on us. We laughed about this heartily, about acting like paupers who were just trying to get a slice of bread and eke out a future, as school after school granted our requests to have these fees waived. We had learned well how to use where we were to get us to where we needed to go.

By the time the spring came, all of us were happy that our efforts were paying off. It was somewhat validating to see how our education and achievement scores were not only competitive with other students locally, but we were making good on securing freshman-year slots at national universities. The boasting began.

"Haaay!" Lorain entered the class during lunch break and started doing the wop. "Y'all are looking at the newest invitee to – drum roll please – Georgetown University in Washington, DC." Now Lorain was in fact a nerd. Anytime, you saw her, she had a book stuck in her face. She knew vocabulary words out the wazoo. We wondered how she managed to keep tabs on all the definitions associated with all different types of words. She had a good gut feeling for context clues and how word roots basically functioned.

She was a geek, but admittedly, so were all of us who were in the advanced, accelerated classes.

Then there was Vatoya, who would turn out to be our class salutatorian. A rather new arrival to our peer group, she had short hair, almost like a one-inch Caesar. She had the black power thing going on. She was personable but so deep, in a good way. She was extremely brilliant and loved doing independent study on literature topics. She could debate you into oblivion and have you contradicting yourself in no time flat. I remember attending a seminar after class one day that she planned and spearheaded on the life and contributions of Eugene O'Neill. She was thorough indeed, and she'd be headed to UC Berkeley in the fall.

Others of us were going other great places. Dondra and Phillipa were going to UNC-Chapel Hill. Peter and Moya were going to A&T in Greensboro. Bunny, which is what we called her, would be at NC State. Chauncey would be at Howard.

I hadn't figured where I'd be going. It was such a hard choice. I wanted to make the right decision. Thankfully, I had a few options and wasn't just limited to having to stay in the nearby area. I asked many for advice, perhaps the funniest of which came from the all-too-unpredictable Brenda. One day, I was lounging in my grandmother's living room, and she walked in, headed to the small bathroom beside the shop where my grandmother did hair. She was putting bobby pins in her hair as I prepared to give her the college list I had to choose from. She held one of the bobby pins between her teeth as she got her hair ready.

"So what are the schools you got acceptance letters from?" Or at least that's what I thought she said through the bobby pin.

She feigned interest as I read the list: "Duke and Wake Forest so far."

Her face brought all types of comedy and jest to what was supposed to be such a serious matter for me. "Well," she said, "Duke's mascot is the Blue Devil and Wake Forest's mascot is the Demon Deacon. Just from those two facts alone, I wouldn't step foot on either one of those campuses." Everything with her was about demons and devils. I realized that this was just her and her saved self. I couldn't do nothing but laugh. So I just had to ponder and pray and just hope I would make the right choice. At long last, there were all these options before me in the form of acceptance letters and invitations for me to make my home at their college or university for four years. I would have a new start at one of many.

Indeed, there was a Duke acceptance. This to me was a no-brainer. I knew I had to leave Durham so that I could force myself to grow. Then there were acceptance letters from areas close to home. Wake Forest. A&T. NC State. UNC-Chapel Hill. And others a bit farther away. FAM-U. Howard. Dartmouth. Brown. UPenn. Yale. Not Harvard. Rejection letter. Their loss. I hadn't conceived that I had applied to so many schools. Maybe it was a function of my anxiety to leave so badly. Maybe I just wanted to be super sure that I would end up somewhere, anywhere. This was a one-time deal, and I had to maximize this moment in time. So after much asking and soul-searching and praying and contemplating, I had made my decision.

It was goodbye to Durham.

And hello to Atlanta.

I was.

Off.

To Morehouse.

Words couldn't express just how ecstatic I was to be leaving. The only real way I saw myself growing was through moving away and starting afresh. Plus, I was getting fed up daily with Uncle Terrence's antics and how the rest of the family kept turning a blind eye to him, even if it put others in harm's way. Simply put, I was ready to go. Ms. Rivers had gone to Spelman and talked Morehouse up a lot during the short time I lived with her.

Before leaving, I had to complete the school term. We only had about a week to go until the year was over, and I was on coasting mode. No more real assignments. I could just relax and get ready for graduation. Dondra and I would normally sit in Ms. Ivey's room during lunch and just talk about life with Ms. Ivey, who was also Dondra's mother and our biology teacher. One day while we sat, Ms. Chalmers spoke to Ms. Ivey on the intercom.

"Ms. Ivey, is Bernard Dillard in there with you?" Since she was the guidance counselor, Ms. Chalmers had access to speak with any teacher in his or her classroom through the intercom system.

"Yes, he's sitting right here." Ms. Ivey looked at me, wondering what type of trouble I had gotten myself into.

"Do you mind sending him down to my office for a second?"

"Sure thing." She bore a hole through me as she stared me down.

"What? I didn't do anything." I was pleading my case without even knowing why.

"Mm hmm. That's what they all say. A guilty conscience speaks first." Ms. Ivey wouldn't be outsmarted.

Dondra laughed and watched me exit the room. I couldn't figure out for the life of me what type of trouble I had gotten into right near the end of the school year. I hated any semblance of turbulence, so I went into lawyer mode and worked on my defense even though I lacked any incriminating details. My mind ran a mile a minute. When I got to the office, I knocked and saw her sitting at her desk.

"Hi, Ms. Chalmers." I gave myself four simple instructions before entering. Play nice. Smile. Endure lashing. Exit.

"Hi, Mr. Dillard. Have a seat." She made it worse because she said all of this without even turning around and acknowledging my presence. She continued typing on her keyboard. Once she reached a decent place to stop, she swiveled her chair around and looked at me.

"So I just wasn't sure if there was a problem." I voiced my concern and kept smiling.

"Well sort of. The problem is that you only have about a week to get a speech together." She withheld details on purpose, as if to torture me with knowledge she knew that I didn't.

"Speech? What kind of speech? Nobody told me about any speech."

"That's why I'm telling you now." She couldn't hold back anymore. "I called you here to let you know that you'll be giving the valedictory response at graduation this year. We calculated all the grades, and as your counselor, I'm letting you know that you ended up with the highest grade point average in your class for all four years. So as I said, you have a week to get a speech together. You should plan on it being about three minutes tops. You're free to go back to Ms. Ivey's room."

"Alright." I still stared at her in disbelief.

"Oh, and I was looking at your records. Did you know you only had one absence?"

With all of the drama I had gone through, I guess this wasn't too much of a shock. I'd do anything to get to where I thought there was peace.

"Wow, no I didn't realize that."

"No, let me clarify. I mean you had only one absence for the entire four years you've been here at Hillside."

Now *that* was news, ridiculous news. "Whoa!" was all I could muster. I hadn't realized that I'd been *that* driven. "Okay. Well, thanks for letting me know." That's all I could think to say at the time. I hadn't expected to hear information of that kind at all. She had already turned back to her computer and started typing again. I turned toward the door and headed out.

"Mr. Dillard?" She had called me again.

"Yes, ma'am?"

While continuing to type and sensing that I had paused to look her way, she kept her attention and eyes straight ahead toward the computer.

"Congratulations."

"Thanks." I left and closed her door, wondering how on earth this reality had come about.

I wasn't too sure what to expect on graduation day. I'd spent the last two weeks preparing some comments. Although I had given speeches before, I had done nothing on this magnitude. The ceremony was to be held at NCCU's Eagle Stadium, and it was interesting to see all of the family come together during this time. I hadn't seen all of them all in one place in a while. It was good to see everyone, though. I had so much support, and they seemed anxious to hear what I had to say at the ceremony. There was grandma, grandda, mom, dad, TaKeva, and Dwayne, Jr.

We poured into the stadium on that hot June morning. I walked behind the marshals and took my place on the stage. I looked out into the sea of classmates and wondered how in the world I ended up with this assignment. Vatoya sat beside me preparing to give her address as salutatorian. As with most graduations, few of the students paid attention to the graduation preliminaries. They were only concerned about doing something memorable in their moment as they marched across the stage. And I knew it, so I wouldn't prolong the moment with offering advice that I knew they wouldn't take anyway.

So I was pretty brief. I ended with a prayer quote that I had read countless times on a plaque that rested on a wall in my grandmother's house.

Strangely, the wind had picked up when I got to this part of the speech. I had to hold my notes in place, but it was very appropriate given my final charge. "May the road rise up to meet you, and may this wind be always at your back." No stuttering. The original quote actually said "the wind," but I improvised, according to the current weather element. I heard cheers and applause. Listeners looked at me as though they thought I had made the wind start blowing somehow for added effect. I didn't. It just happened to start when I got to that place in my comments.

It was good to see our moving onward and upward. All of us had accomplished something exciting and meaningful. Even though some of us made it by the skin of our teeth, we had in fact avoided the statistic that relegated us to being high-school dropouts. And there was a great sense of success in the air.

I guess I hadn't really realized that with all I had overcome, this was just the beginning, in a sense. How naïve I was to believe that the blowing wind would always be behind us to push us into all things great. In the future, the wind would surely do about-faces and blow straight toward us to challenge our resolve. But for now, we'd relish the moment and feel the zephyr's gentle thrust behind us, propelling us each into the futures we were so anxiously awaiting.

---

*twenty*

---

# a conversation with kendra

---

I wasn't exactly sure what to expect as I prepared to head toward Atlanta. The school year had ended, and I'd be headed there soon. I had been accepted to a summer program, so I would be able to take summer college classes, get credit, and get a jumpstart on other freshmen, who would arrive in the fall. As the time neared, I didn't know how I'd be getting there, but things were moving too much in the right direction for those details not to take care of themselves. Keva was finishing up her fourth year in college and decided that she'd be responsible for getting me there in her Yugo. I would have laughed at the option had it not been the only one. The thought of driving on I-85 in her red, less-than-compact car was too amusing. But it would have to suffice. We had to decide on the time that we would head out, given the time I had to arrive. I hadn't visited the campus, but I had heard great things about many of the alumni, so I knew the campus was going to give off a larger-than-life vibe. How could it not? At any rate, we ironed out the travel details.

"Keva, the dorms open up at 11:00. And we gotta take time to stop and all that." I was trying to plan the journey.

"Boy, I'm not stupid. I know how to add and subtract. It takes six hours to get there, so we leavin' at 4 AM so we don't have to rush."

"Four? Keva that's too early."

"Too bad. We leavin' at 4:00." It didn't make any sense to argue with her. She was my ride and had assumed somewhat of the role of mother to me, so I just went along with it. In truth, I was quite proud of her for stepping up and volunteering to drive me to school. She was struggling to find her own way through school. Her recent change of major would increase the time and money she would spend in college, but she made the sacrifice to make sure I would be situated. In her own stubborn way, she determined that I would

158

get to the next phase of my journey. It was almost as if she knew that it was better that I leave to expand my personal and educational horizons. "And make sure you pack everything 'cause we not turning around to come back and get nothin'." She was her usual, bossy self.

I had packed pretty lightly. I had purchased a trunk from Kmart and packed all I had in it. That was all I had. A trunk, a book bag, and a few other smaller bags. Whatever I had, it all had to fit inside of her mini-car. I wasn't sure how it all fit, but somehow we managed. We packed the car the night before, and Keva just spent the night at grandma's house. That next morning when we were to leave, grandma got up to fix us breakfast.

"Grandma, don't fix us nothin'. It's too early. We'll pick up something on the way." I was encouraging her not to waste energy cooking. Otherwise, she would have prepared a full meal.

"Well, y'all can't get on the road on an empty stomach. Take a piece of fruit or something." She was insistent.

"Okay. We'll take some fruit, but don't cook nothin'," Keva chimed in. She barely ate anything when the sun was up. I knew she wouldn't eat any grits, eggs, and bacon that early. "We gotta go, grandma. Bernard gotta be there by a certain time."

"Well, y'all be careful. It's dark outside. When y'all need gas, don't wait until the hand gets all the way on E. Stop when it gets to half a tank. And when y'all stop, make sure you only stop in an area where it's a lot of people and a lot of light." Grandma continued to give last-minute advice to us as if we didn't know these things already. "And don't drive too fast over the speed limit. Cops can hide anywhere, and you don't want to get no tickets. And don't drive too close to other cars. Keep nice distance between the cars. Stay in the right lane, too. Let cars pass y'all. Don't y'all worry 'bout passin' no cars."

"Grandma, okay!" I had enough. "We got it! Thanks for everything." I gave her a hug and a kiss.

We walked out and got in the car, and she followed behind us, dressed in her robe. There was no evidence of the sun anywhere, but the moon shone quite distinctly and brightly. We got in the car, and I rolled down my window because I knew she'd have more to say.

"Keva, be careful coming back tomorrow." She seemed a little concerned that Keva would have to do the entire drive back alone from Atlanta on the next day. "Ursula know y'all on y'all way, right?" My mother's college friend stayed in Atlanta and was happy to let Keva spend the night with her before coming back the next day.

"Yes, she knows I'm coming. I told her I would call her when we were halfway there." She started driving off. "Alright, grandma, see you tomorrow."

"See ya, grandma. I'll see you at the end of the summer." I said my goodbyes.

"Bye, now. Be smart about things, and don't lose focus. I love you."

"Love you, too. Bye."

We drove off, and I could see her silhouette in the rear view mirror, eyeing us as we drove down the street. She was still waving, not knowing if we could see her or not.

"So I'm drivin' an hour and then you drivin' an hour, and we'll keep switching like that. I'm not driving all six hours while you sit over there and go to sleep." Keva started with her demands before we could get out of the neighborhood.

"Keva, I'm not startin' with you this mornin'. It's too early."

"I'm just telling you that you drivin' half the distance."

Right when she said that, I remembered that I left something. "Keva, I don't have my check-in form that they mailed me and also another paper."

"Bernard, where is it? We'n got time to be backtrackin' already. I told you dat."

"It's not at grandma house. It's at daddy house."

"Why is it over daddy house? I thought your mail go to grandma house."

"All my college stuff was mailed to daddy house, and I left it there by mistake when I went by there to get some of my sweaters."

She had the most disgusted look on her face because she knew I needed it. Luckily, we hadn't gotten on the highway yet, so we just went by my father's. The normal late-night visitors' cars were in the driveway. I wouldn't make a disturbance. I would just pop in, get the papers, and pop back out. We were already late and didn't have time to waste. Once I got in, I saw the papers and grabbed them. I didn't really know why, but I started to feel tears forming on my way out but fought them back. I locked the door and headed toward Keva's car. About halfway there, I heard the door unlock behind me.

"Bernie!" My father heard the stirring and wanted to see who it was. Out of all the times he wanted to talk, he wanted to pick the time that I was literally on my way to college. I hadn't anticipated speaking with him. I just wanted to be gone and be on my way. But he had called me and stepped outside into the darkness. He had on his socks and flip-flops.

"Hey, daddy." I was more startled than upset.

"Just wanted to say congratulations, man." I wasn't sure where this was coming from, but I wasn't investing much in a heavy-duty conversation now. Plus, I knew if I did, I'd get emotionally taken in and one moment would eventuate into an hour, which I just didn't have, not right now. "You did good to stay focused and make something out yourself." I just stood, stared at him, and listened. I couldn't stop the tears from forming, though. *Lord, not now. This is not the time for me to break down.* "Keep on doing good, Bernie. Keep your grades up. I'm proud of ya."

"Alright, thanks." That's all I could think to say. I had really moved past the point of anger toward him. That emotion had fizzled out a few years prior. In a weird way, I felt a sense of pity for him. I moved toward him and gave him a hug. Sadly, I couldn't remember the last time I had done so. Doubly sadly, I actually didn't care when it was. "See ya later, daddy. Take care o' yourself."

"Okay, man. Take it easy." He turned his attention to Keva. "Hey, puddin'."

She waved from the driver's seat. "Hey, daddy. I'll be back tomorrow." She was still staying at his home. I didn't know how she did it.

I got back on the passenger's side, still trying to keep my emotions at bay. I couldn't afford to keep crying over another person's choices. I had come to determine that it wasn't healthy for me.

Thankfully, Keva did her part to beat back whatever emotions I was dealing with. Sometimes, I think she knew when I was sinking into an emotional rut and had her own way of snapping me out of it with her crassness. "I sholl hope you got everything now! We ain't got time to be stopping nowhere else!"

"Yeah, I got everything."

Somehow, I think it ended up being more than coincidence that I left those items at my father's house. Maybe every child longs for some semblance of affirmation and blessing from the father, no matter the age. As weird as it was, I felt a strange sense of validation from him and that this next chapter would welcome me with open arms of sorts.

"Bernard, wake up!"

I had drifted off to sleep during my shift of driving. The captain had driven the first hour and was wise enough to stay alert during my shift. "Fool, is you crazy?! You tryin' to get both of us killed?!" It was a question but really an emphatic statement. "Pull over at the next rest stop. I'm not foolin' wichu early this mornin'!"

"Keva, you act like I'm falling asleep on purpose. I ain't never drove no long distance like this before." I was trying my best to justify my tiredness.

"So what? If you keep falling asleep, you ain't got to worry about no Mo'house or nobody else house 'cause you ain't gone make it past South Carolina, let alone Atlanta. Pull over!" She had that permanent frown on her face.

"I gotta wait 'til we get to a rest area, Keva." I wasn't pulling over on the side of the road.

We switched after I had only driven for twenty minutes, much to her chagrin. And she let it be known how upset she was. "You probably doing this on purpose so I'll have to drive the whole way!"

"Keva, whatever. I ain't doin' this on purpose. I'm not that crazy." Strangely, after we switched, I was wide awake.

"Now all of a sudden, you so awake. You ain't sleepy." She was driving again and sizing me up.

I laughed but only because what she was saying appeared to be the truth. I didn't know how I was so wide awake when I sat in the passenger's seat but so tired when I started driving. I had no explanation for it other than I'd never driven far before. All I could do was laugh. I kept being sensitive to her tiredness, though, as I intermittently drove my twenty-minute shifts. That was all I could give. She kept calling my name when I got sleepy and as I kept veering to the side of the road. She didn't sleep a wink. I wasn't sure how she would drive the entire six hours back by herself, but she had been trained to be much tougher than I and would handle herself well. We watched the sun rise and listened to music. Soon, we were right outside of Georgia, with only 169 miles to go.

As we approached Atlanta, the highways opened up to six lanes, and there was a sense of newness that gripped me. I was pretty stoked about it and couldn't wait to see the palatial, mansion-like campus.

"Uh-uh. No way! This can't be it!" This was all I could utter when we pulled into the campus entrance. This was so anticlimactic. I'm not sure what I envisioned the campus looking like, but this wasn't it.

Keva reveled in my disappointment by giving an explosion of laughter. "That's what you get! You should have visited before you decided to come all the way down here."

She was actually right, but I wasn't about to feed into her sense of correctness. I hadn't visited because I couldn't afford it, and no one really mentioned anything about helping me orchestrate a visit. So I had to take what I could get. At least we were traveling during the summer. The prefreshman science program was ideal for me. If my experience this summer was too much to bear, I had a small window of time to change where I'd spend my college years. At the very least, I could take courses and hopefully make a couple of A's that would be applied to my college transcript.

The rust-colored buildings seemed to blend in with the red clay that donned parts of the campus. We drove up to the security station on campus to get further directions.

"Yes, I'm looking for Forbes." I was reading the instructions guide that I had been mailed and talking to the guard to figure out where I would check in.

"Just go straight up the hill and it'll be on the left." He gave back driving instructions. "But after you unpack, you gotta come back down here and park your car over in the lot." He pointed toward the tennis courts.

"Thanks."

After we got situated, Keva and I just walked around campus to see what else it had to offer. Before we knew it, we were on Clark Atlanta's campus. The border was seamless. It all seemed just one big lot. I didn't know where Morehouse started and ended when it came to the big quadrangle.

"Keva, I think this is where they filmed *School Daze*." I offered some school trivia, but she could have cared less.

"So what? Whoop-dee-do."

"Yep. I think that's where Gina got one of her first roles." I offered some more advice, but she trumped me.

"Her name is Tisha, nerd. Why people always think actors' names are their real names? Her name is Tisha Campbell. Gina is her character on Martin, Mr. Valedictorian." She always had to take it there.

"Whatever." She was right.

It was finally time for her to go to Ursula's. I hadn't seen her in ages, probably since I was in diapers. She and my mom went to NCCU together, and she had even lived in the community in which my father lived. Now, she lived in Atlanta as a teacher at Washington High School. Her son and Dwayne, Jr. were pretty close, while her daughter, Bianca, and Keva were the same age. Keva would stay over there for the night and then hit the road alone the next morning.

"Well, looks like I got to meet some new friends this summer and start over, huh?" I was trying to figure out a way to say goodbye without being too mushy. Keva was not the one to go through all of that emotional stuff. "I'll just probably study all day and never go to Spelman. I ain't trying to lose my focus and my scholarship. Plus, look how small I look. Them girls ain't gone want nobody that look like they a freshman in high school when I'm in college."

"Yeah, you do look small." She knew how to put the knife in the womb. "Look, you can be a bookworm if you want to. It ain't all about grades. You better learn how to meet new people and stop being so much of a nerd. You better have some street smarts and not just book smarts."

We walked toward the car. "I ain't no nerd. I just do my work." And I supposed she had forgotten that I had overcome the same family dysfunction that she did. So I wasn't exactly underexposed to the harshness of life.

"Well anyway, good luck, nerd. I'm going over to Ursula's house to get some rest, and I'm driving back tomorrow."

"Well, call me when you get over there."

"Call you for what? I'm older than you. You ain't older than me."

"What that got to do with anything? Stop being so stubborn." We were back to our bickering, even as she climbed into her Yugo. I didn't know how or if she would be able to make the six-hour drive back by herself on the next day, but I'm glad she had somewhere to stay on that night. I was learning that she was one tough cookie and offered advice the best way she thought an older sister could.

I stood by her car as she started to drive off. "Well, see you later. Thanks for drivin' me up here. I don't know how I'm gettin' back after the summer program is over, but I'll call grandma to try to set some'm up. Keva, don't try to do all six hours on tomorrow at one time. You not no superhero. Just take your time. Ain't no rush. I'll call everybody and tell them I made it up here." I was trying to get everything in. Thankfully, I had hugged her before she entered the car, but that was the extent of emotion I would get from her. I was the crybaby because my eyes started watering again as she kept her usual stoic face and gave little response.

As if she had ignored everything I had just uttered, she gave her departing summer words. "Bye, nerd. Do good." That was it. She was pulling off, and all I saw were the brake lights go off and on as she approached Westview Drive. I didn't know how that rinky-dink car made it or would make it back. I could only stare from behind and hope that it had one final trip left in it.

It was great to meet so many positive brothers that summer. I thought I was pretty sharp, but these guys ran rings around me and sometimes made me feel like I shouldn't have been there. One of the guys was from Mississippi and had gotten a near-perfect score on the SAT. He'd go on to become a chemistry professor at Howard and do great research. Others would get MD/PhDs from the best universities in the country and achieve greatness in their own right. And here I was, sharing dorms with them, not knowing if I'd measure up or become anything noteworthy. I figured I'd just take one step at a time and get through this first summer successfully and get the best grades that I could.

Much of the time that summer, we were bombarded with classes and tutorial sessions. It felt more like academic boot camp than anything else. We got a chance to mingle with the girls from Spelman, who themselves were undergoing a similar rigorous onslaught of academics. So whenever we could all get together, testosterone and estrogen were raging everywhere. Thankfully, the counselors were there to help keep a rein on us so that we didn't get out of control.

"Hey. What's your name?" Here was a girl asking me my name, and I was almost shaking but trying to act like I was calm and cool.

"Who, me? I'm Bernard." Not thinking straight, I didn't show the common decency to ask her hers. So she volunteered.

"Okay. I'm Kendra."

"Oh, alright. Nice to meet you." I was lying. I was nervous as hell.

She continued. "So where are you from?"

"North Carolina. Durham. I was born at Duke." I always felt the need to pre-explain where Durham was. I figured Duke was a well-known national university and a nice focal point.

"Why you tell people what hospital you were born in?"

"Well, I didn't know if you heard of Durham. But a lot of people know about Duke."

"Oh." She tried to follow my logic but seemed only more confused. She drank some of the pineapple and orange juice mixture that still had the pulp in it. "Well, I'm from Michigan. Ypsilanti, Michigan." And she didn't even venture to give me a geography lesson. In her mind, it was where it was. If I hadn't heard of it before, it wasn't her problem. Thankfully, I had my own reference upon which to continue the conversation.

"Really? My aunt lives in Kalamazoo. I go visit sometimes but not a lot. It's too cold. I don't see how black people live up there. You know, we don't like cold. At least I don't."

She laughed. "Yeah, that's about a two-hour drive from Ypsilanti. And I didn't have a choice where I was born."

I laughed a dry laugh. Right there, before my eyes, I was having my first real conversation with a girl since arriving in college. And the whole while, I could feel my body shaking with nervousness. I wonder what she was really thinking. I wonder if she noticed how skinny I was or if I seemed too geeky. This stuck in my mind, thanks to Keva's constant use of the nerd lingo. At any rate, I was just happy to have gotten through it without making myself look too off-the-wall.

"Well, I'm sure I'll see you around this summer." Kendra was saying her goodbyes because she and the other girls had to get to their tutorial sessions, and Dr. Dreyfuss was standing there, rounding them up and giving us a don't-even-think-about-coming-to-their-dorm stare. We boys had to walk back to campus and get on with our nightly tutorial and prepare for the next day. As the rest of the guys buddied around with each other, I stuck to myself, proud that I hadn't put my foot in my mouth and embarrassed myself in front of Kendra. It was hard to negotiate this thing without any advice from my father about how to pick up girls. I'd have to just be my best nerdy self and socialize the best that I could.

# twenty-one

# 5′10″, 130

That summer in Atlanta was great. We didn't have the latitude to just venture out into the city because most of us were still under eighteen, and a string of robberies around the campus had recently ensued. Legally, we were minors, so we had to govern ourselves within the strict confines of the program's guidelines. I was glad I had chosen to go down and get a head start on the rest of the freshmen. Granted, the calculus and English classes were gruesome. Because of the challenge in schedules and different summer programs to service, there only ended up being three of us in the calculus class, but Professor Tate taught us just like he taught his other class, which literally had forty-five people in it. He had been trained at University of Michigan but hadn't finished his dissertation, it was rumored. In a few years, he'd have to leave Morehouse because of some contention regarding his credentials, but I always thought it was a political and underhanded deal to have him removed. He was a gifted mathematician and eventually moved on to teach at Jackson State and then Gordon State College.

After the program was over, Keva came back to pick me up. Believe it or not, I was excited to see her. I had missed her uncanny sense of teaching lessons and getting on my nerves. I was shocked to see that the Yugo had made another trip.

"Hey." I was smiling and exciting.

"Mm. Hey." She returned the greeting in her normal bland and unaffected manner. But I could tell in her eyes that she was happy to see me.

As we headed back to Durham, I was able to drive more than I had before. I was getting the hang of sitting down for hours doing nothing, watching life pass me by. I had learned the art of rolling the window down and letting the air outside hit me in the face. She even started to trust me more because she didn't hesitate to catch several naps as I took my turn driving.

Once we hit the city borders, everything looked exactly the same. I wasn't sure how much change I thought a summer would have, but I guess I expected some. We stopped by the restaurant, and I saw my dad. He was doing his normal round of cooking as he always did. I couldn't believe how skilled he was at doing this. If only I had half those skills, I'd be satisfied.

"Hey, dad." I startled him.

"Hey, Bernie!" He was excited. He popped a hush puppy in his mouth and came to hug me. "How was Hotlanta?"

"It was nice, different, but nice. They didn't really let us do nothin'. They made us study and study and study. I got two A's in the classes I took, but it was tough. I didn't know it was going to be *that* hard."

"Yeah, well keep doing it up, man."

I had to grab something to eat. I had missed my normal access to the collard greens, potato salad, candied yams, and all the other fixings. I had traded it in for generic slop on campus. I couldn't get back quick enough to devour the cuisine I had grown up on.

The month I was back, I made a point to go see my mother, who had managed to get back on her feet. She was staying in government-subsidized housing and was making ends meet. Keva and I drove over to where she stayed to see how she was making it. There was no answer when I knocked on the door, so I decided I'd get back in the car.

"Keva, she ain't there."

"Well, let's go." Keva wasn't about to wait for her to come back. It was a one-shot deal with her. Right before I got into the car, I heard a familiar voice from a distance.

"Heyyy, baby!"

I looked around to see where it was coming from. There she was, walking on the railroad tracks. There was a set of them behind her home, and she often used them as a shortcut to go to the store. "Ma, why you walking on the tracks? You know they not safe."

"Shit, I'm a country girl. I'm used to walking on these thangs." After that quick explanation, she went back to her initial excitement. "Hey, baby. How's my baby doin'?" She laid a wet one, a really wet one, on my cheek.

"Dang, ma." I dried it with the shoulder part of my shirt.

She went to kiss Keva, but Keva was having none of it. "No, ma, stop!" She pulled away and gave her signature frown.

"Girl, I tell you the truth, you done had yo' own mind since you came outta me. I don't know why I even think you gone be anything different than you."

We all sat and talked and just enjoyed each other's company. When it was time to leave, we said our so-longs. She was doing pretty well for herself. She had taken up a job at Burger King and had to be at work pretty early the next morning to make the biscuits. But she always looked toward heaven and uttered a prayer when we left. This time was no different. *Lord, protect my chirren. Look after 'em. Don't let nobody do nothing to 'em.* She was praying out loud so we could hear as we walked back to the car. Keva rolled her eyes in her head and let out a loud sigh because it was so embarrassing. In her mind, why couldn't mama do this when we were in the house? It just *had* to be done outside.

"Bye, ma." Keva hurried up and got in the car.

"See ya, ma. I'll stop back by before I go back to Atlanta in a few weeks."

"Bye, y'all." And then she'd start crying on the spot, no warning, no prep, and utter what was indeed a true statement. "My children growing up." If Burger King didn't work out for her, she could always nab a role in some melodrama in Hollywood.

Once I made it back to Atlanta that fall, my confidence had soared. I witnessed the other freshmen's anxieties but shared in none of them. To me, I was somewhat of an upperclassman because I had been there that summer. I was even offering direction concerning some of the campus destinations. Keva had driven me back, and I was getting the hang of driving long distances. I had gotten to a point where I could drive for two hours straight.

I had checked into my room on the third floor of Hubert Hall and met my roommate, who was actually a resident assistant. He hailed from St. Croix, Virgin Islands and had the accent to go with it. Lymuel was very soft-spoken and always walked around in flip-flops, even during the winter months. I guess I was glad that I didn't have a party-going roommate that first year. He was always studying and keeping my floormates quiet. He really didn't have to reprimand us that much. After all, we were staying in an honors dorm. So I just did my work and steered clear of anything that would get me in trouble with him.

After perusing the college catalog that summer, I had decided that my major would be English, much to the disappointment of my grandfather. He had worked his fingers to the bone, building his restaurant business and assumed we'd all major in business management, accounting, or something similar. That, in part, was Keva's dilemma. She was trying to please him concerning her major and not herself. Consequently, she was struggling in her studies. It wasn't until she changed her major that she developed a passion for college and her career. After speaking with my grandmother, she encouraged me to pursue what I wanted to pursue.

"You the one who gone be sittin' in them classes, so you need to choose something that you like." I always remembered hearing that advice, even though I was always stubborn enough to follow my own heart anyway. It was just good to know that I had that kind of support coming from elsewhere.

I loved math but seemed more passionate about reading, so I went with that option. Plus, anything that could assist me in verbal and written communication would help me in any career. I was convinced that being an English major would give me confidence and help me attack my stuttering problem, which still reared its head every now and then, depending on the circumstances. I'm sure I'd develop an appreciation for the classics and contemporary literature. I also loved writings by certain African-American authors like William Wells Brown, Toni Morrison, and all those who wrote during the Harlem Renaissance. I figured this was the time to expand my academic horizons, and English seemed to be the highway to help me in that exploration.

The classes were great, and the professors were second to none. I'd managed to sign up for a public speaking class but dropped it after the first day since I found out we'd have to give extemporaneous speeches. Too nerve-wracking. I was loving the fact, though, that I was not the only nerd in my classes. I was probably the only one who looked like a nerd, but at least everybody there was intelligent, give or take a few. To be honest, I had my mind set on the Rhodes Scholarship as a freshman. I'd researched what the committee looked for in a potential candidate. The academic strength, the athletic prowess, the leadership knack, all of which I had. It was just a matter of time before this dream would be realized. Just like the other goals I had accomplished, this one too would be realized through persistence and focus. In the meantime, I'd just enjoy the college ride and be grateful for this opportunity.

"Hey! Let's go, Dillard. You slackin'! Let's go! Let's go! Let's go!" No one could ignore Coach Green's voice. Even when we were clear across the football field, his high-pitched voice was distinctive, and we had better obey his commands. It was rare that he yelled at me because I always did what he said, but he didn't shy away from whenever he had to do so. "Hey! Dillard, if you don't move up to the front, you gone have to do another one." I heard him loud and clear and struggled my way to the front until we finished. "There you go, son! You gotta keep close contact with the leader. Run up front!" I squatted to rest but not for long. "Walk it off, son. Walk it off!"

Perhaps one of the best decisions I made at Morehouse was to join the cross country and track teams. I wasn't on any type of athletic scholarship but decided that I'd walk on and try to be a part of the program. It was a little boring going from class straight to the library and studying for six hours. I needed something to break up the monotony. Since I had been running track since I was a kid, it seemed like a no-brainer for me to see if I could make the team. I was noticeably lankier than the rest of the guys, but it didn't matter to me. Coach Rumsfeld back in Durham told me that I had heart, so I never really looked at my size as a disadvantage. When I arrived on the first day of practice, I introduced myself to Coach Green and informed him that I wanted to be on the team.

"Hi, Coach. My name is Bernard. I ran track in high school and wanted to see if I could be on the team here."

"Well, you gone have to run cross country first, son, to get yourself in college shape. You gotta have heart to be on this team."

"I ran cross country in high school, so I'm sort of used to it."

"Well, here it's a little different. The distance is a little farther in college, so you gone have to be ready." He was making sure I was ready mentally. "By the way, how tall are you, son?"

"5´10."

"How much you weigh?"

"130."

"Lawd, have mercy. We gone have to get you in that weight room and feed you, son."

lemonade

"Well, I don't know why I'm so skinny because I eat a lot. My metabolism just high, I guess. My grandma be sayin' I must have tapeworm or some'm."

He smirked. "Well, high metabolism or not, you need to gain a little weight."

"Okay."

"What event you do in track?"

"In high school, I ran the quarter and the 300 hurdles."

"What was your time in the quarter?"

"My fastest was a 50 in the quarter, and I split a 48 in the mile relay."

"Well, you gone have to run faster than that here. You not on scholarship, so the guys we got on scholarship run faster than that."

"Alright, no problem." In my mind, I didn't have anything to lose. I wasn't on athletic scholarship anyway, so he could only kick me off the team if I didn't run up to his standard.

"Just meet us out here tomorrow and start this cross country training. We ain't got no time to waste, son."

"Okay. See you tomorrow."

And that was the beginning of a great relationship between Coach Green and me. Once the track season started, I never missed a practice or halfway completed a workout. I did everything that Coach Green asked. A few of those on scholarship teased me because I wasn't cutting any corners, which made them feel uncomfortable. But it was cool. It was all done in fun. I wasn't holding back. If anything, I kept them on their toes. Coach Green even threatened to yank their scholarships because they weren't getting the results he expected. He had his own uncanny way of driving home his point when it came to trying to motivate us, especially those who were on his scholarship dollars and not performing. "Son, what? Y'all gone mess around and let Dillard take ya money. Here he is, a walk-on and running circles around some of y'all. You gone look around one day, and you gone notice that your pants gone be hanging around your ankles and you gone be bent over, hoping you'n get screwed." We would turn away from him, trying our best not to laugh.

But DeSean from Jacksonville, Florida couldn't hold it. He burst out laughing. "Sorry, Coach!" He was apologizing but still laughing. He only did what all of us wanted to do. He just had very little restraint in him.

Coach cracked a slight smile, knowing that his imagery would touch our funny bones. "Son, what? I know it sound funny, but I'm serious as a heart

172

attack. What? This is something that *you* gone have to want. I can't want it for ya. I don't care if you just got one foot. If you here on *my* money, you better hop yo' ass around that track on that one foot and hit the times I need you to hit." He started his responses typically with *Son, what?*

When he said that, DeSean only got worse and started laughing out loud for the second time. "I'm sorry, Coach." He was apologizing again.

But nobody on the team, not even DeSean, had a personality as wild and amusing at Stone's. He was from the Atlanta area and did not hesitate to make it known. Practice to practice, we had no idea as to what Stone would do or say that would have team members in stitches. I tried not to egg him on during workouts because I was so goal-oriented. In my mind, we had to get through the grueling task that Coach had in mind on that day with no distractions, but Stone always found a way to make sure humor was the order of the day at some point. This was especially so during away meets, in which we had to take the bus and stay at some modest hotel.

During these trips, I'd grab my seat by myself in the rear near the window and prepare for the journey. Soon, I'd see Stone making his way down the bus aisle, and I'd feign sleep, thinking he'd find entertainment elsewhere. In my false stupor of sleep, I would feel an undeniable plop in the seat next to me, along with his gotcha type of announcement. "Dillard, just wake right on up! You not sleep. I saw you when you closed your eyes. Just wake right on up! I'm sittin' here whether you want me to or not. Just move over!"

And then, he started to amuse everyone on the bus, as if he were on stage. In his half-munchkin, half-helium-ingested voice, he'd begin singing songs like *Reasons* by Earth, Wind, & Fire or *Let Me Be Your Angel* by Stacy Lattisaw. There was no way the team could keep its composure. Even Coach was laughing. I tried not to laugh but couldn't help it. Stone was a nut. "Man, Stone, just know that you is a fool."

Coach Green always seemed to pair us up when rooming. "Ah, let's see, lemme look at my list. Looks like we got Stone and Dillard roomin' together. I'm sure y'all will be nice company for each other." And he'd smile. He paired us up repeatedly and deliberately. I think Coach had an eye for balance. He knew I was so focused, sometimes overly so. And Stone's personality would help me chill out and learn how to flow with life. On the other hand, some of my seriousness would hopefully influence Stone. For one couldn't play or joke all the time. Perhaps this calculating move on Coach's part would lead to an even exchange in both of our characters. A lot with

Coach Green, as with Coach Rumsfeld in high school, seemed to be less and less about track itself than it did about our developing into real men with real character.

Most times, once we got settled in our room, tired from traveling woes, Stone and I just chatted and talked about goals and God, a few fears and insecurities. When he got into serious mode, he doted over how much support he got from his parents and how he really wanted to be a role model for his younger brother. Although I wasn't able to identify with the exact kind of support core as he and felt a little disappointed that I didn't, I knew we were both on this manhood journey together and would support each other as best we could. After all, we were still young men just looking to enjoy our college days. We'd have the rest of our lives to be grown up. As for right now, Stone would just be Stone, and I would just be me.

I don't think anything could have prepared me, however, for his transition in life beyond college. We lost touch somewhat after those socially formative years, but I caught wind of the fact that he really started making an impact in society. He had become a great businessman by establishing key networks and connections with one of hip-hop's most astute entertainers and moneymakers. He was learning the ropes of that world and making serious moves. He became an author, married his Spelman sweetheart, and was making some acting waves in Hollywood. When I went to see the movie *Fat Albert*, there was Stone on screen, acting just as silly there as he did on the bus. I wasn't expecting to see him in his role, so it was a refreshing and welcomed shock. I just grinned from ear to ear, feeling a strong sense of pride and happiness for him.

He changed his name to a more entertainment-based name, and he eventually was able to get the right connections to become the host of a major MTV reality show in which he motivated the next generation of so-called thugs to refine and re-define their perception of manhood, celebrating the notion that classy is cool. Here was a man who wasn't just talking about moving forward. He was doing it. And he was unlocking the secret to make his personality and business acumen work for him. It was just good to know that someone who I'd been in contact with was managing to fight through whatever opposition was necessary to find his niche. And if he could do it in his own way, then I was encouraged that I'd be able to do it in mine.

I ended up not just making the track team, but I ended up being one of the key team members. The good part was that I was running because I wanted to not because I had to run to keep an athletic scholarship. My times improved greatly in the 400-meter hurdles, and I ended up running the final leg on the 4x400 relay during my senior year, in which relay members ran a lap and passed off the baton. Everyone wanted to be on this relay because it was the most prestigious relay, especially if you ran the last leg, which turned out to be both stressful but exciting to me.

Despite Coach Green's strange way of motivating us, he always helped us realize that it wasn't just about track. He spoke with us frequently about life and being a family man. He showed us by example how to function as men because he constantly brought his wife and children to our track meets and had us interact with them. As confrontational as he could be sometimes, he also showed us his gentle side when it came to acting as father and husband. It was good for me to witness the example he set in that regard. His actions made me wish that I had that type of encourage and nourishment in my developmental years. But I learned how to observe what he did and to tuck it away in my treasure chest of how to make relationships work.

# the maroon and white envelope

eing away from home was liberating. It wasn't hard for me to be motivated to go to classes without someone's telling me to get up and go. I had witnessed a few of my brothers who were struggling with their newfound freedom. Many of them chose to sleep in for their early morning classes. Since middle school, I had been getting myself up and making myself ready to hop on the bus while my father slept. Continuing this pattern in college seemed no different. I couldn't believe I was actually on campus living my dream on the road to graduate and win the Rhodes Scholarship. I could taste it in every move I made. Regarding my pre-Morehouse days, I chuckle at the time in which I wrote a letter to Dr. Benjamin E. Mays while in high school, asking him to give me some advice to assist me in my decision on whether I'd attend Morehouse or not. The secretary wrote me back and informed me that Dr. Mays had passed away some time ago and that she'd included some information about the school to aid me. I'm sure she thought I was one dumb nut.

At any rate, I was here now and didn't want to change what had gotten me to this point. I was consistent with studying and running. But I hadn't found the right place to worship. We had services on campus, but those didn't really fulfill me as much as I would have liked them to. I'd have to find a decent church off campus to help me remain sane and stable and to keep me grounded with principles I had made as a part of my daily life. I met up with a few friends in Hubert one Sunday and decided to journey with them to a church within walking distance.

"So how did y'all hear about this church?" I asked Nevin. Some of us at Morehouse and Spelman were part of the gospel choir on campus and sort of hung out and traveled in a pack to church.

"We actually just got the phone book, opened it up, put our finger on the first name and saw that it wasn't too far from campus. So that's where we're going."

"Are y'all serious? What kind of strategy is that?" I wanted to use an alternate word for "strategy" but resisted.

"Yep. We just gone see what it's about and if we don't like it, we just won't go back."

I didn't really have anything to lose, so I went ahead and took the twenty-minute walk with them. We cut through campus, through Clark, down past Spelman's back entrance, through John Hope Homes, up Hills Avenue, and arrived at a small, unassuming church that sat literally in the middle of nowhere. "Are y'all sure this is it?"

"Well, the address is the one that I wrote down that was in the phone book."

"Um, it don't really look that great from the outside, but let's just check." Carrie, one of the freshman girls from Spelman, chimed in.

I looked at them as we approached the door and let them go first. There was a small foyer at the entrance and a decent-sized sanctuary. We walked down the center aisle to find seats, although I think we were supposed to walk down either side and then fill in from there. The usher missed us and just let us find our own seats. We were early, so we sat down and just waited for Sunday school to be finished. The Sunday school setup was strange. All classes were being held right in the main sanctuary. Different pews were sectioned for each class. Amazingly, class sections managed to drown out what was going on in other sections, as if their section was the only one present.

"What kind of setup is this? Why don't they get confused or distracted by the other classes?" I was asking an honest question. It wasn't like the place was enormous.

"That's the million dollar question." Kinnis had to get smart with me.

Soon, we were preparing for the 11 AM service, and we ended up just sitting where we already were. It was easier. A few people looked strangely at us because we were apparently in *their* seats. But they adjusted because I had decided I wasn't moving anywhere.

Right before the service started, the organist started playing and the drummer started warming up. The drummer was a female and had talent that would put any brother to shame.

"Okay. This isn't too bad." Nevin was voicing his approval. "The music sounds nice."

"You can't judge whether a church is good just based on the music, boy." I was putting in my two cents.

"I know. I'm just saying the music is good."

Once the service started, that place must have gone through a major transformation because everything about it in my eyes seemed fine. Far from perfect, but it was good.

It was one of those old-fashioned sounding churches, but the people in it seemed relatively young, not what one would expect from one of those types of churches. There was a praise service that resembled the sound of a concert. People in the congregation were playing tambourines skillfully as if they had rehearsed with them for years. It was a hand-clapping, foot-stomping, devil-chasing church. At times, they lifted their hands to worship and would get in a nice dance when the drums gave off a serious beat. Before I realized how dignified I was supposed to be acting in such a setting, I was already joining in, clapping, and tapping my own feet.

"Man, I like this place." I had to yell it to Nevin because of the volume of the music during the praise service.

"Yeah, me too." He had to shout it back.

Once the choir prepared to sing, I glanced over at Nevin and the rest of our group. My high was gone somewhat based on what I saw. The so-called choir was comprised of two sopranos, five altos, and three tenors. The dark-skinned lady who had walked to the front to direct them seemed like she knew what she was doing and had dealt with these low numbers in choir attendance before. She seemed unfazed and asked one of the altos to come down more to the front for visual balance. "Um, did the rest of the choir oversleep or something?" I joked to Nevin under my breath and laughed.

"I know. I'm saying. Where the rest of them at?"

When the choir started singing, I sat back in awe with wide eyes. The two sopranos literally sounded like ten. The altos, like ten too. The tenors held their own as well.

"What? How in the world are they sounding like that?" I was floored.

"They sound like a gigantic choir, but they only got just a handful of people." JoAnn had finally added to the conversation.

By the time they had finished, the whole church was standing up, caught up in the worship experience generated by those few singers.

Around offering time, a guy came from behind a door by where the drums were located. I assumed it was a bathroom, but it was actually an entrance from an office area. He had on a robe and a distinguishing pair of what looked like M.C. Hammer glasses. The presider of the service was saying something, but I was still focusing on this guy, who was making an entrance. Somewhat heavyset, he walked up the stairs to the pulpit and walked across and took his chair. This was obviously the pastor. Some of the congregation stood up and sat down when he sat down. I kept staring at the M.C. Hammer glasses because I hadn't really seen anybody in clergy wear them. While staring in that direction, I noticed a lady in my periphery walking alongside the wall, moving toward a seat in the front that was especially for her but a little off to the right, out of the way. Her chair was not as long as a regular pew, but it was longer than a regular chair. A pewette. And it was all hers. She was the pastor's wife. She had a beaming smile and appeared very quiet. Between his glasses and her permanent smile, they seemed a match made in heaven.

Once he finally approached the pulpit, he only stayed a matter of minutes. He had to introduce his sister, who would be doing the sermonic solo. I watched her walk up the stairs and grab the mic. She apparently had just stepped out of an angel's body because the noise that came from inside of her didn't seem real. The range of her notes was unthinkable. She didn't just sing soprano. She sang super-soprano. She dwelt in a musical realm of her own.

"What the ..." Before I finished, I realized we were in church and caught myself.

Nevin stared back and finished my thought, not caring where we were. " ... hell."

"Have you ever heard of her?" She had to be famous. Nobody could not be famous with a voice like that.

"Naw, I ain't never heard of her." Nevin had no clue. Coming from him, that was major because he was a part of a recording group back in his California hometown. So he was in the know concerning up-to-date gospel groups. "Never."

We'd come to discover later that she would become a well-known fixture on the gospel scene, she and her other eight sisters. They would often be compared to the Clark Sisters, but they hailed from Atlanta, of course. Ten children. It was rumored that the father wanted enough sons to staff his own baseball team but got nine girls instead. Funny.

The pastor was very encouraging. As he brought the message, I forgot about the cool glasses and listened to what he said. His wife was on her feet in support of his every word.

During the service, he welcomed us, the first-time visitors. "We are the family church of action, where Jesus is surely the main attraction." He had nice charisma and charm. When he said it, it had a nice ring.

As we left, needless to say, we had been pleasantly surprised. We left and walked back to campus.

"Well, I don't know 'bout y'all, but I think this is where I'll be goin'." I was pretty sure of it.

"Me, too," Nevin agreed.

Carrie and Kinnis seemed pretty sure too.

JoAnn was a little more hesitant. "Mm. I don't know. I'll see. There were some good things and some things that were not so good, in my opinion. I may visit around to see what some other churches offer."

As we walked Carrie and JoAnn back to Spelman, we made it back to campus. We laughed and joked about nothing. I was just happy to know I had found somewhere that I could call a church home.

I had decided at some point to enter the Honors Program in college. As if college itself wasn't hard enough, I made the decision that I'd need more of a challenge academically. I had been invited before starting as a freshman, but I thought it wise to delay entry a year to get myself acclimated to college life. I'm still not sure why I joined because all it meant to many were more challenges associated with the normal academic load. But I was up to taking on the challenge.

After the first year, I was admitted by the program director. She told me to register for the Honors sections of whichever courses were offered that semester. That semester, I signed up for the honors sections of World Literature I and American National Government. The guys on campus were bright, but the fellows in these honors sections were geniuses. I didn't feel intimidated, but I had to be sure to stay studied up to keep pace. The World Lit class was fine, but for some reason, nothing was clicking in the Government class. It seemed as though the more I read, the more confused I got. I would look around the class, and everyone would seem like they were following along, and I felt like a fish out of water.

We only had a midterm and a final exam in the class, along with a term paper we had to write to get our grade for the course. Every day, I was in the library after track practice, struggling to keep up with the reading for the course. You couldn't get much studying in at Club Woody, though. This was the nickname given to our library because it was more of a social meeting place of all the students in the Atlanta University Center and named after Robert Woodruff. I would manage to find a pretty secluded area there, however, where I could study to help me focus. I had managed to unlock academic mysteries in previous courses in high school and so far in college. This course would just be another one I'd have to fight and add to my resume of slain courses. I hadn't gotten any C's on my record up to this point, and I sure wasn't going to start now.

Dr. Michaelson lectured rather matter-of-factly about the American system of rules and governance and how the authority was distributed between the federal and state governments, or something like that. Ideas weren't gelling at all, and I got a D on the midterm. Shortly afterwards, he passed out topics for the paper. All of them looked alien to me, but I'd settle on one eventually. I kept telling myself that I'd figure this course out. But the learning curve was pretty steep, so I had better learn what I needed to and better learn it quickly. The Lord hadn't let me down up to this point, and He wouldn't start now. I put in hour after hour after hour at Club Woody. It was no playtime for me. I couldn't mess around, get a low grade, and possibly lose my scholarship. There was no way I'd end up back home in Durham because of finances. A low grade could automatically send me packing and going home. The college didn't play when it came to its money and your academic performance. Funds were limited, and there were not many of us who had full, four-year academic scholarships.

I had started doing what I knew to help me through this difficult time. I had found some quiet place on campus that I'd visit regularly to help me keep my wits about me. I'd talk to God and just decompress. *Lord, I don't really know what's going on here, but I'm not understanding why I'm not grasping this material. I need some help. Nobody else seems to be having problems with what's being taught, just me.* And I'd just talk and be quiet and talk and be quiet until I got sleepy.

Before I knew it, I had postponed choosing the topic for my paper. I was struggling just to keep up with the regular course material that I didn't have time to write a paper too. I wanted to speak with others in the class, but my pride wouldn't let me. In my mind, everyone else in the class seemed attentive and was hanging pretty strong. They joked amongst each other and appeared to love it. Mostly everyone enrolled was on the pre-law track, so it seemed they had a predisposition for doing well in the course for that reason alone. I wasn't law-school bound. Neither did I want a career in public policy. This was just a course that just happened to be only one of the few honors courses offered this semester.

Five days before the paper was due, I thought I had better begin. Completing a twenty-page paper in five days suggested an insurmountable feat, but I'd do it because things just always happened to come together for me, as I saw it. About two days before finishing the paper, I had an epiphany. I would just count my losses and remove myself from the course. It was better to preserve my GPA and have fewer hours than to play superhero and stick it out, knowing I had bombed the midterm. So I made a break for the registrar's office.

"Hey, Ms. Wilson." I was somewhat out of breath.

"Hey, dear. How are you?" She always was nice to me. I had heard horror stories about students and the rapport with those in the administration office. Thankfully, in this instance, I had a pleasant experience.

"Yeah, there's a course I'm enrolled in. I don't think I'm doing too well, so I think I want to withdraw from it."

She processed what I said and genuinely gazed at me with sad eyes. "Bernard, I hate to tell you this, but yesterday was the final day that you could withdraw from a course." Murphy's Law was clearly in motion for me concerning this class.

"For real?" I was crushed. It was looking like I'd have to stick it out and give it my best effort. "Alright, thanks a lot. Have a good one."

I managed to push out what I thought was a decent paper. I had outside sources and made sure that I didn't plagiarize. I knew I wouldn't get an A on it, but at this point, a D would be just as welcomed. I had never been so nervous about a course in my life. Why was I not getting it?

The paper was to be turned in on the day of the final exam. Naïvely, I had an unction that the Lord would place another, separate paper for me in the bushes that I could recover as I entered Brawley Hall to go take the final.

It would be my ram in the bush, literally. I kept casually looking in bushes on my way to the building to see if some last-minute miracle would happen. The only thing I managed to see at each glance were poorly pruned bushes that were hosts to a few birds as they danced from branch to branch, chirping the theme song for the final-exam war in which I'd soon be involved.

Thankfully, the final exam was multiple choice. I had studied to a point, where I would be able to narrow down to two possible choices and go with gut feeling. After what seemed like an eternity, I handed in my exam. All I could do was hope I did well enough on the paper and luck up on the final to squeeze a C out of the course. It would be my first C ever, but I felt fine with it since I really did give it my best shot.

I packed up and drove almost immediately back to Durham. My grandmother had paid a small amount to buy a car from her sister-in-law, Aunt Cammie. She, with her half-laugh, half-cough, was my grandfather's baby sister and was one who didn't hesitate to speak her mind. She wasn't using her '81 AMC Concord anymore, so I was grateful to have something to drive back and forth to Georgia. So I jumped in the car and made the six-hour trek in what seemed like record speed.

I was just tired and felt like I just needed to get back to my familiar surroundings, even if they were not ideal. At that time, no grades were posted online for one to check, so everyone had to wait until around Christmas when grades were physically mailed to the permanent address. I kept checking the mailbox to see if the report card for the semester had come. I wanted to witness the miracle that had been wrought this semester. For the life of me, I still hadn't figured out why this particular course was so slippery. I'd taken courses before, which I didn't particularly like or care for, but I'd just manage to learn the material and ace it. This one was a different beast altogether. It had different horns, different teeth, different claws. Just different.

I came in one day and saw the maroon and white envelope on the table. Terrence had gotten the mail while I was out and left it for me. The moment of revelation had to be good. I wanted to see how things had righted themselves. I took a shower, put on my pajamas, made some tea, sat quietly, and stared at it. I almost started to pray but realized that what was done was done, good or bad, and no type of prayer would change the ink on the report card. After taking a couple of sips, I convinced myself to see the results of my efforts. I tore along the perforations, grabbed the semi-circle in the middle,

183

and yanked it out. The carbon copy inside served as a final, last-minute distraction. I finally read my marks:

| | |
|---|---|
| *SOPHOMORE ASSEMBLY* | *P* |
| *WORLD LITERATURE I (HONORS)* | *A* |
| *LITERARY FORM* | *B* |
| *INTERMEDIATE SPANISH* | *A* |
| *INTRO TO PHILOSOPHY* | *B* |
| *AMERICAN NAT. GOVT. (HONORS)* | *F* |

# inside the heart of a tiger

I withdrew my membership from the Honors Program faster than a cat could lick its butt, as my grandmother used to say. Never before had I gotten a C, let alone an F in an entire course. Some people thought this would be my breaking point, similar to Uncle Terrence's when he was at Harvard. The difference with me, I suppose, was that doing well academically was something I strove for but didn't define myself by. I never lost sleep because of a good or bad grade. I was just wired to aim for the best, which often resulted in A's. At any rate, I rested throughout that winter, refocused, and pressed full steam ahead and got ready to drive back to the ATL. This slight setback wouldn't deter my goal of getting the Rhodes.

As mentioned, I was now driving the entire distance by myself, not without some driving challenges still, but the Concord felt like a Rolls Royce to me. I had programmed myself to stop every two hours or so, but I still would often drift to sleep. On numerous occasions, as I passed through South Carolina, I would doze off and be shaken awake as I drove on the edge of the highway road. As I drifted off the road, I eventually began driving over the grooves, placed there for obvious reasons. When I woke up, my hand shot out of the window as I lifted it to thank God. Some of the drivers passing me waved back, thinking I was waving at them. If they only knew.

By the time I was a senior, I had bounced back pretty well academically and athletically. I got 4.0s during both semesters during my junior year and had gotten a little taller and heavier, a whopping 142 lbs. I managed to carry my weight on the track team and was appointed captain during my last year. Coach Green must have seen something in me for making me captain because he always talked about my being a leader. In my mind, I was just struggling to make it and taking one semester at a time. He was much more than a coach because he always told us we could come talk to him outside of practice if we needed to talk. And I remember taking him up on his offer once.

As I studied one day, I had gotten word that things weren't going too well on the home front concerning my father and his choices. Plus, my mother was still alone, not making any real progress in life. It seemed to be one of those moments where things were pretty much the same as they had always been, but to me they felt overwhelming. I climbed out the bed, threw on some clothes, and walked out of Kilgore Hall. It must have been 2 AM.

"Yo, you good, man?" I had awakened Ced, my roommate from Richmond. He never knew me to leave during this time, so he wanted to be sure I was fine.

"Yeah, I'm cool, man. I'll be back." I didn't want to talk to him about it.

"Be safe, yo."

I walked up to the campus exit on Fair Street and up to Coach's white house. I started to second-guess myself as I approached the door. It was dark and I was sure he was asleep. Before I convinced myself to turn around, I went ahead and rang the doorbell. I didn't hear it, so I assumed it was broken. In my mind, it was a sign to turn around and go back to bed. As I turned to walk down the stairs, the porch light came on.

"Dat you, Dillard?" Coach was standing at the door.

"Yes, sir, it's me."

"Come on in, son." He held the door open and let me walk in. He pointed me to the couch and directed me to sit down. He sat in what obviously was his chair. "You thirsty?"

"No, sir. Just couldn't sleep 'cause earlier I got some bad news from back home." I didn't go into details but just gave him as much as I was willing to share. "My daddy is not making good choices, and I'm really concerned about him. I'm trying to stay focused here in school, but I just keep thinking about the kind of danger he putting himself in. To be honest, I sort of hate him."

"Mm hmm." Coach was never at a lack of words. So that response threw me off a bit. Sensing his silence, I continued. It hadn't registered that we were sitting in the dark. He hadn't bothered to turn on any lights.

"And I'm still concerned about my mother. She stays by herself, and I just worry about her a lot. It's hard to keep my grades up because I always think about stuff at home." After he let me empty out, he offered a few choice words.

"You know, Dillard. As you get older, you'll find out a whole lot about life. I'm not saying what your father is doin' is right, but you should never judge a man. He may have a lot of pressure on him from whatever direction. And your mother gone be fine. The best gift you can give both of them right now is what? Finishin' up here and graduatin'. It may seem selfish, but son, what?" He interjected his signature saying. "At some point, you gotta do the best thing for you right now, which is gettin' that piece of paper from Mo'house. Some thangs, you gotta leave in the hands of the Man Upstairs. You just gotta make sure you make the right choices for you and make sure you have a good future. Then you can go back and help them when you yourself get stable." It all made sense, but it was just good to hear him say it, I guess.

After we talked a while longer, I was fine. "Thanks, Coach. Sorry to bother you."

"Naw, son, what? If I tell y'all that y'all can come talk to me at any time, I mean it. It ain't just words, son."

"Alright, Coach. See you at practice tomorrow."

And he shut the door and turned off the light outside. At that point, I knew it was true that he was not just some ordinary coach. He had been a godsend to help to navigate my way through some turbulent days.

About a month after then, he made a request that took me by surprise. "Hey, Dillard! Over here for a second."

We had a grueling workout that day, and I just wanted to make my way back to the dorm. We had to run five 400s in practice, but we had to run them in a way that he called the fox and the hound. Somebody had to start out 10 meters ahead of everyone, and the rest of the pack had to try to catch him during the lap. If you were caught, you as the fox had to run an extra one. If you didn't catch the person ahead, you as the hound had to run an extra one. Either way, someone would end up with an extra one.

It seemed to be a lose-lose situation. Thankfully, I was not caught, and I managed to catch the fox on each one. So I only had to run five times. While some of the others ran their extra one, I met with Coach. My body just wanted to go eat and hit the bed. But I just listened as my muscles throbbed in pain.

"Next week, me and my family goin' to my church homecomin' in South Carolina. I want you to come and go with us."

"Really? You really want me to go?"

"Yeah, son. I think it'll be a good trip for you."

"Okay. Thanks for asking. I'll go." I wasn't sure if I agreed because I wanted to go or I was just tired. I knew he wouldn't quit if I didn't agree. So the trip was on.

"I'll let you know more details later, like what time we're leavin' and all of that."

"Alright, Coach. See you tomorrow." I was actually pretty excited to be going. Anything that was a change from the normal, humdrum existence on campus was rather welcomed.

"Phillip, stop hittin' me."

"Angela, you stop hittin' *me*."

"If both of y'all don't stop, I'ma knock both o' y'all out." Mrs. Green was looking backward at both of them from the passenger's seat. Coach knew he didn't have to say anything. His mere presence spoke volumes. They knew how far they could go. He could just focus on driving.

Veronica just laughed at both of her siblings and shook her head. Eddie didn't pay any of them any mind either. It was too early for him to even acknowledge the childish games his younger brother and sister were playing this morning.

I sat in the back seat of the van, laughing to myself at them. I had never really seen his family personally and up close like this. I only saw them at practice and at some meets. It was rather funny to see Coach interact with them. He was definitely the glue that held it together. His children and wife respected him a lot. To them, he was a lamb, but I'm sure the children had witnessed the lion too. We guys on the team witnessed the lion often but for good reason.

After tiring of each other, they thought they'd come and bother me.

"Dillard, Dillard, Dillard, Dillard." Phillip started in, and Angela joined. They called me what they'd heard their father call me. They probably had no idea of my first name.

"Hey, Phillip. Hey, Angela." I'd entertain them for a while since they shifted their attention to me.

But their mother would rein them in. "Y'all leave Dillard alone. It's too early."

Coach was paying attention to the road and reinforced what his wife said by a frequent and stern look into the mirror. His children interpreted it loud and clear.

We arrived in South Carolina that Sunday morning, got a bite to eat, and headed to the church. We sat close to the front, and I sat between Phillip and Angela. The service started regularly, with the prayers, singing, and standing. Soon, the presider made a few comments, acknowledging Coach Green and his family's presence.

"And today, church, one of our sons has returned home, all the way from Atlanta, Georgia." *All the way? These people were acting like Atlanta was halfway across the country. It was only about 200 miles from where they were.* "And he brought his family with him. We so happy to have Clarence Green and his folks back home." The chorus of amens reverberated throughout the congregation. "At this time, we just want him to come up and say a coupla words to us."

Without hesitation, Coach Green popped up and headed to the front. There was a mic stand set up down from the pulpit, so he didn't have to go up on the platform. He just spoke from ground level. "Hello, everybody. It's good to be back. You know, we don't get a chance to come back like we want, but whenever we do, it feels like we haven't even left." Mrs. Green gave Phillip "the eye" since he was playing while his father spoke. I chuckled within myself, but it soon gave way to terror. "You know, it's so good to have my family with me. I brought my wife, of course, and these four knuckleheads. Y'all see how big Phillip gettin'? He ain't no baby no mo'." He was getting relaxed behind the mic and didn't feel the need to be as formal now. "I also brought one of the runners on the track team. He's a special young man. He's a leader and is just like one of my sons." *Really? I didn't know he felt that way.* "He's been a great part of the team, and I thought it would be a great idea for

189

him to come with us to see my hometown." The amens continued. "And at this point, I'd like for him to come up and say a few words to y'all, whatever is on his heart."

Time literally felt as though it stood still. Before I could process any anger that I may have had, I was walking toward the front while everyone seemed frozen in whatever posture they had assumed. To this day, I have no clue what I said. It must have been something about being away from home and being a part of a new family. Whatever I said, it must have been good because Coach and everybody else gave me hearty congratulations afterward.

Phillip started picking on me and started joking about how I sounded like a preacher, but that was just him and his personality. "Dillard, is you a preacher?"

"Naw, why?" I laughed it off.

"'Cause you was sorta sounding like one up there."

"Naw, I'm not."

By the time we ate and drove back to Atlanta, it was evening. I was beat and just wanted to get to bed. Coach pulled up to his home, and we all filed out. Even Mrs. Green was noticeably tired. She was trying her best to gather the gang and make it up the stairs. I gave her a hug and said my goodbyes to everyone.

"Thanks, Coach. I appreciate it. That was a nice trip."

"No problem, son. You did a great job. Get a lotta rest, 'cause we got 'blood alley' tomorrow." He was describing the practice from hell, where we had to do lunges the entire length of the football field and hop up and down onto tables with no running start and with no relief. We also had to do pull-ups for a minute straight, no stopping. The day after a blood-alley workout, walking on slight declines felt like steep slopes. The quads, hamstrings, calves, and buttocks all ached at the same time. He was turning back into his role of pain-wielding coach and letting go momentarily of that of father. I hated this type of practice because he turned into a completely different person, one who wasn't satisfied until he saw pain and anguish in every face, including mine. So I had better be thankful for this rare moment, where I had a behind-the-scenes look at him and his.

"Alright. I'll be ready. See you tomorrow." As I walked back to Kilgore, I knew I held a special place in his family's heart. And I realized that I had seen what few other athletes had: an inside glance into the gentle heart of a tiger.

# clotel; or, the president's daughter

hings back at the church I attended were going well too. The stress of classes would become somewhat exacting, so it was good to have an outlet weekly. I went to Sunday school and the regular services. The Sunday school classes were not the average classes like I experienced as a youngster. The teacher seemed to have been watching me all week and speaking solutions to the stress I encountered. I never forgot the first class. We sat and waited in our section of the pews for our teacher to arrive. Soon, the back door to the office opened, and out came the same woman with the amiable smile. It was the pastor's wife, Olivia Dixon.

"Hello, everybody. I trust that you're doing well. I'm excited about being the teacher for the young adult class. I have a special place in my heart for the college students, so I was glad to be able to get this assignment and be your teacher. Every class must have a name, so we will be known as 'The Pacesetters' because we set the pace, and the others follow."

At least she had a vision and knew what she wanted. We college students couldn't wait to get to her class because she didn't just teach a boring lesson, but she engaged us and spoke to where we were in life. She knew that teenagers' trying to live a halfway decent life was a struggle, especially in college. Many of us were away from home for the first time and were anxious to experiment with all that life had to offer, both good and bad. She helped to become a voice of reason to many of us and kept many of us out of trouble. We liked the pastor, but we loved his wife. She challenged us and made us think more in-depth about what was so casually accepted.

"So we're talking about Daniel on today. Nevin, what you know 'bout Daniel?"

"Well, he was in captivity with those other three guys." Nevin did his best to answer.

"What other three guys?" She pressed further.

"You know, those other three Hebrew guys."

"What were their names?"

"Shadrach, Meshach, and a bad Negro."

We all laughed.

"You know what? I'ma pray for all y'all. What were their names? Anybody?"

"Shadrach, Meshach, and Abednego." I finally chimed in and offered the correct answer so we could move ahead. I knew I was right.

"Were those really their names? Are you sure?" For some reason, she wasn't buying my answer.

"What do you mean?" I challenged. "Those *are* their names. Just look it up." I wouldn't be proven wrong because those names were the ones I heard my entire life.

"Are you *sure* those were their names? Because the first thing the enemy does when he tries to destroy you is to change your name so you'll start answering to stuff that doesn't reflect who you really are." We all were trying to figure out what she was talking about. When we looked it up together, we discovered that she was right. Those weren't their real, original names.

The classes kept getting more and more interesting, and she became a mother to many of us. She nurtured us through rough moments and kept us encouraged. Her husband and she were a dynamic duo, who would take Atlanta by storm, we were convinced. For some reason, I took a particular liking to her because she had an unconventional way of thinking and wasn't afraid to challenge the status quo, the normal perspective that everyone was used to. I didn't find too many like this in the church, but whenever I did, I found myself drawn to them. I adopted her as my "other mother" and just eventually started calling her ma or mom. She didn't have any biological children, so she seemed to welcome the title with open arms and an open heart.

My final year of college was upon me. I would have to maintain a special focus for this year because this was the year I'd be applying for the Rhodes Scholarship. It had been a dream of mine since high school. I had played my cards right, and now the time was upon me to make this dream a reality.

Sure, I had failed a course, but I was convinced that I could spin it as just one more obstacle I had overcome on my way to leaving my mark on society. I was in Durham and set to drive back to Atlanta for the start of this final year.

I was driving back in a newer car. My cousin, who at the time was the Executive Assistant to the "Sister Girl" President of Spelman, had bought herself a car. She gave me her old one shortly after the Concord reached the end of its life. I prepared to make the Atlanta drive again after Brenda gave me some money for the road. As I rode on the highway, I had flashbacks concerning my driving trips with the Concord and laughed as I wondered if this new car would perform the same miracle as the other one did. I still try to process a few experiences that I had with that Concord before it made its way to car heaven.

I-85 South was a beast, and the Concord was now getting on my nerves. The car was falling prey to normal wear and tear, and I had to put up with seven hours of poking along the expressway. I was singing at the top of my lungs to pass time away as cars overtook me in the left lane as if I were standing still. I'd get to a hill and would dread it. I had to press the gas pedal extra hard and turn off the air conditioner to make it upward. Of course, the muscle spasms in the right leg were severe, but I just had to endure it until the trip was over. Without thinking, I just prayed. *Lord, this car is getting on my nerves. My leg is hurting. I need some help.* Thinking nothing else about it, I continued driving, minding my business.

*Shoot, here comes another hill.* As I approached the bottom of the hill, I prepared my muscles to press the pedal again and hold it until I made it to the top. Only this time, as soon as I got to the bottom of the hill, the gas pedal went down on its own. I looked around in disbelief, under the steering wheel, beside me, nobody. I kept singing and acting like nothing was different. The car was old, so it didn't have cruise control, and this was before the questionable reputation of Toyota cars' doing their own thing. Besides, I didn't even have a Toyota. Time after time, the gas pedal would press itself when I got to the bottom of a hill, stay pressed while climbing the hill, and let up once I reached the top. While climbing the hill, I would just sit and chill as the car made its way to the top. I'd have to press the pedal once the hill ended, but I never understood how that miracle came to be.

I'm not ignorant of how silly that episode sounds. I've come to realize that hardly anyone would believe the account. In fact, if it didn't happen to me, I probably would be doubtful myself. My life has always been at the crossroads of things natural and supernatural, and this time was no different. I wanted to see if this newer car, the Chrysler, would do the same thing. So as I drove, I released my foot from the gas pedal as I approached the bottom of a hill. The car went slower and slower and almost stopped. I guess the same thing wouldn't happen with this car, probably because it had its own cruise control. No need for a miracle if the car had what it needed to make it. So cruise control had become my new best friend.

I thought about my method of attack in applying for the Rhodes. I was excited about moving to London and knew I had a strong collegiate background to support a strong application.

I'd have a rough academic load this semester, too. I'd be required to take two semesters of African-American Literature with Dr. Milsap, a renowned genius, who held many seniors back because of how tough this class was. He was from The Bahamas and was one the sharpest people I have ever met. There was no avoiding him because he was the only one teaching the course. On the first day of class, tension in the air was high because everyone knew what was at stake. We waited until Dr. Milsap entered. I walked in and sat beside a bald-headed, light-skinned brother. I'd strike up a conversation to lighten the mood.

"What's up, man. I'm Bernard. Have you heard about this professor?"

"Yeah, man. He's actually pretty good. I took him for an earlier class in the major."

"You what?" I couldn't believe someone actually took his class voluntarily.

He laughed. "Yeah, if you put in the work and study, you actually learn a lot from him."

"How did you do in the class?"

"I got an A."

"Man, you legit. I never heard of anybody getting an A from Dr. Milsap."

He laughed. "I'm Hakim, by the way. I'm from Jersey."

"Oh, aight. I'm Bernard. I'm from Carolina."

194

"North or South?"

"North. What part of Jersey you from?

"Plainfield."

"I never heard of there? What's it near?"

"It's 'bout a good hour from New York City."

"Das cool."

"Yeah, man. I just got back from being overseas for a year. I took a year off to study abroad to see what that's like. I would have graduated this past May, but I figured finishing one year later wasn't such a bad thing, especially since I was given a good chance to broaden my horizons out of the States. I recommend that everybody travels out of the country at some point. We're so Americanized, it's sickening."

"I hear you, man. I totally agree. I'm preparing myself to do just that this semester. I'll be getting my application together to apply for the Rhodes Scholarship to study at Oxford."

He looked at me as if he had seen a ghost. "Word, yo? Me too. I didn't think anybody else really knew about it around here. There's never been one awarded from an HBCU before, but that doesn't mean that we can't try."

"I hear you, man. That's wassup. We should definitely try. By the way, where did you study overseas last year?"

"Oh, I studied in . . ." Right before he answered, Dr. Milsap walked in and brought us back to reality with his overbearing presence.

"We'll talk later, man," I whispered. It was important to hear every-thing the professor said from day one if you wanted to make it out, and I wasn't about to be distracted for one second.

Hakim and I kept each other encouraged during the course and during the application process. I would frequently run into him after track practice as he rode his bike on campus.

"Wutup, Hakim?"

"Chillin', yo. How's the application going?"

"It's going alright. I didn't realize how long it was. And all the recom-mendations you gotta get for it is crazy."

"Well, just keep at it, man. It'll pay off."

"Aight, man. Lemme get inside. My coach wore us out today, man. I'll see you in class."

"Peace."

I had to hurry and grab something to eat in the cafeteria because I couldn't miss *Fresh Prince of Bel-Air*. Will Smith knew he was crazy, along with Hillary, Aunt Viv, and the butler. Some of the brothers and I laughed at how stupid Will was and his comedic timing. Afterwards, I'd get back to the application, but this was a welcomed break, where I could let loose and forget about school. Some of the girls came over to the room to chill and watched it with us.

"Man, Will is ridiculous." Dante fell out laughing. We were watching the episode in which Will was lip-synching. He was performing Jennifer Holliday's *And I'm Telling You* from *Dreamgirls*.

"Dat fool is stupid," Sherice yelled in agreement.

"I honestly don't see how the rest of the actors can keep a straight face while they filming. I would be breaking down all on the set. They would be like 'cut.'" I added my angle.

"Look at him. He just fell all over Uncle Phil and beatin' on him while he singin'. He is retarded!" Tichelle was talking and laughing. We were laughing so hard that we were on the floor, gasping for air.

Afterwards, we walked the girls back to Spelman and got back to work. I would finish up on the application, which was going pretty well. I had to complete so many components and get six recommendations. I had handed out the forms to several professors, my coach, and Olivia to have my pastor write a letter. As the deadline approached, I made sure I had all the components and placed it in the mail a week before it would have been late. Hakim told me he made the deadline too. At this point, it was just a waiting game.

In the meantime, we still had to keep up with the hellish load that Dr. Milsap was requiring. He made each of us read a separate book by an African-American author, write an analysis, and give an oral report to the class. This was the assignment that historically made students cringe. If he sensed you were summarizing the book, he stopped you while you were talking and requested that you take your seat. "The assignment was not to provide a summary," he would say in his distinct tongue. "Any high-schooler can summarize. This is an analysis. Show me how you are thinking, not just regurgitating." So everyone in the class sweated when his time came to present. I was no different.

From the list he disseminated, I had chosen to read *Clotel; or, the President's Daughter*. It was a great book, but I had to make sure that my paper met his requirements. I dug and dug and tried to dissect the work until I ended up with what I hoped was a good analysis. The truth, though, was that you didn't know until it was too late, until you were interrupted and asked to sit down. Once we started reading the reports, he required that two students read per period. Eventually, my day of reckoning came. Charlie and I would present and have to hope for the best.

As I walked into class, I realized I hadn't been this nervous in a while. I could feel the tightening of my stomach muscles again, so I knew I'd be stuttering, at least in the beginning. Thankfully, Charlie was going first. When Dr. Milsap walked in, he wasted no time. "So we'll be hearing from Charlie and Bernard today. Charlie, you're up first."

Charlie seemed rather comfortable and made his way up to the class podium with no hesitation. He started his talk. "Hello, everybody, I'm Charlie Cox, and I will be presenting on the book I read. The title is *Iola Leroy or, Shadows Uplifted*, and it is by Frances Harper. This novel gives a chilling account of what it was like to be a mulatto during slavery times. Iola is mixed. She has a black father and a mixed mother. She realizes that, even though she looks white, she is indeed black." Before he could go any further, Dr. Milsap interrupted.

"Charlie, stop! I can't listen to any more of this. The assignment is not to offer the class a summary of your novel. That's low-level thinking. Also, please be sure to get the facts of the novel straight. Iola's father was not black. He was a white Mississippi slave owner and a man of means. Please have a seat."

Charlie looked so distraught. Even if the rest of his paper was a hard-core analysis, he had dropped the ball. With Dr. Milsap, you had to convince him early that it would be worth listening to. He had no time to waste. "Mr. Dillard, you may rise." It felt like I had to throw up.

I went ahead and grabbed the paper I wrote. The podium seemed a mile away. "You got this, man." Hakim was trying to encourage me, but nothing he could say would allay my fears. I was glad that I didn't have to speak extemporaneously. I would have been a wreck. He simply just wanted us to read what was on the paper.

"H-Hello. My n-name is B-Bernard Dillard, and I read *C-Clotel; or, the President's D-Daughter* by William Wells Brown." *Relax and get yourself together*, I told myself. I continued.

"In 1853, W.W. Brown takes a s-serious swipe at the socio-political culture of his day through the p-publication of this novel. Although one c-cannot assume that novels reveal intimate details about the author's life himself, it becomes difficult to ignore the p-parallels between Brown's own life as a f-fugitive and that of his chief female protagonist, Clotel, who is the alleged offspring of P-President Thomas J-Jefferson." I didn't even look up. I kept shaking, stuttering, and reading. Before I knew it, I had managed to get to page four, the final page, with no interruptions.

"In closing, the r-reader witnesses striking s-similarities between Brown's personal life and Clotel's f-fictional one. Through the eyes of Clotel, Brown s-s-seems to chronicle the frustration and annoyance he experiences in h-his own life. Whether he addresses ..."

"Stop!" Dr. Milsap interrupted me. I could hardly believe it. I had never felt so insulted and belittled. I almost made it to the end. He went forth, explaining the reason he butted in. "This is the kind of paper that everyone should aspire to. Notice how he is not summarizing the text but giving an analysis of the text. This is the type of higher-level thinking that I am looking for." Hakim was smiling. I wasn't. I was barely looking up at the class, just wishing I could read my last sentence so I could sit down. Even in the midst of this compliment, I just wanted to finish and get out of class. "Mr. Dillard, continue."

"Whether he addresses interracial r-relationships, the ills of slavery, or the c-corruption of politics, Brown presents a fresh p-perspective through which he explores the ch-challenges facing the African-American family. Thank you."

Feeling sweat trickle down the side of my face, I hurried to my chair to sit down before the professor had a chance to change his mind about how well he thought I did. Before I knew it, Dr. Milsap was in the front of the class, teaching the day's lesson. My underarms were drenched, and my heart was still beating fast.

"Way to go, bruh." Hakim offered congratulations.

"Thanks, man. I'm just glad it's over. It's t-terrifying up there."

"It's good training, though. Good job."

He always managed to see the bright side. As for me, I was just glad that I, like Brown, had just survived my own form of oppression. Indubitably, this was indeed a Pyrrhic victory, but it sholl felt good to be free.

———— *twenty-five* ————

# staring at the sky

I guess I hadn't really noticed it as much, but the campus was a beautiful place. The grounds people had taken a certain pride in maintaining the lawns and gardens. Frequently, I'd just walk and enjoy the greenery but would then soon be reminded where I was as I approached the red clay, not too far from the flowers. There was no real need to buy white shoes for obvious reasons. The dust was too undeniable. The infamous Georgia red clay had lived up to its reputation and didn't disappoint. As I looked down to make sure I avoided all the dirt, I hadn't realized that I almost bumped into Hakim, who was riding his bike toward my direction.

He startled me. "Hey, man. What's goin' on?" He was sweating.

"Just chillin', man. 'Bout to head to the room."

"Oh, aight. Yo, I just checked my mailbox. I found out I made it to the next level in the Rhodes, man."

"Really? I haven't checked my box yet." For some reason, I was getting nervous.

"You should check it. I'm sure they would have to mail responses out to everybody who applied."

"I don't know if I even want to check, man."

"Go see, man."

"Aight. Lemme go check."

I didn't know why I was sweating so much. I'm sure everything would be fine. Everything had been pointing me in this direction for the past three years. I felt like it was my destiny to get it, at least past Round One.

As I opened the box, there it was. The letter. I also discovered a letter from grandma and some announcement about some seminar on campus. I just stood there staring at the outside of the envelope, beating myself up for not asking Hakim to describe the envelope his came in. Was it a regular-sized envelope or one of those large ones? At least that would have taken away from the mystery of it all. The one I had was a regular envelope. It didn't feel like it had any enclosures. Just a simple letter. But I figured they had no real reason to invest much in postage, even for those who managed to make the Round One cut. So I'm sure things would be fine. As I stood there, I must have debated in my mind about five minutes concerning the letter's contents. I had spent three years building up to what seemed to be such a defining moment. I would have no more of the suspense and opened the letter, which embodied the following basic sentiment:

*Dear Bernard:*
*Thank you for submitting your application materials for the Rhodes Scholarship. The Rhodes Committee had its initial meeting and decided on the candidates who would proceed to the semifinal round of the Award. As you are well aware, competition for the Scholarship is stiff each year, and we wish strongly that we were able to make more awards than our budget allows. Unfortunately, we were not able to confirm you as a semifinalist in the Rhodes competition. We wish you continued success in all of your academic endeavors.*
                                                    *The Rhodes Scholarship Committee*

That was it. Three years' worth of toil, planning, and preparing myself to win the coveted scholarship. And it was gone. In a matter of five sentences. I just walked to my room, fell on the bed, and stared at the ceiling. Thankfully, Ced wasn't there. I tried to imagine a Plan B. Naïvely, I didn't think to have one. At least I would have an entire semester to figure something out before graduation.

In fact, by the time graduation rolled around, I had decided that I wasn't ready to become a wage earner yet, so I did the grad school thing. I applied and got accepted to Harvard's Graduate School of Education. I rejected the offer because I wasn't ready to leave Atlanta yet. I'd stay in the city and work on a master's in education. I'd probably teach for a few years and move on to the next phase of life.

Hakim had become the big man on campus. When the chips fell where they did, he had succeeded in his quest to win the Rhodes Scholarship. He became the first Rhodes Scholar to come from an historically black college or university. The press he got was extraordinary. Article after article was written about his achievement. The nation seemed to turn its head in

Morehouse's direction even more than it already had. It was indeed a moment of pride for all of us. Although there was a sense of disappointment
that I felt, I couldn't help but feel happy for someone who made history,
someone who I interacted with on a daily basis. He took it very much in
stride, too. He never got arrogant about winning. He was the same old,
high-yellow Hakim with the baldy.

I had to be pretty proud of myself for trying. After all, I would be
graduating from college. I'd be the first male in my family to do so since my
grandfather finished Tuskegee. My uncles and older brother, for whatever
reason, had fallen short. My other cousin, Oscar, who was a year ahead of me,
actually took a little longer to finish. He started out at Florida A&M but
had to transfer to North Carolina A&T because of financial difficulties. This
added a few years to his pursuit, but he managed to finish shortly after I did.
So I had nothing to be sad about. I was just glad to be finished.

It was great to see my family make the journey to Atlanta to support
me. It was refreshing to see everyone. Mama, Keva, Dwayne, Jr., grandma and her sister, Aunt Jolynn. Daddy made it, too, which was very nice.
Tensions among the travelers simmered a bit. There was no need to open
up cans of worms that would engender strife. So journeyers only socialized
with those in whose cars they took the trip. The goal was to travel to Atlanta
and help me celebrate this momentous occasion. Graduation would be held
on Sunday afternoon, so we all decided to attend church services that morning. I sat where I normally did, and the family was interspersed throughout
the congregation as space allowed. There was normally standing room only
during services, so they would just have to find the best place to sit. With
the crowd, I hadn't heard the confrontation between my mother and Aunt
Jolynn, which had its roots in my upbringing. Apparently, Aunt Jolynn
sat close to my mom and couldn't resist the urge to comment on what she
thought she knew. "Vicky, I just don't see how you could leave Dwayne, Jr.,
Keva, and Bernard when they were younger."

Shocked, my mom took the high road but not before making Aunt
Jolynn think. "Don't worry about my decisions. You don't know everything
that happened. I don't see how Thomas left Cindy." Thomas was Aunt
Jolynn's son, who had left his wife Cindy for a younger hottie for no logical
reason other than the fact that he was bored with his humdrum life. Cindy
had stood by him through thick and thin, but he left and started another family, producing more kids and all. Aunt Jolynn didn't seem to think

anything was wrong with that but didn't hesitate to challenge my mother with situations that Aunt Jolynn knew very little about. And my mother, who could snap in a heartbeat, let Aunt Jolynn know in no uncertain terms. Out loud and in church, she grunted, "Let me move my seat before I end up cussin' in this church." She moved her seat and later told me about the confrontation.

"Mama, you don't have to justify any of your decisions to anybody. The Lord was well aware of what happened back then, and He knows the true story of how daddy acted. Aunt Jolynn hasn't been told the whole truth over the years. She thinks she knows what happened, but she really doesn't."

"I know, but it just pisses me off that everybody got something to say about it, and they don't say shit to Dwayne about his ass and what he did. He got children all over Durham, and they don't seem to see that." She didn't mince words and sometimes exaggerated a bit, but I knew what she meant.

"Well, don't worry about it. We're here to celebrate my graduation. So let's just do that and move on with life." It was sad that Aunt Jolynn had dampened the mood with her pettiness because of misinformation concerning us that she had been fed. But all was settled, and we focused back on the positive again.

That afternoon was such a time of happiness and unbelief. Of course, this was something I had worked hard for and looked forward to for four years. But to be a part of it was beyond words. As we marched from King Chapel to the campus quadrangle, I just tried to take in every step, every moment. So many of my brothers throughout history had taken these steps. They had made this same walk toward the beginnings of making their mark outside of the college's hallowed halls. Over the years, many had blazed trails in so many avenues of life. Politics, entertainment, medicine, education. And here I was, not knowing exactly where I'd make a mark but was at least willing to make one.

I arrived in my seat and took it all in. The ceremony was full of pomp and circumstance. After all, this was Morehouse College. I got somewhat impatient because of all of the bells and whistles, but I just tried to remain focused and keep the right perspective. I'd be walking on that stage in no time. Our speaker was A. Leon Higginbotham, a judge who was teaching at Harvard's Kennedy School of Government at the time. As one might expect, I remembered absolutely nothing of his speech. After he said, "Good afternoon, men," I tuned him out. I knew he had finished once I heard the clapping of my brothers.

After some time, Hakim took the microphone. He was addressing us not for his Rhodes win, but he had managed to maintain a solid 4.0 grade point average throughout his time at Morehouse. As a result, he was speaking to us as our valedictorian. This was his time, and he made the best of it. By the time he finished, the class members stood and gave him a roaring ovation. In particular, he made us English majors stick out our chests in pride. Surely, this couldn't have happened to a more deserving and humble person.

When the time approached for each one of us to cross the stage and grab the degree, I was surprisingly calm. As I stood at the bottom of the platform steps, I listened to the pronunciation of my name. He slaughtered my middle name, but anyone else who had the same task would have also butchered it. I still wasn't sure what possessed my mother to give me such an off-the-wall middle name. I have never heard it before and will never hear it again, unless I one day bequeath it to my son. I took a moment just to take in the moment, and I then made my way toward the top of the stairs. I clutched the leather casing and heard my folks in the distance, screaming and yelling. I could tell my mom's voice anywhere: "Alright, Bernard!"

The feeling was more than I'd imagined. I had joined the ranks of a great brotherhood, and I was grateful to God for the opportunity. Once I returned to my seat, I looked upward and realized that I had been simply staring at the sky for some time. It was indeed blue, speckled with a few clouds. I wasn't sure what I was looking for, maybe a glimpse of Him who had held me together and guided me to such an historical and pivotal juncture in my life.

————————— *twenty-six* —————————

# what had i gotten myself into?

fter graduation, I decided to stick around Atlanta and attend grad
school there. I thought about the impact that Ms. Rivers had on me
as my teacher in middle school. I never forgot how she allowed me
into her home to stay, and I became excited to pay it forward.

I moved to the Decatur area, attended classes, and worked part-time in
catering. This job was eye-opening, to say the least. I was amazed at how
people treated you when they thought you were a nobody. If there is anything
I've learned in the food industry is that you always should be nice to those
handling what you consume. I can remember how rude many of the guests
would be toward me. They had no idea I had a college degree and was currently enrolled in grad school, and I didn't make it a point to tell them. It
was a lesson to see how people came across when they thought you were just
somebody without an education, hopes, and dreams. As I wore my black and
white tuxedo uniform, there were many times that those sitting at dinner
tables would brush me off and send me to fetch coffee like a dog fetching
slippers. Thankfully, I had enough integrity not to add any of my own extra
"ingredients" in with their drink. I just vowed never to treat anybody less
than human if they had jobs that were not seen as important in other people's
eyes. I learned that every human being, educated or not, is important and has
his or her own significant role in society that makes it function and go 'round.

After finishing most of my degree requirements, I was able to seek a real
teaching job through provisional certification. This meant that I had basically completed all of the coursework but still had to fulfill the student teaching
requirement. In a perfect world, I would be able to find a teaching job that
would serve as my practicum experience but would allow me to get paid at
the same time. It was obviously meant for things to work out as such because
after speaking with a principal, I was hired on the spot while finishing up

my last year in grad school. Beth Johnson, the principal at Renfroe Middle School, saw enough promise in me to take the chance of hiring me as one of her sixth-grade teachers. I was ecstatic but then realized about a week before school started that I had absolutely no experience in running my own class-room and wondered just how I would come across to the students since I was so young and looked it. No one or no course could have ever prepared me for what I'd be in for during these next two years.

"Mr. Dillard, Rontrese hit me!"

"Mr. Dillard, how old are you?"

"Mr. Dillard, you look young."

"Mr. Dillard, tell Toby to stop talkin' 'bout my mama."

"Mr. Dillard, I left my homework on my kitchen table."

"Mr. Dillard, can I go to the bathroom?"

"Mr. Dillard, if B.B. don't stop, I'ma slap 'im."

I was in a daze trying to make heads or tails out of the situation into which I had placed myself. The mayhem I was experiencing with my own crop of children, as I called them, was real. Sixth grade was such a vulnerable age group that had its own peculiarities. Much like the middle child, kids at this point in life were going through so many identity problems and issues. And I was given the task to help them navigate their way through them. I had chosen to work with this age group because of the impact Ms. Rivers had on me. Many a day, I wanted to hunt down Ms. Rivers and give her a huge hug. I didn't know how she as well as other teachers did it. I was fresh out of college, single, with no kids, and I was still getting worn out.

I had discovered that these students were so fragile and inquisitive. The responsibility as a teacher weighed heavily on me. I always strove to be fair but firm. I realized how much they depended on me for safety in and out of the classroom. I'd have to maintain a watchful eye for students who were reserved, abused, hungry, ignored, and emotionally deprived. And at some point, I'd have to find time to teach the math. Since there were very few African-American male teachers, many of the students gravitated toward me as a father figure. How would I help them in this regard, especially since I hadn't had the best example? I felt so inadequate but seemed to do okay with the on-the-job training. I'd discovered that I didn't have to be perfect, but I just had to be myself and show genuine care.

I was only about ten years older than they, so in many ways they saw me as a fun teacher. It was always a chore to maintain strict boundaries while being friendly. I managed this by being absolutely horrifying to them during the first week of school. I didn't smile once during that week, and my answer to everything was "no," even if the request was a legitimate one. All of them hated me with a passion that week, but it at least gave me the upper hand and gave me room to loosen my grip as the year progressed. In hindsight, I was probably too mean. They were already intimidated because this was their first year at a new school. So I had to milk this advantage. As they entered the class, I had my script ready in my head.

"Come in, find your name on your desk, have a seat, and keep your mouths shut." One could hear a pin drop as they filed in. They scurried about and obeyed. I dubbed myself Rambro, the black version of Rambo. It wasn't my normal disposition at all, but it was a necessary evil. I continued, laughing internally but displaying a hard exterior. I wrote my name on the board. "The name you see on the board is my name. If you can't read what it says, ask one of your friends during lunch to tell you what it is." They looked around in disbelief that I didn't verbalize my name. "This is sixth-grade math. You will meet the other teachers on *my* team later who will be teaching you the other subjects." They had to know I meant business. I kept up the shenanigans.

"Everyone, stand up!" They obeyed. "The ground you are standing on means that everybody is starting at the same starting point." Someone had used this same example with me at one point. They used it as motivation to say everyone was starting at the same level with an A in the class and that if we stayed focused, we'd all excel. I implemented my own twist. "At this point, everyone is starting out with the same grade in this class, an F. You haven't earned anything yet, and I'm not giving out any free grades. Whatever you earn in this class is the grade you get. If you want an A, you have to work hard to earn it. But as of right now, you haven't earned any-thing, so everyone's grade at this point is a big fat zero. Have a seat." I could see that I had them wrapped around my finger. A few of them were on the verge of tears, but this was the only moment that I had to show that I meant business. I would always be able to lighten up during the year, but there was no way to start nice and end mean.

By the time Thanksgiving came, they were laughing and joking with me but still had that indelible mark in their minds of how mean I could be. By the time we hit Christmas break, they were off the chain. Indeed, my classroom gave off a sense of organized chaos. They never got out of control but never hesitated to keep vying for my attention often in the form of picking fights with each other.

"Mr. Dillard, I was minding my business and then Zane hit me." Lonnie made it his mission to tell whenever someone did something to him but never disclosed his role in initiating it.

*So hit him back* was what I wanted to say. "So what did you do to start it?" I knew it was more than met the eye. Lonnie was quiet, so Zane gave his side of the story.

"I tried to ignore him like you said the last time, Mr. Dillard, but Lonnie be playing too much. He was talkin' 'bout my mama, so I hit him." Zane was looking frustrated.

"Okay. Well, when ignoring him doesn't work, I told you to let me know and don't take matters into your own hand. Since you couldn't restrain yourself, Zane, and since you always manage to start the mischievous ball rolling, Lonnie, both of you have silent lunch."

"The *what* ball?" Lonnie inquired.

"Don't worry 'bout it. You got silent lunch." And that was that. At least for then.

On occasion, I lapsed into a character I created when teaching. My alter ego was named Joe, and he appeared without notice. He was unpredictable when he taught. He could place one foot on a desk, grab the string from the overhead screen and place it across his nose, and the like. Whatever he did, he sent the class into a tailspin of laughter. Neither the students nor I, for that matter, knew when Joe would appear. This helped to keep the students attentive and guessing. Students who ordinarily seemed to be bored with academic stuff were paying attention and doing work. I was glad. Periodically, students would ask before class if they would see Joe on today. Since I didn't know, I couldn't answer. Hence, they attended regularly in the hopes they would have a chance to see him. Thankfully, whenever Joe showed up, he didn't disappoint.

In addition to the regular math lessons, I was instrumental in teaching students about how to manage money. My classroom management system was based on the notion of the Dillard Dollar, which was basically fake money that students could earn to purchase things in the Dillard Store that I would buy on my limited teacher's budget. As vain as the concept was, I have to admit it was pretty ingenious. I cut out some green paper in the form of paper money, placed my image in the president's slot, did a little artwork, and handed them out to students for staying on task, performing well on tests, and helping each other around the class. I was happy that parents started contributing items to the store for students to buy. Students were in charge of running the store and the class bank, adding interest to classmates' accounts if the money was left for at least a month. It was refreshing to see young people understand stuff about money that even adults can't quite manage to comprehend. I have always been concerned with the level of understanding that the next generation has about money, its power, and its worth. Further, I always wanted students to understand that in order to appreciate money, it has to be earned and not just given to them. Many of them seemed to learn the lessons I taught them in this respect and hopefully carried them into their adult lives with their real jobs and personal money.

The only regret I had about teaching was leaving the school when I did. After I left the school, another African-American male took my place. At first, he seemed to have a good rapport with colleagues and students alike. I got word, however, that about two years into his teaching assignment, he crossed the unthinkable boundary and was indicted on charges of having inappropriate relations with one of the students, another male. If I would have stayed longer, I feel like I could have shielded that student. I was very protective of students in my classes and those in that age group in general. I guess I held a special place in my heart for that age group since I had been taken advantage of around that age. My heart was heavy for a while after learning about that. In fact, I wrote a letter to the principal, apologizing for my indirect role. If I had only stayed one more year, things could have worked out differently. But such was life.

In all, teaching at Renfroe was a rewarding experience. By far, teaching at that level was the most difficult job I have had to date, but it has also been the most rewarding. I had and will always have a deep sense of appreciation for teachers. I can barely express the weight I felt on my shoulders to make sure I kept my crop of children safe and ready to face the world. I am humbled by the sacrifices of so many people like Ms. Rivers, my grand-mother, and others who opted to make their living by molding and shaping the lives of others, who often struggled to find out where they fit in the grand scheme of life.

After teaching, I didn't remain in Atlanta much longer. In addition to teaching, I had remained supportive of the ministry with which I was affili-ated. The leader had a strong vision as to what he was trying to achieve, and I was excited to be able to contribute what I could. As part of his goal, he wanted to run a Christian school, which was right up my alley. My training, education, and experience would be ideal for such a vision. I was honing my skills at this point so I could be a great asset to what was in store.

Unfortunately, things didn't go as smoothly as expected. Many of us in the ministry had become disappointed because the marriage between him and Olivia had gone southward. I couldn't express how disappointed I was because both were very close to me. It felt as though I was going through the turmoil again I had experienced as a child with my own mother and fa-ther. They had so much promise as a couple, and many looked up to them as a model team. As I've gotten older, I've learned the wisdom of esteeming those in leadership positions but not making gods out of them as if they can't be human and make their own choices.

Shockingly, Olivia had been asked to leave the church. After all she had sown and given mentally, financially, and otherwise, she was now treated as some infidel, who was conspiring against the well-being of the ministry. A lot of us college students were devastated because she had helped to keep us focused during our study years. She had invested a great deal of strength, energy, and prayer in us, and many of us were saddened about the split. After she left, she managed to find the resolve to start her own ministry. A few of us left the old ministry to help her with hers, including me. Hence, Life Enrichment Ministries was conceived and on its way to making an impact in the community.

This was one of the most challenging decisions I've made in my adult life. Never could I have imagined the sacrifice and grit that go along with starting a ministry from the ground up. No seminary school can prepare someone who wants to undertake a task such as this. It becomes strict on-the-job training. I had no qualms, as many do, with aligning myself with a female leader. So many females had already impacted me as I grew up. So I was used to their being able to step up to the plate and make a difference.

Of more importance to me were the quality of the leadership and that the leader ranked high on the integrity scale. I was solidly convinced that Olivia had both.

We started the ministry in her living room and eventually moved into a storefront. I sowed a great deal of myself in so many aspects. Mama Olivia had now become Pastor Olivia and would eventually become Bishop Olivia, and she didn't seem to miss a beat in this newfound place of leadership. But to me, she'd always don the Mama moniker. Her focus and dedication demanded respect and helped keep the ministry vibrant and alive. Though she was single now, she maintained a high standard of leadership and remained steadfast in her convictions. We all took note and celebrated what God was doing in her life.

After a while in Atlanta, however, I sensed that it was time for me to move on to the next phase of my life. I felt as though my mission in Atlanta at this point had been accomplished. Somehow, I had managed to stumble through a changeover from boy to man, bereft of any significant male steering. Many times, it seemed like I was wading aimlessly as I navigated through those adolescent murky waters. But here I was, ready to embark upon the next phase of my life. I packed up my SUV, said my goodbyes, and hit the road again. It was especially hard to bid adieu to Olivia because she had sown so much into me as much as any natural mother would. Strangely, I still knew that it was time for me to move on so I could keep heading in the direction to which my purpose was taking me. I wasn't quite sure what the next chapter would be, but at least I had a plan. And it was time again to pursue it.

# zigzag

From Atlanta, the drive to the DC area would be about eleven hours, so I decided to drive half of the distance and spend the night at home in North Carolina. Whatever I couldn't pack in my Ford Explorer, I just gave away and paid Olivia to be my property manager. During my final years in Atlanta, I was purchasing a home and thought I'd just rent it out to make a little more money.

I had arrived in Durham to get a little rest. I'd only be there for a night and would then move on. As I expected, my grandmother had changed the sheets on the bed and gave me a big hug as I entered. Of course, Uncle Terrence was his usual self, giving great conversation at the outset and resorting to his nervous laughter as he walked down the hall. Aunt Brenda would arrive soon, too. We'd chat for a minute before I retired. I really just wanted to eat, relax, and sleep. A brief conversation wouldn't hurt, though. And conversations with her were never dull.

"So you're moving again, huh?" She was fishing for more details.

"Yep, time to move on. My job in Atlanta was being phased out. I knew for a good year, so it gave me some time to prepare." After my teaching job, I had gone back to work at Morehouse as a program coordinator. The job was funded by a federal grant by the Department of Defense and only lasted for three years. I would have to have a professional plan in place after that. During those three years, I had decided to take a college math course each semester, especially since my job gave me the benefit of tuition remission. Before I knew it, I had finished all of the courses for the math major and would pursue graduate school in it.

"Well, that's good. The Lord had to move you away from Atlanta somehow." Brenda offered her viewpoint as to my departure.

"So I'm sort of excited about starting over. Years ago, I didn't have any idea that I'd be moving to the DC area to go after a PhD in math. I never really heard of that many people doing it, but there's nothing else I can think I want to do right now."

"Well, ain't nothing to it but to do it."

"Yep."

By that time, grandma had entered and informed me that there was some food on the stove. She never failed to alert me of the presence of food on the stove or in the refrigerator. I told her thanks but that I had stopped on the road and picked something up. She quickly went in for the kill. "You talked to your daddy?"

"Now grandma, you know I haven't called him. I just got in. And when you ask if I talked to daddy, you should always ask me if I talked to mama too." She only seemed to be interested in whether or not I had spoken with her son. I always had to remind her to ask me about both of my parents. "Plus, he never returns any of my calls anyway, so I'm not breaking my neck to contact him when I come." I was tired of driving miles and miles and miles to get home and then of being expected to drive all over Durham to see relatives. If they wanted to see me, they could drive a few minutes to see me at my grandmother's.

"You making more out of it than you should."

"Maybe, but at least you know where I stand regarding it." Life wasn't normal until we both engaged in a mini-argument. That was it. It had come and gone, and I was headed to bed.

I awoke to the smell of bacon, eggs, and the like. My grandmother always prided herself in cooking breakfast before I got on the road. There was an air of excitement in the air for me. I always liked pursuing new challenges, and this was no different.

"Morning." I walked over to the kitchen and kissed her on the cheek in part to relay that there were no hard feelings about our discussion on last night.

She had already squashed it and moved on. "Hey, baby. How'd you sleep?"

"Great. The bed felt great. Like old times. I'ma head into the shower and get on the road."

"Well, breakfast will be ready in a second."

"Kay."

I hadn't realized how much I had missed her cooking. After wolfing down what she prepared, I got ready to hit the road. Brenda gave me some money before I left, which was always a welcomed departure gift. She made her way out but not without her usual farewell. "I call you blessed."

I made my way out, saying goodbye to Terrence. My grandmother followed me out and sat on the porch as I made my way to the vehicle. I kissed her and thanked her for everything. She gave her normal advice as she fanned herself while rocking back and forth. "Don't drive too fast, and if you feel yourself getting tired, just stop. That city ain't goin' nowhere. Just take your time."

"Aight. I'll call you when I get there." And I left. Through the side view mirror, I could see her stretching her neck as far as it could go so that the car stayed in her view. I snickered to myself and said to myself that she was a trip.

I realized that I had to pass by mama's house on the way to the interstate, so it made sense to stop by there before making the journey. I pulled up her driveway and blew the horn. Nobody came out, so I knocked on the door while the nosy neighbors watched. I noticed the door curtains shift to the right and then a scream.

"Hey! My baby at the door!" She fumbled to open it. The key was always lodged in the lock from the inside, but she still couldn't manage to open it. Finally, the door swung open and she grabbed and hugged me tighter than I'd expected. "Lord, my baby!" Without any hesitation, she started crying.

"Mama, stop all that."

"Dwayne, Jr., Bernard out here." She made an announcement as if millions of people were listening. Dwayne had moved in with her so she wouldn't have to live by herself. In her mind, she was able to make it by herself and never hesitated to let him know on occasion.

"Hey, man." Dwayne greeted me but didn't move from his reclining position on the couch.

"Wassup."

"Baby, I can't believe you moving to DC. You just all over the country, ain't you?" She was expressing her excitement. "You just doin' it up, goin' back to school and erthang. We gone be calling you doctor in no time. Hell, I'ma go back to school and get my master's. Hell, I still got a good mind."

"All over the country? This just the second place I moved to. I ain't all over no country." We both laughed.

We caught up as much as we could in the short time we had. Knowing I had a decent drive ahead of me, I made my way toward the door. She attempted to stall me as best she could. "Wait, come on in here in the kitchen and let me give you some of these canned goods."

"Ma, I don't want no canned goods. I gotta go."

"Naw, come in here." She started grabbing canned potatoes, string beans, and anything else she could reach in the cabinets. She shoved them into plastic bags and kept looking for things to give me. "You can take some o' these too." She had a nerve to give me some packs of Stove Top stuffing.

"Aight, ma, thanks. Gotta go. See ya, Dwayne."

He hollered a "see ya" back at me.

She followed me outside and started bragging about me to the neighbors. "Hey Gert, this my other son, Bernard. He movin' to DC. He tryin' to become a doctor, girl."

"Mama, please. You ain't got to tell that lady all my business." I spoke under my breath.

"Shit, you my son. I can brag on you if I want." She was just as quiet in her response. Because of the awkwardness of the situation, I felt compelled to speak to the neighbor. "Hello, ma'am."

"Hello. Good luck. Your mama a real good neighbor."

"Okay. Nice meeting you."

My mom walked me to the car. Like clockwork, she started the waterworks again. She started talking to God so that I could hear. "Lord, protect my baby. He moving to another city. Lead and guide him. Don't let nothin' hurt him."

In the middle of her prayer, I started laughing, which caused her to stop praying and crying and to start laughing along with me. She chastised me.

"See, Bernard, you playin'. I'm serious. It's a lot of things out here that can hurt you."

"I ain't said nothin'. I'm just laughin'. Anyway, lemme get outta here."

As I pulled out the driveway, I could see her begin to cry again. She stood in the yard and waved at me. I couldn't help but start laughing to myself. I waved back, watched her shrink through the mirror, and felt a tear slide down my left cheek.

I arrived in the District in about five hours. I had only stopped once in order to gas up. I had gotten into a groove of driving and didn't want to keep breaking my concentration by stopping more than I should. This new city seemed to have a different feel to it. It was no Atlanta and definitely not a Durham. I was surprised at how close three territories were to each other. One could easily live in Virginia, Maryland, or DC and work in either of the same three areas. I had merged onto the beltway and eventually saw the Capitol building in the distance. I couldn't believe I'd be living so close to all things political. I'd spent quite a while in Atlanta, and this was just the change I needed. I'd be in for at least a five-year commitment, and this didn't seem like too bad of a place to settle.

To be honest, I didn't know what possessed me to go after a PhD in applied mathematics. In retrospect, I must have been pretty arrogant or delirious to attempt such a feat. Part of it was that my old job was ending, and the other part was that I was still young and had some time to figure out what I really wanted to do in life. Now that I was in the mix, however, there was no turning around. I'd never been one to back away from a challenge, so I was in it for the long haul.

Thankfully, I had outside funding so I didn't have to worry about working. I could just focus on my studies and give it my best shot. Classes were a bit tough because I had chosen to focus on statistics, although I hadn't taken any statistics classes beforehand. It just seemed to be a fairly robust field in which I could use my skills. So I had to take a few pre-graduate courses to get me up to speed. My professors all looked like Einstein. Old, crazy hair. They all seemed to speak a foreign language to me, so I had to dedicate countless hours in the library to stay up with the rest of the class. In my mind, that was my job, so it was fine that this was my plight.

Between classes, I'd make it a habit of watching reruns of the Martin Lawrence show. Through all of my stress, those episodes helped me stay focused and reminded me not to take this phase of my life too seriously. Mama Payne was the worst, who never seemed to get along with Gina, despite Gina's many efforts to make peace. And Mama Payne just always went in for the kill, especially during the Thanksgiving episode.

"You still shuckin' dem peas, big face?" She was relentless and always knew the right words to say to get under Gina's skin. I kept watching old episodes as if they were the first time I'd seen them. It was a fact. Martin Lawrence was stupid. His comedy hit home with me more because he had grown up in the area not too far from where I was living now. So it was good to live in the area where he seemed to base a lot of his characters, especially that hoodrat, Sheneneh Jenkins. She helped me get through many a stressful time. I had gotten through the first year pretty well, but I knew this was just the beginning and that I had to up my game if I were to survive this process.

One of my buddies from back in Durham was also pursuing his doctorate at the same school. We had both finished Morehouse, too. We hung out, laughed at Martin together, and tried to keep each other focused throughout this grueling ordeal. Never in a million years would we have thought that we would be having a conversation about the recent developments in the DC area.

"It doesn't even seem like this should be happening here." Brad was just as shocked as I was. People in the DC area were frozen.

"Man, this junk is crazy. Who would have thought this would be happening in DC?" I was in my office venting to Brad while he worked on one of his papers for his class. I was trying to focus on some ungodly statistics homework problem but kept being distracted by the streaming news online. "See listen at this." I turned the volume up. ABC's Peter Jennings started talking:

> "It was a terrifying situation for thousands of people. Gunmen in the neighborhood killing individuals in a methodical way. When the news got on the radio and the television, people were too frightened to go outside. It happened again and again and again. This is what it's been like in Montgomery County, Maryland, which is basically part of Washington. We have a reporter there tonight. Carl?"
>
> "Well, Peter, virtually every law enforcement agency in this area, including local police, FBI, US Marshals, and Secret Service is looking for whoever is responsible for the worst murder spree that has ever happened here, including the murder today at the service station behind me. The shooting started yesterday at 5:20 PM. A bullet went through the window at Michael's, narrowly missing a clerk inside. It was the only

miss. At 6:04 PM, a middle-aged white man was killed outside of the supermarket. This morning, the murders resumed. At 7:40 AM, another white man mowing his lawn. At 8:12 AM, an Indian man, gassing up his cab. Minutes later at 8:37, an Hispanic woman sitting, reading a book on a bench outside of a restaurant. Just over an hour later, at 9:58 AM, another single bullet, another victim. A woman cleaning her car at a gas station. Altogether six shots, five apparently random victims within sixteen hours. Police are stunned."

I couldn't listen to any more, so I turned the volume down. "This is just ridiculous. It probably ain't nobody but some angry white man trying to make a political statement. Or some terrorist that's trying to do Round Two of 9/11. Man, they done shut down school activities, soccer games, and everything. They even got me bouncing around and hiding around trees while I'm waiting for the campus shuttle to come pick me up."

Brad laughed. "I know. It sholl can't be nobody black. They wouldn't be able to keep no secret like dat. They start feeling like they can't make no mistake and be done told Pooky or somebody else in the hood that they ain't missed a shot yet. Just hang their own selves."

"Right. They need to hurry up and catch him, though. Sad part about it is you don't have no idea who gone be his next target. He all over Virginia, Maryland, and DC."

"Be funny if it was a woman."

"Yo. I didn't think about that. That would be wild. Be on some Annie Oakley vibe."

Here we were, minding our business, trying to further our education, and somebody was offing random people in and around the DC area. I never thought I'd live in any city where I'd have to worry about whether I'd live, simply walking from point A to point B, or just sitting, or waiting for the bus. Of course, the odds of my getting shot were slim to none, but so were the people's odds who actually *got* snuffed.

"Well, I'm 'bout to head home, player. I had enough of this stupid stat problem that I can't figure out. I'ma call it a night. You can stay here if you want. Just lock the door."

"Naw, I'm leaving too, man. Gotta head home and give Lori a call. She trying to plan something for this weekend, so I'ma see what's up with her."

We left the office together and headed to our cars in the darkness. Admittedly, I had a little pep in my step and walked to my car in a zigzag pattern, as if running a football play.

Brad decoded my behavior quickly. "Boy, you stupid!"

"Well, if he out here, he ain't gone hit me. It's hard to hit a moving target. He'll never be able to stabilize that gun and focus on me." We hurt our sides laughing. "And if I come up to a red light, I ain't stopping. That's just what he wants. No motion. If the cops stop me, I'll just tell 'em I didn't stop because the sniper out here somewhere, and I just wanted to make sure I kept moving."

"Yeah, right. That cop'll be snigglin' and grinnin' and writing you a ticket at the same time you bobbin' and weavin'."

"Whatever. At least I'll be livin'."

We got in our cars and prepared to head in our separate directions. I made one last farewell. "Aight yo, I'll holla at you tomorrow. Don't get shot!"

I retired, enjoyed the weekend, and woke up on Monday and turned on the TV. I couldn't believe my ears as I listened in disgust. The sniper had attacked again, but this time he had crossed the line. He had attempted to gun down a middle-school student in Bowie. It seems like it was a direct attack on the police chief, who had guaranteed that students would be safe. This was obviously a vigilante who had no sense of restraint. I was hoping and praying that the culprit would be found very soon. More and more, it seemed as though people in the city were united because of this sense of terror. I chuckled a bit because people didn't seem to mind joining forces to pray now. Those who wouldn't have thought to pray in any other circumstances joined hands and called on God in a flash. They wanted protection and their normal lives back, and prayer became the "in" thing to do for that harrowing month of October.

Thankfully, our prayers were answered, much to everyone's delight and utter shock. Brad and I surely ate our words because when they released the images of those responsible, the shooters weren't white, Arab, or of any other stereotype that seemed to fit this kind of crime. They were a black guy, who was an ex-serviceman and who had joined the Nation of Islam, and his black protégé from Jamaica. Here was a black duo that brought the entire tri-state area to a standstill. As the saying goes, who woulda thunk it? The fact that people could now exhale was tempered by the undeniable disbelief that such a crime spree was organized, planned, and executed from a couple of Joe Blows. At any rate, it was good to get back to some type of day-to-day normalcy.

I hate to admit, though, that it took me a little more time to let go of the zigzaggy walking pattern I had so cleverly invented for my survival.

# sooner than i thought

As much as I relied on comedy to help me deal with the stress associated with this new challenge, my ultimate strength would come from finding a good church home and staying connected to the Lord. Mama Olivia had suggested a church that she knew well in Baltimore. The people there had become a second family for her as she dealt with the pangs of her divorce. She spent a lot of time between her home in Atlanta and the Baltimore area with her friends there. This was a lifeline of sorts to her, and she wanted me to share in the life-giving realities by being a part of that ministry. So I agreed.

I made the forty-five-minute drive each Sunday, in spite of how tired I was. The people there were great, and so were the services. They reminded me so much of services I was used to back in Atlanta. I worshipped God freely there. I lifted my hands, praised God, and got renewed for another week. I buddied up with a lot of Olivia's friends, and they treated me as their own son. Instead of making the drive to Carolina, I'd start spending Thanksgiving at Nellie's, one of Olivia's closest friends. Between eating until I was stuffed and struggling to put up the mammoth Christmas tree, visits there were always joyful and provided constant laughter.

Admittedly, though, I was tiring of the near hour-long drive each way every Sunday. On some occasions, I almost fell asleep at the wheel. If only it was a little closer where I lived, it would have been ideal. After some time, I decided to make a decision and attend a church closer to where I lived. Olivia wasn't too happy about it, but I just had to follow what I thought was the right leading.

"Mama, that drive is just too far. It's a good service and everybody's nice, but I can't keep making that drive. And we get out sort of late, too. There's about three messages that are given during service, so we don't get out until about 3:00 in the afternoon." I was explaining my case to her.

She made her signature comment when she didn't really agree with what was being said: "Ah hah."

I continued. "So I decided to start going to the church down the street from where I stay." The church was on Rhode Island Avenue and was pretty popular nationwide. The Bishop was a good minister, but his wife was great. She had a way of encouraging you to aim high and do better in life. She was a regular on the national preaching circuit and had a way of hyping you up and then saying, "Y'all sit down," as if she had nothing to do with why we were on our feet.

"Well, okay." I could tell Olivia knew she wouldn't change my mind. She always honored my choices by not smothering me and by allowing me to make my own decisions. Of course, she had assumed the role of an adopted mother in my life, but technically she was my pastor and only gave me sound advice about what she thought would help me spiritually. I was always thankful, though, at her trust in my ability to make my own decisions and be my own man, dealing with my own consequences, good or bad. "Thanks for letting me know."

I made it back to Atlanta to visit often. On this particular occasion, I would venture back to make a surprise visit to see Olivia and other extended family. She was celebrating her pastoral anniversary, so I thought I'd come back unannounced to make her day. I normally stayed with her and her family when I visited. There was no need to stay in a hotel and waste money. This time, I wouldn't stay in a hotel or with her. Staying with her would spoil the moment. So I contacted some friends who lived outside of Atlanta, in Alpharetta. We had hung out on occasion when I lived in the city, and I thought it was a good idea to bunk on the couch, still saving money.

"Ey wassup, Gino." I had called to make sure I could stay overnight and head back on the next day. I decided to drive from DC to Atlanta. I wasn't too keen on paying for an airline ticket for such a short visit. My SUV would hold up fine for the journey.

"Wutup, Dillard. Yeah, you can bunk here, man. We ain't gone be doing nothing but chillin'. How is DC?"

"It's aight. Nothing to write home about. I be spending all my time in the library studying so I don't fail these classes. So I haven't really gone out into the city to hang out that much. But it's okay. Found a good church, so I'm good."

"Aight, yo. Well, just hit us up and let us know what time you think you'll be headin' in."

"That's a bet. Thanks for lettin' me stay."

"No doubt."

After getting all the details about the Saturday afternoon anniversary program, I planned my visit. I'd get in on that Friday night, head to the festivities on Saturday afternoon at the church and surprise her. She would have no clue and would be crazy excited.

It was good to see old faces at the church. The storefront building was holding up fine, and the people were still down-to-earth. I was excited to be able to see Mama. We kept in touch via phone and email, but nothing could replace the face-to-face interaction between mother and son. As the afternoon progressed, I fit right into the worship. It was good to be amidst all of my Atlanta friends and family.

As the praise service continued, she entered and took her place onto the pulpit. She was hanging strong despite all of the drama concerning her divorce. Her name, actions, and motives had been misrepresented somewhat by her ex-husband, but she took the high road, started her own ministry, and moved forward. She lifted her hands and joined the celebration. She never caught a glimpse of me because I managed to blend into the crowd and remain unspotted.

Around offering time, we would prepare to walk toward the front row by row and drop our gifts into the basket. She stood by as everyone came up and blessed them with a handshake or comforting pat on the shoulder, praying for their finances. As the usher motioned for my row to proceed, I stayed low-key and walked up as everyone else. By the time I reached the front, our eyes met, and she paused a bit wondering if she was seeing correctly. Once she processed who I was, she let out a loud shrill, which scared some.

"My son is home! My son is home!" She gave me a gigantic hug and wouldn't let go. I likewise was ecstatic. The offering had been held up by a mother-son reunion. I was happy to be back, and she was happy that I was home.

She eventually explained to the rest of the newcomers what all the excitement was about. As she took the microphone, she doted on me, which always made me uncomfortable. I wasn't one who sought the limelight. I just liked working in the background to make things happen. Needless to say, my uncomfortability did little to stop her from putting me on blast and telling about all of my achievements. "And pretty soon, we'll be able to call him 'doctor.' That's my mathematician! That's my boy!"

As I blushed from my seat, the congregation clapped for me and continued to wish me well. After the service ended, we said our hellos and goodbyes again and went our ways. It felt somewhat strange because I wasn't staying with her as I usually did. I had to make it back to Alpharetta to hang out with my boys but not before having dinner with Mama and the gang. We shared our usual laughs and did some serious reminiscing. They always joked about how much I ate as a student during my Morehouse days and how I never seemed to gain any weight. "He was just a human trash compactor" was several of the usual refrains I endured. But the jokes were all in fun. I told them I'd perhaps see them sometime again in the spring. It was winter now, around early November, so I doubted I'd make it back before the year ended. It was just so good to see everyone. I hated leaving, but duty called and I had to keep it moving.

"Well, y'all be good! It's always good seeing you. Keep me in your prayers." I was noticing how Mama was shutting down a bit. She didn't like these type of send-offs. She did well to keep her emotions in check, not letting them control her, but I could tell she didn't want me to leave.

"I'll talk to y'all next time. See ya soon." But I didn't realize soon would be sooner than I thought.

After dinner, I made the forty-minute drive back to Alpharetta to chill out the rest of the night. Gino and Khalif were roommates and were watching football, so I thought I'd join them. Jessica, Khalif's girlfriend, had just left and said she had to get ready for work. The Falcons were up by two and there was one quarter left. Sunday Night Football reruns were my passion, and I wasn't about to miss the rest of this one. This was probably the one sure inheritance I got from my father.

"How was the function?" Khalif was eating some takeout.

"Man, it was good. I ain't seen them people in a minute."

"Das wassup, man. It's good to have good folks."

"It's some food over there, man." Gino chimed in.

"Naw, we went out after church and ate. I'm stuffter than a mug." They both laughed at "stuffter."

As the game finished up, I had drifted in and out of sleep. I didn't realize how tired I was. One of the moments I woke up, I thought I was still asleep because of what I saw. Khalif was smoking, but he wasn't smoking a cigarette. In my grogginess, I overhead Gino warn Khalif not to get me involved. "Yo, don't let Bernard try any of that. It's too strong."

I was fully awake now and wondering what they were talking about.

"Don't let me try any of what?"

"Yo, don't worry about it, son. Just chill out and go to sleep."

"Dawg, I'm a grown man." I guess I didn't want them to feel like I couldn't hang with the big boys. Besides, I was three times seven plus. "If I wanna try it, I can try it."

"Naw, Bernard, you don't want to mess with that stuff. Me and Khalif used to it. If you don't really smoke, it might not be a good look." He walked to the back and headed to the shower. "Yo, Khalif man, I ain't playin'. Don't let him smoke none of that."

"Yo, man, I heard you the first time. Aight, aight."

I had never backed down from a challenge. I wasn't ghetto, but I wasn't a choir boy either. I could hold my own. Or so I thought.

"Khalif, pass it over here." I wasn't going to be defeated.

"Naw, man, you good. It *is* a little strong. It got me buzzing."

"Man, stop playin'! Lemme see it." I reached my two fingers out to grab what I thought was just a white joint. After going back and forth for a good minute, he gave in.

"Man, damn, here!" As long as I heard the shower running, I was cool. I knew Gino wouldn't co-sign on my decision. So I had to hurry up and smoke it. Strangely, I was smoking like a pro. I had heard that smoking really wasn't smoking unless you inhaled the smoke and not just blew it out. So as I dragged on the joint, I inhaled deeply so it entered my lungs. I didn't feel anything, so I continued and passed it back to Khalif. He started smoking and passed it back to me.

I repeated what I did the first time and made a brave assessment. "Man, what Gino talkin' 'bout. This ain't nothin'." I heard the water stop running, so I gave it back to Khalif for good and laid back down, feeling absolutely nothing. As I watched TV, the picture started getting dimmer and then clearer. "Khalif, can you fix the TV? Somethin' wrong with the color and picture."

"Bruh, what you talkin' 'bout? Ain't nothing wrong wit' dat TV."

"It's going in and out. And it's spinning."

That's when Khalif realized that he shouldn't have let me have any part of the smoking experience. As I lay, it felt like all of my functions stopped for two seconds and then resumed again. I started a sentence, paused for two seconds, and then finished it. When Gino came back in, he saw me lying in a daze and slurring something that was supposed to resemble a sentence.

"Man, Khalif, what the hell. I told you not to give him none of that shit. That shit is *strong*. You don't know how strong that shit is."

"Yo dawg come on. Shit, he a grown ass man. If he too stupid not to realize he shouldn't have it, that's on him."

"Yeah, but that ain't a regular joint, yo. That got some extra shit in it."

I had managed to sit up, but the world around me kept starting and stopping. I could hear and then all of a sudden I couldn't. Mere silence. Then I could hear again.

"Bernard, you aight?" Gino was looking at my eyes. Khalif was laughing. "This shit ain't funny. He goin' in and out."

I managed to get my phone and start walking. I couldn't die like this. Those two-second pauses felt like what I thought was death, and I wouldn't go out like this. I was barefoot and shirtless and thought maybe I needed some fresh air. It didn't register with me that it was twenty-nine degrees outside. Frankly, I didn't care. I opened the door and walked outside in just my pants. To me, it actually seemed like it got hotter the more I stayed out-doors. As I made the call, some lady who was bundled up from head to toe, stared at me as if I had lost all of my senses. She looked at my bare feet and bare chest and noticed how I was shaking as I was trying to dial the number. She almost said something, but I interrupted her when the phone connection was established.

"Mama Olivia?"

"Hey, Bernard. How are you?"

"Not too good. I smoked something. But I think it was some extra stuff in it, maybe some cocaine. Can you come get me? My car is here, but I don't think I can drive."

I could hear her give a faint sigh. "Where are you?"

"I'm out here in Alpharetta." I gave her the address and what landmarks were in the general surroundings.

"I'm on my way." As she was heading out of her home, her brother, Frank, was just coming home from hanging out with his fiancée, Quita. "I need you to come ride with me. We gotta go get Bernard."

"Where he at?"

"In Alpharetta."

"Dang. He all the way out there."

"Mm hmm."

It seemed to me like an eternity waiting for them to arrive. I called about two times in between to see if they were really coming. My own SUV was in the parking lot, but I was in no condition to drive.

I had gone back in to try to gather myself, but the room was still dancing and the TV hadn't gotten clear yet. Khalif was in a daze himself, but he was more experienced in how to handle it. Whatever zone he was in, he was navigating it well. His eyes looked heavy, but he was enjoying every second of it.

Gino was more concerned that I was freaking out. When I came back in, he encouraged me to put on some socks and my shirt. But I was hot, or at least I thought I was. It was amazing how the substance altered my sense of reality when it came to my own temperature. I understand now how people could die outside in the cold if they were stoned. Nothing was normal when it came to my perception of that. "Yo, dawg. Your body shaking. Ain't you cold?"

I just sat down, wondering why I decided to do this. I didn't know why I felt like I had to prove my manhood by proving this point. I had remembered Len Bias, who decided to try drugs one time when he was heading to the NBA. Even though it was his first time experimenting with them, he paid the ultimate price for that decision, having been found dead before his life in the NBA started. How could I have been so stupid?

I put on my shoes and shirt and just waited. Soon, the doorbell rang and Frank came inside with his huge, intimidating football build. When the door opened, he just walked in, grabbed my bag, and motioned me out. I told Gino and Khalif that I'd see them later, not realizing that this would be my final time contacting or interacting with them. I got outside and tried to maintain my sense of sobriety. "Thanks, Frank, for coming out here to get me, man."

"No problem, man. You just gotta be careful."

I saw the headlights on Olivia's car and saw her silhouette in the passenger's seat. As groggy as I was, I just wanted to get out of there and head home. She had contacted one of her other adopted sons, Jaan, while they were on the way. Apparently, he met them halfway to come to pick me up, and he left his car parked somewhere. I wasn't sure how they worked out the details. All I know was that Jaan was driving my vehicle while I sat in the passenger's seat. Before I knew it, we were all on the expressway headed back to Atlanta.

Honestly, Jaan was the wrong one to be in the car with me as we made our way back. He was given to be overly playful, and this time was no different. I knew he would say the very thing that would trigger a response from me that would seem as though I didn't understand the gravity of the situation.

As he drove, he began his shenanigans. "So, Bernard, have you tried drugs before now?"

"Nope."

"What did it feel like? Does 'high' feel good? Like, do you feel good right now?"

I couldn't do anything but burst out laughing. This was not my personality, but the effects of what I smoked just made me want to laugh at the silliest comment. "Man, I don't know what I feel like. I can't believe I did this." I continued laughing.

Jaan started laughing too, which made things worse. He managed to ask another question in his fake voice of concern. "So who were those people you were staying with? Are they in the church?"

"I don't know what they in. They just friends I knew when I was living here. I thought they were cool."

"And they're the ones who gave you those drugs?" He asked it in a funny way on purpose.

The question sounded funny, so I started laughing again. I couldn't compose myself, so he continued. "I can't believe you got Mama out here running you down all over greater Atlanta." Why did he have to say "greater"? That just made me lose it even more. "Bernard, why are you laughing?" But he was very deliberate in saying things that he knew would keep me over the edge. "You know she's in the other car right now praying for you and your destiny. She don't play that. Homey don't play that." I couldn't regain my composure because he kept trying to make me laugh intentionally. "You know she's a prayer warrior. You know she talks to God, and He listens to her. You know she loves you if she got out of her bed to come all the way out here and pick you up."

"Yeah, I know. I feel bad that I had to call her."

"Who you tellin'? You should have just called me, and I would have come and gotten you. But you called Mama?" It was a question but more of a statement of shock.

"Well, it made since to me 'cause I thought I was about to die."

He laughed and shook his head. We finally arrived where Jaan parked his car and switched drivers. I think Frank drove my car from there to Mama's house, but I can't remember. Before I knew it, we were pulling up to her residence. I had to gather myself because there would be no joking and laughing with her as with Jaan. I had to pull it together.

I walked in and followed her instructions. "You can take the bed upstairs. There's a towel and soap in your bathroom. I'll see you in the morning." I wish she would have just lit into me. I could have handled it better. She had this knack for being calm in heated situations, and I hated it. I would have rather she start yelling and upbraiding me for making such a bad choice.

"Okay. I'll see you in the morning. Thanks for coming to get me."

"Mm hmm." Her voice ended with a slight crescendo at the end.

When I woke up in the morning, she startled me. She was sitting on the bed by the pillow, staring at me. I couldn't tell if she awakened me when she sat or if I came to on my own. I was even-headed now and knew this conversation wouldn't be like the interchange between Jaan and me. She started in.

"So you okay?"

"Yeah, I'm fine. When I said 'See ya soon,' I didn't realize soon would be *this* soon."

She didn't acknowledge the joke. She just sat and stared at me. "So, why do you think you did it?"

"Mama, I don't know. I was just in the moment. I thought I could handle it and didn't think it would lead to all of this. Maybe I just wanted the challenge. I don't know what I was thinking."

"Hmm." She looked down a bit. "Well, I *will* say this. If you don't know why you decided to try a substance that you had no knowledge about, then you really do need some serious help. To go from never trying drugs to all of a sudden doing it just because you wanted a challenge is something to think about. You've overcome enough challenges already. And given your family history, you should be very aware not to put yourself in situations that would cause you to repeat what you've seen as a child. That's some serious generational stuff that you're up against."

"Yeah, I know."

"Well, it's not enough to say, 'Yeah, I know.' You have to realize that you are a man of purpose and destiny. And you have to know that the enemy will do everything he can to make sure that your purpose and destiny are aborted. You do have greatness inside of you and great potential. But potential don't mean a thang if you sabotage your own destiny yourself by making silly choices."

I remained silent and just processed what she said.

"Well, I'm heading out." Today was Sunday, and she had to get herself together to preach. I told her I'd be there after I got a little more rest. "You know I love ya. But I love ya enough to tell you the truth, boy." She popped me on the head as if to try to symbolically knock some sense into me. I felt like a brief laugh was fine. She smiled and laughed a bit too. "I'll see you when you get there." Her mother, Frank, and she headed out the door. I heard the two beeps of the home alarm system as they opened then shut the door.

I decided that I'd get up, wash up, write a note, and make the drive back to DC. I called Mama as I drove back. She told me I could have waited to leave when they returned so we could have had a sensible farewell, but I had just decided to jet. That weekend was indeed an eye-opener. I thought I was coming simply to help celebrate someone else's achievements. However, I had learned what was probably one of the greatest lessons of my life. I realized that I never had to do anything to prove manhood to myself or others. I didn't have to prove it with drugs, sex, money, or anything else society used as a measuring rod to quantify masculinity. As I traveled on I-85, I just stared blankly in front of me, just thinking and resolving within myself that this lesson need not be learned twice.

# jericho walls

---

School was going relatively well. I was conducting some research with my advisor. She was from Israel and one of the leading minds in applying statistical thought to business fields and biosurveillance. I was presenting my research at top venues like Georgia Tech and the National Institutes of Health. I had finished most of my coursework and still had one final major exam to pass. Aside from school, however, I was beginning to realize that perhaps I was hiding behind books and not dealing with me as a person. Over the years, I had found great solace in academic success. It started out as wanting to do well in school so that I could move away and not feel trapped by the circus around my childhood surroundings. Over time, it became a safe haven for me and afforded me an out. I was busy studying, so marriage could wait. The truth of the matter, though, was that I felt somewhat inadequate and slightly embarrassed about what I had gone through, those lessons from Lydell. I wasn't willing to take the risk to open up my emotional self to women for fear of rejection.

How could they really understand the baggage that comes along with being violated sexually, especially by another male? As kooky as it sounded, I had determined that they would laugh and ask me all kinds of questions as to why I let it happen. So I just decided to stay quiet about it and let time take care of it, until I finally got the revelation that time doesn't heal all wounds. There is no magical element of time that is responsible for healing. In fact, I learned that insecurities escalate over time unless considerable effort is placed on making healing happen. I had decided that enough was enough. If no one else would take the lead in helping me work through this reality, I'd help myself. I would admit myself to counseling and discover what it was that was making me tick.

I can't remember how I found the facility. I wasn't sure if I saw a flyer in the city, or if it was advertised on campus, or if I became proactive and Googled for it. I had made initial contact with the center, and my heart raced even as I just spoke on the phone with the representative. Never before had I spoken with anyone about this other than my aunt in Michigan, and it was actually creeping me out. I just knew I had to follow through and give myself a chance at having a relationship with the ladies. I had to stop being my own hindrance. True, it wasn't my fault, but it was my life and my responsibility to get where I wanted to go with it. I would let the phone ring and find the right words somehow.

"Hello." The lady sounded a bit hood and was chewing and popping gum. Just my luck.

"Um, yeah, good morning. My name is Bernard, and I wanted to speak with someone to set up an appointment."

"Which department you want? Sexual assault? Vape? Incest? What?" She meant rape.

I hadn't really thought about their having different departments. Were there really that many cases such that they had to have all of these separate branches? "Um, well I guess I can speak to someone in sexual assault. I have never done this before, so I'm not sure who I need to speak to."

I heard papers shuffling in the background, almost as if she were prepping herself to read. "Okay, well sexual assault is like the big term that almost includes erthang. Rape is more narrow, like a specific thing that happened sexually. Incest means . . ."

"Ma'am, you don't have to go through all of the terms." I couldn't bear to listen to her so-called scripted definitions. She was in fact trying to interpret her own reading of the definitions. Sad. I could see where Martin Lawrence got his subjects from when he decided on Sheneneh.

"Oh, 'cuz you was seeming like you didn't know who you needed to speak to." Another gum pop.

"Alright. You c-can transfer m-me to the area for s-s-sexual assault." My palms were sweaty, and I had begun stuttering again. Signs of nerves.

"K. Waymint. Hold on one sec." She sang the word "one."

I was hoping this wasn't a sign of things to come. I had finally decided to address this, and I'd wind up speaking with a cast member from the Victims R Us reality hour.

The seconds waiting seemed an eternity. They really needed to fix the way they operated. I'm sure people hung up the phone during this waiting time. I'm sure nerves would set in, and the conversation with the first receptionist wouldn't help the situation. I decided I'd hold and fight through any feelings to retreat. I'm glad I did.

"Good afternoon. May I help you?" This new voice was a woman's voice, very soothing. It was night and day compared to my conversation with Ms. Bonequasha.

"Y-yes. I w-wanted to sp-speak with someone a-b-bout s-setting an app-pointment for s-s-sexual ass-sault." I couldn't believe this stuttering started again. I honestly felt stupid, but the woman maintained her composure.

"Alright, great! We'd love for you to come in and meet with us. One sec. Let me grab this pen. Okay, let me get some info from you. How are you doing, by the way?" I could tell she sensed my nervousness.

"D-Doing p-pretty w-well. J-Just trying to h-hang in th-there."

"I hear you. Aren't we all." It was a statement, not a question. "Alrighty. I didn't catch your name. You can just give me your first name."

"B-Bernard."

"Alright, Bernard. And we need a phone number so that our counselor can reach you." I was a little disappointed because I thought she'd be my counselor. She was just the one who set up the appointments. After I gave her the information she requested, she promised that the counselor would contact me within twenty-four hours.

"Okay. Well, I'll w-wait for the c-call." I wasn't sure what else to say. I was so uncomfortable finally talking about this.

"Well, thank you so much for calling us, Bernard. We look forward to meeting with you. Have a blessed day."

"B-Bye." I wasn't sure what I was about to get into, but deep down, I knew I had made the right decision.

When I awoke the next day, I felt a strange sense of being refreshed. I knew I was about to embark upon a necessary, though unpredictable, journey. I was actually excited about starting the process, even though I was a bit anxious and didn't know what to expect. After it was all over, I was bound to end up in a place that was better than I currently was. That would be a good thing. So I was pretty happy when the phone rang and discovered it was the call I was expecting.

"Hello." There was no stutter.

"Hi. I'm trying to reach Bernard. This is Judge calling from the P.G. County Abuse Center."

"Okay. Judge who?" I thought my counselor was an attorney.

"No, my name is Judge. I get it all the time. My name is Judge Taylor."

"Oh alright, man. How's it going? Glad you called."

"I'm doing great, man. I just wanted to reach back out to you. I received a message from our department that you'd like to come in and get the process going concerning some things you've experienced."

"Um, yeah, in a nutshell."

"Okay. Well, when do you think you can come in? We can talk a little more specifically about things when you show up. I'll actually be the counselor working with you, so hopefully we can build a sense of trust between us so you can move forward."

"Alright. Sounds good. I can probably swing by this week if you're available."

"Great. How does this Thursday sound, say after lunch around 2:00?"

"That'll work, man. I'll see you then."

"Fine." He gave me the actual address and mentioned that I'd have to park in the parking deck, where I'd have to pay an hourly fare. The session would only be an hour per meeting, so it shouldn't get too expensive, he promised. "See you on Thursday, Bernard."

"Okay. See you then." A part of me still couldn't believe I was going through with it. All it took was a simple phone call to start the ball rolling. A simple phone call.

By the time Thursday came, I had begun to get nervous again. It was one thing to speak on the phone with people, but now I had to become a face to them. I arrived at the parking deck and made my way inside the building. I caught the elevator and got myself together as I made my way upward. I felt my heart beating faster because I didn't know what to expect. I just had to keep assuring myself that things would be fine.

When the elevator door opened, I saw the lady who must have been the first receptionist I spoke to when I called. Her hair was flawless, and she had on some weird-colored fingernail polish. Within seconds, she confirmed my doubts when she spoke.

"Hey. Can I halp you?"

"Yes, I'm trying to find Judge's office. I have an appointment with him."

She kept her right hand on the table, and motioned the finger on that hand to the right, as if to point me in that direction. "Jes walk 'round the corner over there and keep goin' and goin' and goin' down the haw-way. You'll see it over on the right side when you get down there." The infamous gum-popping started.

I'd just resolve to find it on my own, given the shoddiness of her directions. "Okay. Thanks."

"Mm hmm. Anytime." More gum-popping.

As I made my way down the hall, a part of me felt like it was walking the plank. Clearly, everyone would know why I was there. I stuck out like a sore thumb, pretending that I knew where I was going and seeming more confused with each step. The door to the office was locked, but a friendly voice from a woman who was walking by gave me some gentle instructions. "Just pick up the phone on the wall, and the receptionist will start speaking with you." And she continued on in the direction she was walking.

"Thanks."

"No problem." She said it like she had a mouth in the back of her head because she didn't miss a beat in her walking world.

I lifted the phone, and it rang automatically.

"Hello, this is Judge's office." It was the voice of the nice woman again.

"Yes, this is Bernard. I have an appointment with Judge."

"Hi, Bernard. Grab a seat right outside, and Judge will be out shortly."

"Alright. Thanks."

I grabbed a magazine during the wait and also to keep from having to look at people who walked by my general area. It felt like every eye in that wing of the building was on me. They knew I didn't work there, so I had to be visiting for the other reason. Indeed, I was making more out of it because whenever I glanced up, people were minding their own business, not even realizing I was there. What I was feeling was my own sense of paranoia. Surely, I was experiencing my own type of illusion of grandeur. I was reading some issue in *Ebony* about how Mo'Nique was on the come-up. I was so enrapt in the article that I hadn't realized that Judge was standing at the door, holding it open, trying to get my attention: "Bernard!"

"Hey, Judge. You are Judge, right?" He was an African-American guy, who looked in his mid-thirties. He had a short Caesar cut and wore a pair of frameless glasses.

"Yeah, come on in. That must be a good article, man. I called you about three times."

I grabbed my stuff and tried to continue with the humor. "Maybe while I'm here, I probably need to get my hearing checked too. It might be wax." We both laughed.

I entered, and the door closed behind me. I followed him into his office, and he gave further instructions. "Just grab a seat, man. Let me grab something over here."

I sat down and just observed my surroundings. To the left were a race track, some Lego pieces, building blocks, and other toys. Sadly, his clientele obviously included little boys who hadn't managed to escape this harsh reality. I started to tear up a little because of this, but thank goodness Judge was one of those whose job it was to intervene and help them gain some sense of normalcy back.

"Okay. So let's start. Apparently, the directions were fine because I see you made it."

"Yep, I'm here."

"So, why don't I tell you a little about me." He thought it wise that he break the ice and give me a sense about who he was and why he worked here. "I'm a PhD student at George Washington University in Psychology. I'm studying psychology as it relates to any type of abuse, especially in the African-American community. I've noticed that different types of abuses occur in our community. Unfortunately, although these terrible things happen in our community, we as a group tend not to seek out professional help because of shame and embarrassment. So that's my focus. As part of my practicum, I'm volunteering here at the Center to offer as much help and support as I can."

"Oh, okay. That's admirable." That was the only response I felt I could give at the time. Here we were, two African-American brothers, both pursuing PhDs in our respective fields, a rarity in its own right. But here was one brother reaching back to help another one gain his emotional stability back so that he could move forward in the maze of life. "Well, it's nice to meet you."

"So, why don't you tell me a little about you and give me more of an idea about why you're here."

After going through the easy biographical material, I eventually had to talk about why I set up the appointment. "And I guess I wanted to go ahead and deal with the fact that I was subjected to sexual abuse when I was smaller. I never really talked to anybody about it except for my aunt. I figured that if nobody else would get me help, I would get me help. I also didn't have the best relationship with my father either, so I just often wonder if any of those things have anything to do with why I put a fence up around women and don't let them into my world. I mean, I have friends who are women, but it seems like if anything tends to move anywhere close to a serious relationship, I clam up and resort back to my familiar world of being alone. So I don't know the right answers, but at least I think I know the right questions."

"I see. Well, one thing you can be assured of is that whatever we discuss stays here. You don't have to worry about my revealing anything you mention. I just wanted you to be aware of that. You took a bold step by coming here, so I applaud you for that. And to be honest, I don't want you to think that I have all the answers to every question you have. At the end of our sessions, you will still have to deal with life. But hopefully, you'll know a little more about yourself and you'll be better equipped to navigate through life with some key survival tools."

"Alright. Sounds cool."

After more small talk, we decided that meeting once a week for an hour was a good plan. I'd plan on coming for an entire semester. We'd then re-evaluate to see if more time was needed. "So I got a homework assignment for you, brother."

"Dang, already?"

"Yeah, bruh, we're off and runnin'." Judge laughed as he grabbed his notepad. "This week, pick up something you can journal in and write anything you can remember about the first six years of your life. You might can't remember every single thing, but just write about anything you can remember. It doesn't have to be complete sentences. They can just be random thoughts. But commit to placing them on paper. When you get back on next week, bring it with you because I want you to read from it. Deal?"

"Alright, man. That's a plan. Will do."

"Well, looks like our time is up. I'll see you next week around this same time if it works for you."

"Yeah, that'll be good. I don't really have anything to do on Thursdays, so we can meet on those days at 2 PM."

"Alright. Lemme walk you out. It was nice meeting you. I think we're gonna have some great progress."

"Thanks a lot, Judge." On the way out, I bumped into the friendly woman who initially set up my appointment. She was walking out the office area and didn't see me. She was gorgeous. "Hello, ma'am. How's it going?"

"Hi, Bernard. Glad you made it in." She knew it was me, I guess, from the appointment book.

"No problem." I said goodbye to both of them at the same time and looked forward to returning.

I made my way down the hall and made the left, heading toward the elevator. Ms. Hotmess was still sitting at her desk. From what I could see, she was on the computer, playing solitaire. I pressed the down button and heard her say, "Bye."

"See ya later, ma'am. Have a good one."

As I entered the elevator, I knew I had made the right decision. As I felt the elevator head downward, I felt a huge sense of relief because maybe the walls I had built up over time, these Jericho walls, were heading downward too.

Only time would tell.

# shannon, the lady's man

ords can't express how excited I was to be taking myself through this process of discovery. Never had I given thought into processing this aspect of my past and how it was affecting me in my day-to-day realities. Judge and I met weekly to discuss how things were going. He encouraged me to journal to give myself a voice and to process what I felt. There was no need to worry about grammar. I'd just write. I couldn't believe just how much I'd written over time. Many of the entries dealt with my father's unpredictable and occasional rage, while others dealt with school. Judge encouraged me to read out loud to him on certain days.

"How's journalin' goin'?" He was prepping for today's session.

"It's going great." I waited for him to ask the obvious.

"So you feel like readin' today?"

"Yeah, I can. It's cool." So I began.

*I can remember my grandmother saying, "I just don't see why Vicky left." I could. If I were her I would have jetted too. After all, didn't my grandmother know how evil her son, my father, was? Didn't she know of the many times he hit her? Didn't she know that he brought food home when he felt like it? Didn't she know my sister had to iron my clothes because he was too stoned to do so? I guess that's why I grew up hating my mother. I guess when you're a child, you tend to believe the adults. After all, they must be right, right? I'm glad that as I got older, I came to figure out the truth. My sister taught me a lot, how to read, I think. She let me sleep in her bed when I got scared at night. "Keva, I gotta use the bathroom." So she'd walk with me to the bathroom in the dark. I also remember playing with the kids in the neighborhood but*

*not quite fitting in. Often the butt of jokes but still respected. I didn't really want to fit in to be honest. Liked just being a kid. Seems like my sister took up for me a lot when the kids picked on me. But she dogged me out when in the house. I guess she always had my back when it really counted. Sweet girl. Quiet. But had a survivor instinct. I can't remember the first time/age the molestation occurred. All still a blur. Lured somehow over his house. Said he would teach me how to make out with girls. Lay on couch. Told it would feel good. Grind until he cums on the cloth. Then, I go home. Weird feeling. I didn't like it. One of my brother's friends. I wonder if I did anything to make him think I wanted to do this. Happened over the course of years, I think. Into my pre-teens. Prayed hard, cried a lot. Prayers must not be heard because nothing changed. God must be dealing with someone else's problems.*

"Wow, Bernard, that's great stuff."

"Really?" I figured he'd have to say this to all his clients.

"Yeah, it's good when you're able to take time and put all of it on paper. It forces you to think about it, even if it doesn't make sense to you. It can be very therapeutic."

"Okay."

"So how have you been doing with your relationship with your father now, and how are you with intimacy?"

"Well, I don't really talk to my father that much. I used to call him on his birthday, but I really don't anymore. I normally call him on Father's Day, but that's about it. I asked myself why I was the only one reaching out. My phone works both ways. It dials out and receives calls. I guess he hasn't figured out how to use the phone to check on me to see how I'm doing."

"I see." He gave me space to talk.

"And man, I ain't even gone lie, when it comes to intimacy, I haven't put myself in that position. One part of me doesn't even want to come out of his shell to invest the time into getting to know a lady. That means eventually I'll have to tell her about what happened. And I don't know if you know black women, but I feel like they might use it against me if we have a crazy argument or something. May think of me as being less than a man. That sounds crazy, don't it?"

"Naw, I understand where you coming from."

"And another part of me believes that the Lord will send me the right person when it's the right time. So I feel like the intimacy will eventually come when I click with the right person."

"Okay, okay. I gotcha." I could tell he didn't necessarily agree with my perspective, but he just listened and kept his game face on. "I hear you. But sometimes, you have to get out of your comfort zone and place yourself in situations to meet people. Do you necessarily believe that you will only meet your woman in church?"

"Well, not really? She could be referred by someone else, but I would hope that she would love God and goes to church. And honestly, Judge, it's really not a big deal for me if I end up being single. Maybe adopt kids. I think I'd be a good father. I just don't know if I'd be a good husband."

"Okay. Just don't limit yourself. You could meet her in the grocery store or in the gym or at school or in the library, anywhere."

"That's true." I hadn't really realized how much of a pattern I allowed myself to follow daily. I never really deviated from my everyday pattern to try to meet women in different settings. I had become so programmed into doing the same thing. Of course, school had its own set of demands, but that didn't mean that I couldn't venture out and place myself in different settings.

"Well, if you're okay with it, I'd like to focus our sessions on your trying to improve relations with your father and meeting females. I think these are reasonable ideas that are well within your power to work on. As horrible as it was, it's not just about the molestation. It's about picking up from where you are, moving on, and not becoming a prisoner to it. If you can conquer the aftermath of it, maybe you'll be able to help someone else who has gone through similar pain."

"Yeah, that's true. Well, how do you suggest we move on?"

"Well, concerning the dating, maybe you can just place yourself in a different setting this week. You don't have to force anything. Just deviate from your normal routine. If a meeting occurs with someone, fine. If not, you haven't lost anything."

"Aight. I can do that. I'll figure out where I'll go sometime this week and let you know how it goes."

"Give me another week or so to come up with some ideas about your father. I know you may be upset with him still, but maybe you need to just communicate it to him so that you can address it and move on to live your best life."

"Well, I've already forgiven him for things he did and didn't do. Honestly, I have. I have realized that he is his own man and that I still have to love him for him."

"Yeah, but it might not hurt just to let him know how it's affected you, nothing over the top, nothing life-changing."

"Okay. We'll see. As for now, I'll just focus on what we just discussed. I'll see you next week." I got my things and headed out the door. I'd have to get back to meet with my advisor. As I left, I witnessed the most heartbreaking sight. Right outside the door waiting was a little boy, no more than eight, who was waiting with his mother, both preparing to meet with Judge. The little kid seemed so sad. I couldn't help but tear up as I left when I saw them and made my way to the elevator. I never have understood and guess I never will understand the mindset of someone who takes advantage of someone else who is so powerless and so helpless.

I was pretty excited to place myself in situations to get closer to females. I hadn't realized just how much I had enclosed myself into a solitary world. I was actually pretty content with being alone. Between studying, jogging, praying, and hanging out with occasional friends, I had grown accustomed to enjoying a certain sense of privacy and aloneness. Nonetheless, this would be a welcomed change.

After much consideration, I decided that I'd do something completely different. A basic meet-and-greet would be too boring and predictable. I wanted to meet different people in a world where no one was separated into classes or stereotypes. I could just let my hair down and relax. I had decided that I'd hit up a nightclub in the city. I liked good music and, quiet as it was kept, loved to dance. Since I was in the Chocolate City, there would be no shortage of choices for me. Friday was upon me, and I couldn't wait until after class so I could get myself together and go to Dream, the most famous club in DC.

I got my fresh cut at Ebony Barbers in Silver Spring and took a nap before heading out. Around midnight, I hopped into my SUV and made my way onto the beltway. I took the New York Avenue exit and twisted and turned until I reached the club. Women were running across the street in their heels and the guys were managing to walk somehow while their pants sagged almost to the ground. Maybe I was overdressed because I had put on a pair of dress pants and church shoes. It was almost shameful how out of touch I was with the dress code. I was told that I couldn't wear sneakers, so I probably went overboard in my interpretation of what to wear.

After about thirty minutes, I managed to find a parking space. Doing so was part skill and part luck. No one really paid for parking in the lot on New York Avenue. Most people just drove around until they found a space somewhere in the nearby neighborhood. Thankfully, I did just that.

By the time I got in line, it was extending down the block. I had never witnessed such controlled chaos. It seems like every black person in DC was flocking to this club to release the pressures built up from jobs, relationships, and other stresses. This was the time to chill out, drink, carouse, and just have fun.

"Hey girl, wassup. I ain't seen you in a hot minute." Some woman with a short skirt was speaking to another lady behind me.

"Hey, Miss Thang! Don't you look kee-yoot! I love them shoes, girl. How Li'l Ronny doing?"

"Girl, he in the fifth grade. Can you believe it? Just growing up too fast for me, chile. He gone be in high school 'fo you know it."

"You ain't said nothing but a word, girl. Trust me, I know. ManMan just started his freshman year at Anacostia. He think he a man now. I told him, 'Just 'cause yo' name ManMan don't mean shit. I'll still beat yo' ass down.'"

"Okay, bitch! You gotta let 'em know!"

I just stayed quiet and endured the conversation. At least the line was creeping closer toward the entrance. As we got closer, I heard two more females in front of me talking. They were disgusted at what they saw. Some guy had stepped out of line for a second and was leaning against the wall. When I looked down, I saw a stream of water coming from where he was standing. He was leaning against the wall, relieving himself and was quite discreet about it. In fact, I wouldn't have noticed it if the girls hadn't said anything. But I guess this was DC, and people marched to the beat of their own drum here.

By the time we got to the front, I was just relieved. I couldn't believe that people did this every week. At $20 a pop, this would eat my budget up. I tried to stay positive, though, and just agreed to take the night for what it was worth. Maybe I'd meet a cool female, and it would be fine.

Once I got in, it was really nice. People were chilling, drinking, laughing. It was too packed downstairs, so I decided to climb the thirteen stairs to check out the goings-on above me. One of T.I.'s songs was thumping through the speakers, and everybody was singing with him while they held their sex-on-the-beaches or Long Island iced teas and waved them in the air. I'd go ahead and order a Long Island iced tea, too, just to loosen up. That was definitely a mistake because I started feeling light-headed no more than five minutes after I started to drink. I ended up just putting the drink down and hoped it would wear off soon. I hadn't eaten anything either. So the last thing I needed was to get sick because I had no food on my stomach.

I found a place beside the bar to stand. It was out of the way where everyone had to walk, but I could still see what went on. I saw this one girl on the floor, who was crazy cute. She was on the light-skinned side but not too much. She stood about 5'5. Nice body. At least she looked good from afar. Plus, the lights on the dance floor were doing the disco-ball thing, flashing on and off really fast. So I wasn't sure if she was so-called fine through those lights or if she really looked like Godzilla when they turned the main lights on. I chuckled at myself at this notion. As I stared at her, I was bumped by mistake.

"Oh, damn. My bad, yo." A black guy with a Ralph Lauren polo shirt was walking one way and was staring at some girl who was walking the other way. He didn't see me standing where I was and accidentally stumbled over my shoes. Some of his drink got on my pants. "Man, my bad. I didn't even see you right here, B." He didn't call me B because he knew my name and was abbreviating it. It was just a term that most guys called each other. "I gotta chill out looking at these bitches. My girl already don't want me here. I ain't trying to end up in the dog house."

I could tell he was living more on the tipsy than sober side. "It's all good, man. You cool. I feel you, though. These ladies are looking right. Seems like they don't want to give us the time of day, though. They take all that time to hook themselves up, but when you tell 'em they look nice, they ignore you. If you don't say nothin', they be feeling all rejected. It's crazy."

"Word. It *is* crazy. Where yo' bitch at? You had to get away from her, too?" He was prompting more small talk. "Yo dawg, my bad. I'm Shannon." He shook my hand.

"Oh, aight. I'm Bernard, man. Naw, I'm single. I'm trying to see what I can maybe find here." I started laughing to disguise my discomfort with being single. "Just ain't found the right one yet, man. They seem too complicated." I had to say whatever I thought made sense at the moment.

"Damn right, kid." He sipped more of his Patron mixture. "How I'm 'posed to know what they want when they don't e'en know what they want they damn self? Keep lookin' yo. You'll find the right one." He leaned against the bar. "You ain't drinkin' shit?"

"Man, I was but it had me spinning. I had to put it down. I don't even really drink."

"Oh, aight." There was this weird pause. Why didn't he go on and do his normal thing. He felt it necessary to keep up small talk with me. "Yo, what's that cologne you got on? I gotta make my girl buy me some o' dat."

"Light Blue." He must had caught a whiff when he accidentally bumped me.

"So you from around here? I don't think I seen you around here that much, not that I'm here every week." He started laughing.

"Naw, man. I just thought I'd come out here and see what's the big deal about this place. I drive by it all the time. So I thought I'd try it out." There was no need to get into the real reason I was there, how it was a mini-experiment I agreed to in order to test out my social skills with the ladies. In fact, he was taking up too much of my time. I'd have to find a way to break away and get back on mission.

The music had turned into the famous DC-Baltimore go-go music. Everyone seemed to go into a frenzy. All I heard was a chorus of "I'ma I'ma I'ma freak, I'ma I'ma I'ma freak." Everybody seemed to be anticipating this part of the night and went berserk as they danced and sang along to it, including Shannon.

"Awww!" He started dancing in place to the up-tempo beat.

I just watched everybody. Everybody was gyrating and getting it in. At least the alcohol made me think everyone was gyrating.

"Yo, this the shit." Shannon was definitely getting his dance on. He was talking to me at the same time, but I couldn't make out what he was saying because of the loudness of the music.

I bopped in place a little. The music *was* hot. It put a movement in you even if you didn't really want to move. I was trying to listen to what Shannon was saying but couldn't. Between his dancing and the music and everybody else shouting, I could barely understand him. All I kept hearing was something about his being mad. Mad this, mad that. So I tried to listen closer.

"Who you say you mad at, and why? You mad at your girl?" I was trying to prompt him to be clearer.

He clarified his position quite well this time. He got closer to my ear and cleared up any remaining confusion I had regarding what he said. He whispered just loud enough for me and only me to hear. "Naw, no disrespect son, but I was saying that you mad sexy, yo." As he said it, his body language gave off like he was motioning for me to look at the female passing by. To the outsider, this would justify his need to be close enough to whisper.

I was trying to comprehend what I thought he said. Maybe it was the effect of my drink. Or the loud music. Or the chaos period. So I asked him one more time what he said. "Huh?"

"I'ma just put it out there, son. You mad sexy. I'm just sayin'."

Here I was on a homework assignment from Judge, trying to put myself in a position to meet women, and the one that I managed to attract was a guy who boasted all night about his girl at home and undressed the females with his eyes all night in the club. I couldn't do anything but laugh. Literally, I laughed and shook my head. "Man, come on, now." That was all I could get out at the time. I'm sure someone else would have exposed him or verbally assaulted him or worse. That just wasn't my style.

He seemed to be thrown off by my laughter and thought he'd say something to fill in the awkward moment. "I mean, it's all good. I'm just sayin' I saw somethin' I liked and just wanted to go after it. Erbody in here grown. I'm just keepin' it a hunned, B." Interpreted, he was keeping it real. "I ain't never seen you in here before, and you just caught my attention." He sipped from his drink again. "So I just wanted to see what was up, nah mean?" Without realizing it, he seemed to be digging a deeper ditch with every word leaving his mouth. In my analysis, he frequented this place quite regularly, enough to know whose face was new and whose wasn't. And what of his woman? One could assume she was in the dark concerning these club-borne advances.

"Oh. I see. Well, I think I'll pass on that one, Shannon. Nice meetin' you, though." I pretty much took this turn of the discussion as my cue to call it a night. "I think I'm 'bout to head on out and hit the sack, man."

He was still bouncing to the music and trying to act as naturally as possible, given the way the conversation had progressed. "Aight, yo. You sure you don't just wanna just hang and kick it. We can still be boys. Smoke, drink, chill, whatever." He didn't know I'd learned my lesson already with smoking. That surely wouldn't be happening again. "I didn't mean to make you wanna be ghost, my nigga."

I was deducing this wasn't the first time he had pulled a move like this. He seemed to know what was appropriate to say after being rejected to ease the tension. But I was a little disappointed that my initial experiment would have to be cut short. I really was tired and wanted to get back to Cherokee Street.

"Nah, I'm cool. For real. It was gettin' to be sorta too much in here anyway for me." I chocked this up to being just my luck. I did conclude, however, that the incidental bumping earlier on may not have been incidental at all. Perhaps it was a calculated move on his part from the outset. Honestly, I knew this wouldn't be the setting that I'd be able to meet women anyway. I shook the lady's man's hand and offered departing words. "Aight, man, I'm out. Take it easy, and stay safe." I wanted to tell him to think about what he was doing as it related to how it could possibly affect his woman, but my advice-giving self was not up to it. My mind was on my car, my bed, and myself.

I left him standing there, headed downstairs to the exit, made it to my car, and drove home laughing to myself as I drove on the darkened 285. By the time I reached College Park, I pulled into my parking space, went into 4712, kicked my shoes off, pulled off my clothes, and got under the covers. I didn't know why, but I kept laughing. At some point, I drifted off into oblivion because when I finally awoke and noticed the clock, it said 9:13 AM.

# two thursdays from today

During the next counseling session, I made my way into Judge's office and prepared to fill him in on what had transpired over the weekend. "Wassup, Bernard? So how did things go this weekend? What did you do?"

I started laughing. "Maaaaan!"

"Oh Lord, what happened? Did you have all of the chicks falling at your feet?"

"Well, I wouldn't say that. Judge, I went to Dream so I could . . ."

"You went *where*?" He cut me off as if he had the inside scoop on some type of information.

"Dream."

Judge fell out laughing. "Man, are you serious?" I mean, I ain't judgin' you or nothin', but I can't help laughin', man. You ain't even gotta tell me the rest."

"Man, I got hit on by a thug."

"Bernard, man, I could have told you that. That club is known for rolling like that. A lot of DL men go there to find hook-ups. They feel like it's a safe place for them to go because it's a mixed crowd, and they can do what they do without a lot of fanfare. My bad, man. I should have told you that."

"No need to apologize, man. It caught me off guard just like it's catching you off guard. Thanks for letting me know beforehand." I couldn't resist sarcasm.

"Well, I had no idea you were going *there*."

After we laughed a moment more, we regained our focus and continued to set some more personal goals. "Well, maybe you shouldn't really expect to meet ladies at the club anyway. It's just so much going on there that it's hard to see who someone really is in that type of atmosphere. I did want to transition, though, and start thinking about your relationship with your father. I know you've forgiven him already and don't really have any pent-up anger toward him. But it may be nice for you to reach out to him just to see what he thinks about his role as a father. It may help you as you make more moves in life, especially when you become a father yourself. Maybe it'll give you some insight into what not to do."

"Yeah, that makes sense. I'm actually going home for Christmas, so we have a good month or so to do something. I don't know what, but something."

"Well, you've been writing in your journal, so you have been able to get some things off your chest and at least put them on paper. I was thinking that maybe you could write a hypothetical letter to him. Just spill it all out. When you finish the letter, you can actually mail it to him if you want, but you don't have to. At least you will have an opportunity to think about what you say before you say it. I've seen men contact their fathers by phone when they get older, and it just turns into a shouting match. Nothing is really accomplished. You can't guarantee that he'll read the letter, but the odds are that he will because everyone likes reading something handwritten to them. Something about the psychology of it all. They feel more special, more thought about."

"Aight. I can work with that. I never thought of doing that before. I probably won't send it, but it'll give me a chance to organize my thoughts and process it some more." I thought this would be a great exercise. Judge really had some great ideas to help me internalize and make sense of the experience.

We continued with the sessions, as they got closer to the date that I was supposed to hypothetically mail the letter. I'd bring in portions of the letter that I wrote that week before. Judge encouraged me to write whatever I felt and not to hold anything back even if I thought it would be offensive.

"Yeah, I'm actually looking forward to it. I think it'll be good, I guess."

"I hear you. Oh yeah, I almost forgot to mention this program for the counseling participants that we have every year. I wanted to see if you'd be interested in being a part of it. It's called *Take Back the Night*. It's a time where all of our clients come out in support of each other and take part in a ceremony that basically says you refuse to be a victim and that you are taking control of your life in spite of being sexually abused. If you want to share a few words on that day, we really encourage it. Some of the TV stations may be present, so we always let you know that it's possible that they'll do a story on it, and your face will be on the news. It may not, but it might. Just something to think about. You don't have to make a decision now, but the program will be in a month or so."

"Okay. I'll think about it, even though what happened to me with the assailant always happened in broad daylight. So I wouldn't know anything about taking back the night." I laughed.

"You know what?" Judge caught the joke and chuckled.

"Anyway, I probably will do it. I just need time to sleep on it."

"Aight. Well, we can discuss it further in the future. You can start working on the letter to your father. See if you can have some of it written by next week."

"Aight. I'll get up with you later."

During the next few sessions, I read to Judge the different thoughts I wrote to my father. He thought there were some instances where I needed to clarify my feelings. He also encouraged me to say what I really meant and leave no room for gray-area interpretation. I agreed. Pretty soon, I was to return home for Christmas, so mailing the letter shortly after Thanksgiving was our set time for sending it if I chose to. It would allow my father time to read it, process it, and meet with me. My strategy would be to send the letter, go back home for Christmas, and take him out for dinner and let the conversation flow. Nice idea, at least in theory.

As the days to Thanksgiving approached, I resolved that I'd mail the letter after sending a copy to Judge for one last perusal. He thought the final draft was great. In it, I actually told my father about the molestation, although I didn't tell him who had done it. I just thought he should know. I also told him of the ensuing battle I was undergoing with school. I was in the midst of a big fight that could leave me without the PhD. I didn't want to play the race card, but I couldn't ignore it either. I had informed him that if things didn't work out, I'd probably be moving to either New York or L.A. to pursue some semi-career in modeling or acting. It had always been a quiet dream of mine, and I was getting no younger. Essentially, I filled him in on what was going on with me and how I had processed my childhood with him at the helm of parental leadership.

"Bernard, this is a good letter." Judge encouraged me to go through with the mailing. "You really are a good writer. You do a good job in putting words together to express your feelings."

"Thanks. Yeah, I'm definitely mailing it. When I go home for Christmas, I'll just take him out for dinner to see how he reacts. It's amazing. I've never gone out to dinner with him. I'm sure it'll feel strange."

"Well, I think it's the right decision. Even if he doesn't respond in a way that you think he should, at least you've done your part to inform him. You'll be in a better position to move on with your life and not feel stuck."

"Yeah, I hear you."

On the day before Thanksgiving, I drove around the corner to the post office before heading to the gym at Bally. I glanced at the letter one final time before dropping it in the box. I just sat in the car, wondering if I was making the right decision. I hadn't realized how long I sat there because the car behind me blew its horn. I stuck my hand out and waved as if to apologize. I quickly dropped the letter in the blue device and drove away. I felt a little nervous as I left. How would he respond? Would he feel like I was blaming him? Would he shut down? Would he get upset? Even though I didn't know the answers to these questions, any feelings of angst that I had gave way to satisfaction. At least my voice would be heard. Deep down, I knew I'd made the right choice. In about a month, I'd see what the chain reaction would be.

I had been making a casual effort since my Atlanta days to try my hand at modeling and acting. One of the secretaries at Morehouse had asked if I had considered it and encouraged me to pursue it. She had done it for a while and thought I had a good look for it. This wasn't something I had heard people talk about, so I was a little hesitant to go after it. It was, after all, a fickle industry and had a reputation for being cutthroat. I had found a photographer, though, and took some initial Polaroids and mailed them in to agencies with no success.

After I moved to the DC area, I continued to pursue these as time allowed. Pursuing a PhD swallowed most of my time, but I still had moments where I could try to work in this other aspect of my life. I landed a few local agencies, which submitted me for work here and there. They pushed me for all types of opportunities such as modeling, commercial, and print work. A new agency in the Annapolis area contacted me and wanted me to come in to meet the owner. As I sat in the waiting room, the assistant booker, Rory, kept walking by and staring at me as if he knew me. Finally, he broke the uncomfortable silence.

"Have you been in here before?"

"No, this is my first time."

"Okay. It seems like I know you from somewhere."

"No, not to my knowledge. I don't think I've seen you before."

"Oh, alright. Man, you have star quality. It's just something about you that stands out. That's why I kept staring at you. Have you done any work in the industry before?"

"Nah, man. I'm pretty much new to all this. Thanks for the compliment, though. Maybe you can find some good work for me and *turn* me into a star." We both laughed.

Soon, the owner came out and introduced himself. "Hi, Bernard. I'm Yabin. Come right in." After he told me about his agency, he promised that he'd submit me for everything he thought I qualified for. "So what do you do?"

"I'm in grad school right now, so I have a lot of free time. I have a scholarship, so I'm not working. I can focus on school and do this type of work on the side."

"That's great. We actually just got an announcement concerning casting this season for this HBO show. Rory, what's the name of the show that we just got a fax about? They're looking for someone to play in the library scene?" He was asking his assistant about this new gig.

"It's called *The Wire*. They pretty much do all of the filming in Baltimore, so they use a lot of local talent."

"Well, go ahead and send Dillard's headshot and resume in for it."

Surely, he was posturing. He had just met me and was giving off like he really had legit connections. I knew he was just trying to impress me. "If they call, will you be able to get to Bmore?"

I played along with it. "Oh, yeah. I have a car, so it's nothing to get there. It would only take me about forty-five minutes."

"Alright, well stay by your phone. These calls can come in at any moment. So you'll have to be ready to move."

I wanted to respond by saying, "Yeah, right," but I let it drop. If something came of it, it would be all the better. I left more of my contact information and made my way back to campus for class. "Thanks a lot. See you guys later."

Rory was the first to respond. "Okay, Dillard. Nice meeting you. We'll be in touch with you whenever a client wants to see you. Keep your phone close."

Yabin concluded. "Take it easy, sir. I look forward to a great working relationship with you."

I almost had to run to my car to speed back to campus. I had class in twenty minutes and wasn't sure if I'd make it.

The next day, as I sat in class, I did my best not to fall asleep. I loved Linear Models as a topic but didn't care much for the professor. I looked around and saw the sea of Asians in the class. They all seemed to like statistics and flooded almost every class that offered material in this vein. I was the only non-Asian in this class but was somewhat used to it at this level. Friends told me I looked Asian anyway when I smiled, so in some ways, I guess I fit right in. The only grade we received in the course was based on a presentation that each student had to give, so I had to make sure I paid attention and not miss a session. While I was in class, I felt my phone buzzing more than normal.

"Can't they just leave a message?" I whispered to myself. After a while, the caller finally got the revelation, stopped calling, and decided to leave a message. The long vibration signaled just that.

When I left class, I heard the message and realized Rory was calling from the agency. I called to see what all of the buzz was about, literally.

"Hey, Rory."

"Dillard. What's up, man!" He seemed ecstatic. "Man, they called for you. They want you to come and audition for the part on *The Wire*."

"Rory, stop playing. Are you just saying that?"

He laughed. "Man, we don't play about business. I'm serious. They want you to come in. Can you get to Baltimore tomorrow morning?"

"Yeah, I don't have class tomorrow morning."

"Alright. I'm going to email you the details in a few. Don't blow this, Dillard. If you can't make it, let us know now."

"I can make it." I wondered what all the hoopla was about.

"After the audition, give us a call and let us know how it went."

"Aight. I will. Talk to you later."

As I drove to Baltimore for the casting, I casually looked outside and just thought to myself how things were playing out in my life. Things always managed to work out, despite a few challenges here and there. Overall, this was a good life, and I saw myself as being rather blessed. My early years were trying, but I stuck it out and was about to become a doctor. Not bad. And now, here I was embarking upon acting. I hadn't spoken with anyone concerning this goal. It was one of those aims I just pursued on my own. I didn't have time to listen to those who felt like I couldn't do it for whatever reason.

Once I got off the exit and pulled into the parking lot, I entered the entrance for Pat Moran and Associates and signed in. Countless people were there trying to scratch their acting-bug itch. Soon, they called my name, gave me a little prep for the reading, and let me go for it. I was reading for two roles, both of which were of inmates. Typical.

"Man, shit, we locked up. We best not believe that, right?" They listened as I read the role in my southern accent. I had been conscious of covering it since most roles wanted a non-regional dialect. I guess my nerves took over and the southern drawl won out. I managed to mask it the second time they asked me to read after they gave me a little direction after the first take.

"Okay, thank you." The casting rep sent me on my way and rushed in the next guy. She may as well have said, "Don't call us. We'll call you."

I took it in stride, however. It was my first audition ever, and I knew that no experience was a wasted experience. At least I was in school and not in dire need of securing a gig to keep the rent paid. I had to hurry and get to class, which was to start in about an hour. I made my way to the expressway and just watched the road come to me.

About five minutes into the drive back to campus, I was startled when my phone rang. "Dillard, they loved you. They want you to come back in on tomorrow and read for the actual director." It was Rory from the agency.

"Rory are you serious? They couldn't have called you that quick. I just left a few minutes ago, and there were still people there in the waiting room when I left." I was hoping this wasn't a prank.

"Well, I don't know 'bout all that. All I know is I just got off the phone with Alexa, and she wants you to come back for a second reading."

"Alright. I'll be there. Is it the same place?"

"Yep, but they want you there at 2:00, if possible."

"Okay. I can make it. This is wild."

When I went back on the next day, I guess I was a little more nervous because I knew they'd be screening me closer. I was on their radar and had to be on my p's and q's. Just as I took a few deep breaths, the director got my attention. "Dillard, you can come on in."

I wanted out. I had no prior coaching and was starting to doubt myself. Maybe I should just stick to what I knew best. Being a nerd and doing math. In the meantime, I'd just go through with this second reading and get out of there. I was now staring at about six people, including the director, who all sat on a couch and sized me up. I had memorized the lines but felt myself forgetting them the more they gazed at me.

The director must have felt my nerves because he broke the ice. "Hi, Dillard. Glad you could make it back. We'll just have you say the lines for us. Just do as you did the first time. Make it as real as you can. Any time you're ready, you can start."

I could feel my stuttering trying to emerge again but somehow fought it off. I gave it my best shot, treating them as if they were invisible. I relaxed in my chair, spread my legs in gangsta fashion, and tried my best to give the best inmate reading I could muster. I glanced at the director, who had a slight smile. "Alright, thanks for coming in again, Dillard. Are you in the area?"

"Yeah, I live in the DC area, so the drive is not too bad."

"Okay, we'll be in touch with your agent if we go with you. Thanks for coming back."

"Alright, thanks. I'll keep my fingers crossed." And we both exchanged grins.

As I drove back to campus, the phone didn't ring. That's how it was. It seemed to ring off the hook when I wasn't expecting communication. Now that I was hoping for a call, there was no way it was going to ring. I would have to get focused and get to class. The date for my presentation was coming up two Thursdays from this day, and I had to be ready. I made it to class on time and endured the frequent stares by all of the Asians in the class. I felt like they were talking about me because of how they looked at me and spoke to each other in Chinese whenever I was near them. It seemed to resemble the kinds of stories I heard females talk about at the nail salon when one worker spoke to her co-worker in their unique language about the filthiness of the client's feet. I had gotten used to it by now and just wanted to get the presentation over so I could move on.

By the time I returned home from the day's hustle and bustle, I vowed to just chill out that night on the sofa and catch some laughs with Conan

O'Brien. As I watched, my phone indicated that a message was waiting. I hated my Verizon service. It had a mind of its own when it came to calls. It was hit or miss. This time, it was miss.

As Conan did his notorious invisible string-and-hip motion, I listened to the message. "DILLARD, THEY LOVED YOU AND SAID YOU GOT THE PART!" Rory was screaming. "They're sending the official script to us and want to film your part of the episode in two weeks, two Thursdays from today. Give us a call back in the morning. Way to go, man. You're a star!"

I hung up and felt like Charlie Brown after Lucy moved the football. I was completely stunned that two important events in my world had been scheduled for the same day at the same time, and I would now have to make a choice.

# **and that was that**

I couldn't believe the show's episode was shooting on the same day that I'd have to make my presentation. The odds of this had to be close to 0.01%. Whatever probability defined the situation, however, was of no importance because it was indeed happening. I was reluctant to call my agent because he was on such a high. How could I tell him that I wouldn't be able to accept such a coveted role? I decided to wait and maybe speak with my professor to see if there was any way he'd consider moving my presentation date. I was sure he'd view the circumstance as though I was just trying to delay due to being ill-prepared. I would be just another student who was trying to get over.

Any hopes I had were dashed, though, because no sooner than I asked, he said that I couldn't change dates. The schedule was too tight, and it was too late to ask someone else to switch dates with me. Besides, I couldn't think of any of the students who would be willing to change with me anyway since I sensed a certain animosity with most of them in the class. So I just decided to bite the bullet, be a grown up about it, and break the news to Rory.

"Hey, Rory."

"Wassup, Dillard. Congrats on the role. Everyone in the office here is talking about how amazing it is that you got the role. Your very first audition and you booked it. You're a star!"

"Thanks, Rory. I'm not sure if I'll be able to take it, though. I gotta give a presentation in a class, and the grade I receive is strictly based on it. Out of all days, guess which date I was assigned to present?"

"Dillard, no, you have got to be lying."

"Wish I was, man."

"Well, I won't call and tell them yet. Just try to work it out. Talk to your professor."

"I did already. He wasn't hearing it. He don't understand nothing 'bout no acting and all that. He all about the math. They don't play in PhD programs. They expect you to adjust and shut the rest of the world out just to get some dumb degree."

"Well, it'll work out. I can't call and tell them this. We'll talk."

"Aight. I'll talk to you soon."

That next Thursday, I went to class highly upset, not at anyone in particular, just mad. Professor Maddox came in and told Quaxing that he could start his talk. "And next week, Bernard will be presenting on his topic, Generalized Additive Models." My talk was already done, so I could have presented on that day, but it was what it was, and I just flowed with it.

As Quaxing made his talk, the professor kept butting in and taking over. Quaxing had only spoken for about five minutes. The professor had become motivated and inspired and clearly caught the student unawares. He felt compelled to provide an extemporaneous lecture about something the student had mentioned in his introduction. As he spoke, Quaxing stood at the podium looking rather lost and confused, wondering when the professor would quieten and let him continue. He must have been rather disappointed because it didn't happen. By the time the professor realized it, the class time had expired, and he made the most welcomed announcement.

"Well, class, it looks like I got a little carried away and didn't realize the time. Quaxing, we'll let you give your talk on next week. And Bernard, this will push you back a week. You'll give yours the Thursday after next."

As everyone scurried out, I grabbed my leather bag, headed for the door, and just whispered out loud the first thing that came to my mind: *Thank you, Jesus*.

"Yo man, Rory, you ain't gone believe this. Things are gonna work out. I can take the part in *The Wire*."

"What?! That's wassup. I was getting a little nervous trying to figure out what I was gone tell them. We'll get back with you after we get more details."

"Aight cool, man! Keep me posted."

It was good to know everything would work out. They sent the agency the script, and I eventually received it. I didn't tell anyone about the gig. They'd just have to see it if they watched the mini-series. I was not one who was a spotlight guy. I'd just take the experience in tow and learn from it. No bullhorn here.

In fact, when the day of filming came, I went about as if it were a normal school day: prayed, showered, ate, the usual. When I arrived on set in Baltimore, I got to my trailer and just waited for further instructions. It made sense to read over my PowerPoint slides for my math talk on next week. A lot of this show biz stuff was hurry up and wait. Soon, they were calling for me for hair and makeup. The barber lined me up and I had some foundation placed on my face. The scene was being shot in some Baltimore prison, an easy find, I'm sure. My scene was with Larry Gilliard, Jr., who portrayed D'Angelo Barksdale, a high-ranking drug slinger in his family. I had to take all things in stride and act like all of this was normal for me. No one knew that this was a role I got from my first-ever audition. I was a fish out of water but faked it pretty well.

When they said "Action," I took a deep breath and sort of felt the stomach get in knots again. *Oh, please, no stuttering today.* I told myself to calm down and go with the flow. I figured it would be appropriate not to look into the camera, although no one told me. I assumed the camera was just to be a fly on the wall, observing us. It was on a dolly and moved like it was on a train track. It was very distracting, but I continued to imitate everyone else and act like it wasn't there. Soon, I said my lines, "Man, shit, we locked up. We best not believe that, right?" It was over, well at least that take. We must have shot it about twenty times. Larry kept struggling with a few of his lines, and we'd have to start over. And the director gave me suggestions about how to change up what I said with emphases on certain words some times and other words other times.

During a slight break, this one extra asked me, "So, man, how you get this speaking role?"

"Man, you won't believe it. I just went to the audition and read for them and they called me back. God just gave me a little favor, man."

"Oh aight, that's wassup. Keep at it."

Soon, the scene wrapped, and we all clapped. I told everyone goodbye, headed to the SUV, and drove back to the apartment. I started pinching myself to see if this was real. I had just filmed an episode for a series. It seemed like this fairy tale ended just as quickly as it had begun. I'm sure it wasn't really a well-known show, so I didn't expect much. My nose was always stuck in a book somewhere, and I was too cheap to pay for cable. Soon, I found out just how much people loved that show because my phone started ringing off the hook once it aired.

A friend from New York called and chastised me. "Boy, why didn't you tell us you got a role for that show? That show is the truth!" A friend from Durham had reached me and left a message. "Bernard, we saw you on *The Wire*. You did good, boy. Congratulations!" Even Keva called and chimed in in her own way. "Hey, nerd, Art stopped me at the gas station and said he saw you on some ghetto show on HBO. Congrats, nerd." She never ceased to be herself. She interjected "ghetto" on her own.

It was a great moment, highly unexpected, but it felt pretty good to get bit by the acting bug. But after this, it would be back to normal.

I started my sessions back with Judge again. "Man, I know this gone sound crazy, but I swore I saw you on this HBO show last week."

"Yeah, it was me."

"Man, I thought so! You were great, man. I wanted to tell my girlfriend that you were one of my clients, but then I caught myself and remembered that our sessions are confidential. I just wanted to tell somebody, man!" He was beaming. "I can now say I know a movie star."

"Judge, you a trip. It was just one role. It's not like it's recurring."

"Yeah, but man, not everybody in acting gets even one speaking role ever. You should be proud."

"Yeah, I am." I shrugged it off and just wanted to get to today's counseling session. "Well, you know I mailed the letter to my dad and will be going home for the holidays. I think I'll try to meet up with him when I go back and see if I can have dinner with him."

"That's admirable, man. Just stay open and realistic. Even if he doesn't respond the way you think he should, at least you're making what you think are the right steps to make your life more meaningful. Keep me posted on what happens. Oh yeah, have you given any more thought to participating in the *Take Back the Night* program?"

"Yeah. I'll probably do it. If I can help one person, I guess that's all that matters."

"Alright cool. That's really brave of you. It may feel a little weird, but I know you'll feel good about the decision to speak. We'll talk more about it later. We'll meet in about two weeks. We'll have a chance to talk about what happened between you and your father."

"Kay. Well, have a good holiday and all that jazz. I'll see you when I get back."

"Peace, Mr. Hollywood!"

I smiled and moseyed on out.

Admittedly, I was a bit nervous as I made the trip home that Christmas. I normally just stayed with my grandmother, went to visit my mother, hung out with Keva, and made the journey back. I didn't worry about trying to spend time with my father since he was preoccupied and had his own issues to work through. I had determined that I wouldn't set unrealistic expectations when it came to dealing with him. I had cried my last tear concerning him way before now. But now, here I was making him the primary reason for taking the trip. I had no real idea what would happen, but at least I'd know I'd make a concerted effort to spend time with him.

After the four-hour drive, I settled in and handed out a few hugs and kisses to grandma. "Hey, man." I noticed she had started walking slightly more bent over. She never hesitated to grasp me tight and lean her head into my chest. "Boy, you getting taller by the minute."

"Hey, lady. Well you getting prettier by the minute."

"It's some food on the stove, or you can swing by the restaurant and get you something."

"I stopped on the road and got something, so I'm not really hungry. I'm supposed to be going by to take daddy out for dinner."

"Oh, really?" She perked up. She was happy to hear I would be spending quality and deliberate time with her son. "That's great! Where y'all going?"

"I don't know yet."

"Well, y'all have fun."

I called to let him know that I'd be there around 7:00 to pick him up. By then, I'd know where we'd go to hang out. He assured me he'd be ready.

As I drove toward the house where I grew up, there was a strange apprehension I felt as I surveyed the neighborhood. I couldn't believe how small the community felt now. When I was a child, it seemed so huge. Now, blocks seemed so tiny. I drove up the driveway and felt the tightening in my stomach again. So many memories. I cracked the door, stepped out, and looked around.

"Bernie, is that you?" Mr. and Mrs. Phillips were trying to make out if I was the one stepping out of the car. Other than my father, they were the only ones who still addressed me by my nickname.

"Hey, how's it going?" I walked to the street and gave them hugs. "I'm here visiting, seeing how daddy's doing."

"Oh, okay. Well, it's pretty bad sometimes. It's a lot of stuff going on over there, Bernie, a lot of traffic in and out. A lot of loud noise at night and everything."

"Yeah, I know." I wasn't even embarrassed. "I grew up in that mayhem." I could talk to them honestly about this since they had been our neighbors for so long. "Well, hopefully things will get better. Lemme head up here and see how he's doing."

"Okay, Bernie. It's good to see you. We glad you making something out yourself."

"Alright. See you guys later. I still remember those clothes you all gave me and all those apples. I won't forget your help."

They started laughing. "Yeah, Bernie, we remember the clothes and apples too. Keep hanging in there."

As I walked away, I couldn't help but feel as though they talked between themselves about how I overcame that madness as they had done about my challenges when I was a kid leaving their house with the bag of clothes they gave me.

After knocking on dad's door, I just looked around outside. The house seemed so small from what I remembered. There were the plants and the spot where I, on purpose, used to stand with my little umbrella in the rain. It was my own entertainment. There was the mini-ladder that I used to climb, that was attached to the carport. I climbed it one time and got stung behind the ear when I tampered with a wasp's nest. I chuckled. The nest was still there. Soon, I heard someone unlocking the door from the inside.

"Hey, Bernard." Some man answered the door. "Your daddy stepped out. He said he'd be back in a sec."

I didn't even inquire as to this mystery man was. "Well, he knew I was coming to pick him up at 7:00. Why would he leave?"

"He just had to make a run."

I walked away without saying another word and waited in the car.

I just sat and waited. And waited. And waited. And waited.

I looked at the clock and it said 9:00 PM. Two hours had gone by and nothing. I couldn't believe I had set myself up again for disappointment. I started the car and prepared to leave. All of a sudden, the door to the home opened, and it looked to be the same guy coming to the car to relay another silly message. But it wasn't him at all. Around to the passenger's side of the car was none other than my father. He had been inside the house the entire time. He opened the passenger's side and spoke. "Hey, Bernie."

*Whachu mean, "Hey Bernie!" I been waiting out here for two hours for you, and you come in here talkin' 'bout "Hey, Bernie."* Well, at least that's what I wanted to say. I kept it respectful. All that managed to come out was, "Hi. I've been waiting for you for some time. Where were you?"

After giving me some lame excuse, I decided to drop it, keep focused, and get to where we were going. We didn't talk much, just empty words to fill space. I tried to catch him up on what was happening with school but knew he wouldn't be able to understand the details about which I spoke. I brought up the role I had recently got, and he seemed to be glad about that. "Uh oh, you'll be getting an Oscar in no time." He laughed. I didn't.

Once we arrived at the restaurant, we just sat. I didn't want to bring up anything in the letter I wrote. I wanted him to initiate any discussion concerning it, so I was prepared to go the whole evening and have no words about it. At the very least, this would be quality time that I'd be able to say that we had. I just caught myself staring at him and his visage. His face was getting slimmer and slimmer. By his frail makeup, it seems as though he had been doing a lot of suffering.

One thing that wasn't suffering, though, was his appetite. He put away his food in no time, literally leaving nothing on the plate. During the meal, he would casually interject, "Man, this is great!"

"Good. I'm glad you're liking it." He was so right about it. The food was delectable.

We just sat, had small talk, and enjoyed the moment as best we could. A high school friend happened over and spoke. "Bernard Dillard, man I ain't seen you in forever."

Once I turned and recognized him, I stood and offered a hug. "Wassup, Art. You're right. It's been a minute. You lookin' good, man." I turned toward my dad. "This is my father. We're here just grabbing a bite."

"Hi, Mr. Dillard." Art shook his hand.

"Hi, sir." He shook with a nice grip and continued stimulating his gums with his toothpick.

"Bernard, I recently saw Keva and told her I saw you on TV. She didn't seem as mean as she used to be." All three of us laughed because we all knew his reference was well-founded. No one was ignorant of her award-winning personality.

"Yeah, man. Keva is still Keva. She just moved back here recently from coaching at Xavier University in Louisiana. She's back at Hillside now coaching the girls' basketball team. She's doing pretty well."

"Alright, man. Well I ain't gone hold y'all up. Tell her I said 'Hello' again. It's nice meeting you, Mr. Dillard."

"Okay, now. Take it easy."

"See ya later, Art. Good seeing you." As he left, I clarified who he was. "Yeah, he graduated with Keva. He ran track too. I hadn't seen him in a long time." I guess it was good that he stopped by because he seemed to be the catalyst in getting the discussion going between my father and me.

"Oh, really?" Daddy was responding. "So he was at Hillside too, huh?"

"Yep. Coach Rumsfeld used to wear us out. They took me under their wing, though. They were seniors and I was a skinny, lanky freshman. If something happened to me, they knew Keva would be all up in their face."

"Yeah, that's Keva." He knew his daughter. "And yeah, you were a skinny li'l something. I didn't know if you were gone gain no weight or what. By the time you was a senior, you got a little taller, though."

"Really?" I didn't realize he had noticed.

We talked off and on about nothing. It was time for the restaurant to close, so I decided that it was time to drop him back off at home. There was no conversation about anything from the letter, but it was just good to spend some time with him.

As we drove back, I could tell he was ready to get back home and relax. We approached the driveway, and there were cars in the driveway that had appeared since we had left. So I had to just pull alongside the side of the curb and drop him off without turning into the driveway.

"Well, alright, this was nice. I guess I'll see you a little later." I was saying goodbye. No emotions. Just goodbye.

He cracked his door opened, and placed his right foot on the ground outside. He then said something I never would have anticipated. "Oh yeah, Bernie, I got your letter, and I read everything in it. I'm glad you hung in there and making something out yourself. This my first time being a father. If I had to do it over, it's a lot of stuff I woulda done different. I apologize for everything I didn't get right. I hope you do a little better with your kids." So to the point and so matter of fact.

"Alright, thanks." I had no idea how to respond. The timing of it caught me so much off guard. So I just flowed with it. "I'll keep all that in mind."

"Okay, Bernie Wernie. Take care of yourself." He was calling me that five-year old name again. I'd never outgrow it.

"Okay. See you later."

He closed the door, limped uphill to the door, and disappeared into the night.

And that was that.

# scared as hell

I had gotten back and shared with Judge the experience at home. I had no feelings in particular about it. "I'm not even sure what I expected to happen, man. He said what he said and that was it." I'm sure I came off as detached, but I was doing my best to be honest.

"Well, I think it was important for you to deal with it head on." Judge was re-affirming. "At least you can move on and not feel like you haven't gotten closure on the matter."

"Yeah, that's true, I guess. More power to him. I guess he's doing the best he can do."

"Indeed. So you know what's next week, right?"

"Mm hmm. I remember. That program you want me to speak at. It's cool."

"You still okay with it? You don't have to do it if you don't want."

"I know. I'll probably go ahead and do it."

"And you can bring anybody for support."

"Yeah, I'll probably bring one of my best friends. I don't have any family up here, so he's the closest thing to it."

"Well, you only have to speak for three minutes or so. Other people will speak too."

"Aight. That's cool. Let me run to class. I got an exam next week and need to be there for the review."

"Okay. I'll call and let you know the details for next week."

"Peace."

That week seemed like it went by in a day. Judge told me to just say what I thought was right. I was to be at the facility around 1:00 that afternoon. Brad stopped by the apartment and rode with me there.

"So, how do you feel?" He was attempting to gauge my comfort level.

"Honestly, I'm scared as hell."

He burst out laughing. "Yeah, it's probably natural to have cold feet about something like this. Not too many are willing to speak out about this. Friend to friend, I'm proud of you, man."

"Thanks. That still don't change the fact that I'm still scared as hell." We laughed some more.

For some reason, I felt like a victim again. I felt like everyone's eyes were on me, even though I was only one of the speakers and the only male. At least the local stations didn't come as Judge said they might. I don't think I was at the point yet to make my journey known on such a wide scale. When the time came to speak, I wish I hadn't agreed. I had some notes but decided against taking them with me to the podium. When Judge introduced me, I must have walked a thousand steps from where I was to where I had to go. I couldn't help but feel as though the eyes staring at me were judging me.

In my mind, they were poring through a bevy of questions concerning me. *I wonder what specifically happened to him. How old was he when it happened? How many times did it happen? How is he dealing with marriage? I can't believe he's the only male speaker.* In my mind, these were the conversations going on behind the audience's smiles. Smiling was what they were supposed to do. So I just concentrated and looked at Brad the whole time. I still can't remember what I said. The time seemed to fly by. Before I knew it, I had returned to my seat and wished to go home. Brad patted me on the shoulder and was laughing. "Boy, you stupid."

I wondered what he referred to. Apparently, I had said something funny at the podium and couldn't remember what it was. "What?"

He just kept laughing and congratulated me again for following through with it.

After the program was over, people came up and spoke with me, letting me know how thankful they were for my courage to come forward. A part of me felt like they felt compelled to do so and really didn't mean it. I wasn't sure why I had become so defensive and questioning of everyone's motives. I just wanted to get out of there fast.

"Yo, Brad, I'm out. You ready?"

"Whenever you are, man."

As we left, we ran into Judge. "Bernard, we appreciate your doing this. We really do, man."

"No problem." I was getting ready to say "Anytime" but caught myself before saying it. It wouldn't have been true. "I'll see you for the last session on next week. This is Brad, by the way, one of my friends from back home."

They exchanged greetings.

"We headed back to campus, man. I'll holla at you on next week." I couldn't get out of there quick enough. We entered the car and hopped back on the Parkway. "Man, I feel weird," I told Brad.

"Yeah, I can imagine. You did the right thing, though. You never know who was in the audience and benefited from what you said."

"I guess."

We listened to 95.5 FM as we rode back. We didn't say anything more. We listened to Lloyd Banks' *On Fire* for most of the journey back to the apartment.

I thanked Brad for helping me make it through this. After he went back home, I lay on the couch and simply stared upward and remembered that I had to do laundry.

# take a bite!

orcing myself to get psychological support for these childhood events was one of the most important but toughest decisions I'd made in my life. Although this phase was technically coming to an end, I was happy I had dealt with it unflinchingly and would not ever use it as an excuse to stay in life's slump and slum. The last counseling session with Judge was more formality. We'd have small talk and encourage each other to pursue whatever direction we'd take.

"So, what will you do after school?" Judge inquired.

"Man, I don't know. I think I may have been bitten by the acting bug, so I may move to a big city to pursue it."

"Are you serious? Out of all this time you spent in school, you just gone give it up for a maybe situation?"

"Perhaps. I can always get a job based on my education. I may explore and do something I always wanted to do. Who knows? We'll see, though."

"Well anyway, man, this has been a good experience. I learned a lot. I hope you learned a lot."

"Yeah, I did."

"What do you think was the biggest lesson you think you learned?"

"Never try to pick up a lady in a club."

He fell out laughing. "Yeah, man, that *was* hilarious."

I smirked. "Nah, honestly, I guess I'm stronger than I originally thought. I always wished that somebody would help me process this mess. Since nobody else did, I figured I had better help myself. It really does take courage to confront this type of issue, especially as a male. So I may be a lot of things, but a coward ain't one of them."

Judge nodded quietly and offered a confirming smile. "That's what's up."

"I'll just keep at life and learn how to make the most out of where I am."

"Well, man, it's been my pleasure to have helped out as much as I could."

"Well, I'll probably shoot you an email every now and then to see how you're doing. Hopefully, you won't have that many more clients."

"Yeah. Sad thing is that unfortunately, statistics concerning this type of abuse are climbing. I just hope people, especially males, have the courage to seek help and not hide in a corner as though it's their fault."

"True. I hear ya. Well, thanks again, Judge. I'm glad you helped me out. Let me get out of here. I'm dealing with some more drama at school. Long story. Take it easy, man."

We did the man-hug. Right hands made contact. Left hands patted the back while right hands served as a barrier during the hug.

As I approached the elevator, I said my final goodbye to Ms. Isittimetogetoffyet.

"Oh okay, bye!" She was still playing her usual solitaire.

I got on the elevator, never to return to that facility again.

After that episode of getting help for myself, I even managed to have more meaningful conversations with Keva concerning mama's leaving us. We hadn't really discussed the ins and outs of that experience to each other. We had been so busy soldiering on and coping the best way that we knew how. While going through it, we didn't have time to be weak or spineless. But now, we had some breathing room and just tried to make a little sense out of the past.

I called her just to see what she was doing, and she answered the phone in her typical manner when she knew I was the one who was calling. "What." It was indeed a statement and not a question.

"Keva. You shouldn't answer the phone like that. I could be in trouble or in danger or something."

"Well, if you were, I would hope you had better sense than to call me 'cuz I wouldn't be able to help ya, wichu being all the way up there. Better call 911."

I couldn't resist laughing. "Anyway, I'm just up here thinkin'."

"'Bout what?"

"How we grew up. I guess the older I'm gettin', I guess I can understand a li'l bit better why mama had to leave. I guess at first, I thought she wasn't really concerned about what we had to deal with."

"Mm." Seems like Keva wasn't biting or in for a conversation about this. But I was wrong. "Well, I can't say I would've stayed either, Bernard. You just learn how to deal with stuff the best way you can. If somebody was hittin' on me, I don't know if I'd be able to stay around either. Knowin' me, I prolly would kill somebody if they put they hands on me, so I guess we better be glad he still livin'. And wichu doin' all that cryin' comin' up, she probably figured it just won't good all the way around for her to stay. Maybe she thought you would have a breakdown or some'm. Chile, I 'on't know. I ain't tryin' to leap in other people mind to figure out why they do what they do. I can barely keep tabs on myself."

I had never heard Keva talk this semi-rationally before. I had better just listen. "At the end of the day, daddy gotta deal wit his choices, and mama gotta deal wit hers. If they can look at themselves in the mirror and don't feel any guilt or whatever, then good. Mo' power to 'em. But my guess is mama will feel less guilt than him. She tried to make it work, but I guess it just won't in the cards. But what you gone do? Just sit around and mope all day 'cuz things didn't work out with them? I know I ain't."

"Naw. I didn't say that. I'm just sayin' as I get older, I can see it from a different perspective. I guess I used to be mad at her 'cuz it just didn't seem like she was trying to move us outta there. But I guess things have a way of working themselves out. When you a child, you don't think about no big picture. What you see every day *is* the big picture."

"Mm hmm. I guess so. People gone do what they wanna do and when they wanna do it. You gotta let grown folks make their own decisions and their own choices." There was a pause. "Well, lemme go. I just got off work, and I'm starvin'. Them people at my job 'bout to make me go Denise on 'em." We both laughed, understanding the inside joke that only we and Dwayne, Jr. would comprehend.

"Kay. Bye, fool."

"Mm hmm."

She had a way of bringing it all in perspective. Perhaps she had figured out that truth at a young age, much earlier than I, Captain Save-A-Couple. In fact, I mailed my mother a letter, explaining my frustration over the years with her decision not to come and rescue us. I had mentioned that, as a man, I was able to view her choices from a different angle. While I still may not have agreed with what she chose, I informed her that I respected it and hoped she was able to gain some sense of peace out of what had to have thrown her own life into a tailspin. I told her about the conversation that Keva and I had and how we were able to try to visualize all the drama from her perspective. I guess I was hoping her decision to leave us there was a calculated one, not haphazard.

When she wrote back, she wrote on what turned out to be customary for her. She never could seem to find a regular sheet of paper. So there it was: a written-on envelope stuffed inside of another mailed envelope.

*Hey Baby (be alert). Here's a $20.00. Got your new address and phone no. Bernard (mom), Dwayne, Jr. and myself we are allright. Paying bills. What you and Keva talked about is true. The situation had been weighed out, long ago. Don't you worry. Manny is fine (trucking). You enjoying your living in your new house? Love you, Mom. 12:15pm.*

She had responded and had even found the time to put in the status of her current boyfriend, who drove big rigs throughout the southeastern U.S. In my mind, I guess it was good to perceive that somehow, she thought about, even if only remotely, a strategy for us that included our victory. Maybe at this stage, I was just being naïve or falling prey to wishful thinking. But perhaps these meetings with Judge seemed to offer one last benefit that I had not initially sought: a forgiveness for and a better understanding of my very own mother.

Studying for this last qualifying exam for my doctorate was getting insane. I had tried passing it four times earlier, only to receive a pass at the master's level. We had to pass three of these exams to get the degree. I had passed two already at the PhD level, but this last one was my kryptonite. This was my final attempt. My five years of study had boiled down to whether I'd successfully demonstrate an adequate enough level of understanding of Mathematical Statistics. I turned it into my job. I studied from nine to five every day during the winter break. I virtually had no social life and only took breaks to eat and run a few errands.

I even had my own personal tutorial via phone with one of the researchers at AT&T Research Labs in New Jersey, who was a prominent statistician. I had an internship there four years prior and had stayed in touch with some of the most cutting-edge minds in the world. We spoke regularly, as he gave me general pointers about how to answer certain types of questions that might appear. I also had a personal one-on-one tutorial with Ed once a week. He was a past PhD hopeful at the same school, who passed two of the three exams and left with the master's degree. One of the exams he passed was the one with which I was struggling. He too was a Morehouse graduate and was now working at the Census Bureau and knew my pain and plight all too well. I was now in a similar situation as he was, trying to get through this last exam.

On the day of the exam, I got up early and drove to campus to make sure I wasn't rushing and adding extra pressure. Once I got the exam, I said a silent prayer, which must have lasted a good fifteen seconds. I wanted to make sure the Lord was listening. I knew he wouldn't bring me to this point and have all of my years of study wasted. I looked over all of the questions and went straight to the Bayes' Theorem problem. Finding the likelihood functions was not too difficult, so I thought I'd start there. Before I knew it, the time had expired, and I had attempted all of the problems. In about three weeks, the letter with my results appeared in my student box. The PhD passing score had been set at thirty-five. I received a twenty-eight. My heart fell into my stomach. After five years of sacrifice, that was it, just like that. I would not be receiving the PhD. I'd leave with the master's. This type of failure was the type that people shot people in theaters for. Or on buses or trains. I was just glad to realize that no degree would ever define who I was. It was just a means to an end. Although this was a hard pill to swallow, given the amount of time I invested, I tried to keep the right perspective so I could grow from the letdown and perhaps encourage someone else who would go through the same trial.

My last semester there was really just preparation time for me to figure out my next move. There was no reason to remain in the DC area. I had applied to the RAND Summer Associate Program, which was a highly competitive internship for PhD students across the country. Out of the hundreds of applicants they received, they only chose about twenty-five recipients to do summer research, either in Arlington, Santa Monica, or Pittsburgh. When I had called to inquire about the program, the representative immediately told me to have a Plan B because of the stiff competition.

"Odds are you probably won't get it, so you should always have a contingency plan for the summer. They really only choose the top tier of graduate students who have cutting-edge research."

"Okay. Thanks for letting me know. But just in case, can you tell me how to apply?" She didn't know I was given to be stubborn about matters like this.

"Yeah, just go online and fill out all documents there." She was in a rush.

Past recipients of the internships had been bigwigs like Condoleezza Rice. My research seemed pretty interesting to me. I was applying my statistics training to monitoring non-traditional data streams, which was a hot topic in current bioterrorist research. Because of what America was dealing with concerning terrorism at the time, I thought it would be a good fit for the kind of research RAND was currently embarking upon, especially since it was a major think tank whose main purpose was to facilitate scientific and policy research as it related to national security issues.

Around March, the thin decision letter appeared in my apartment mailbox. I knew they only sent these thin letters to rejectees. I was sure that those who were accepted received some mammoth package, providing details concerning what happened at the next step in the internship. I had gone through this before with the Rhodes. I ripped open the envelope, just to confirm what I knew deep down.

*Dear Mr. Dillard:*

*We here at the RAND Corporation are pleased to offer you one of the limited slots in the Graduate Summer Associate Program. You will be assigned to the Arlington, VA office, where researchers and other representatives will contact you concerning the next step in this internship. Congratulations! You should be proud of your achievements. We look forward to a great summer.*

*The RAND Corporation*

Not only was I in a sense of shock because of my acceptance on the heels of a disappointing end to my graduate career, but I was also in shock because I could still live in the same place and not have to relocate to Santa Monica or Pittsburgh for the summer. I could just hop on the DC Metro and get off near the Pentagon. I'd just save money throughout the summer while I contemplated my next move. God was still good and still in control.

Out of those chosen from the nationwide search, RAND had only chosen two African-Americans that summer. Along with me, there was Jatori, whose cubicle was right across from mine. He had gotten a law degree from Howard and was presently pursing a PhD at UPenn in political science. As focused as he was, he was battling a debilitating muscle disease and would eventually wage a serious battle online for his cure to garner support for his uphill journey. We really didn't talk that much, except during a rare stint of down time. We managed to talk about how weird this work environment was and how somebody could easily go crazy working in this place day in and day out.

In addition to trying to learn the R programming language, I spent most days researching modeling and talent agencies. The researchers I'd been assigned to had been whisked away to Iraq to try out some of their research there and left me holding the bag to prepare for a mandatory presentation I had to give at the end of the summer on clustering theory and its application to research I did there.

The summer's end was marked by a great research experience and a hefty financial stipend. My presentation was a success, even though I was shaking in my boots while making it. I had met some great friends and was able to spend a lot of time walking around Pentagon City Mall, the basement of which housed our offices for the summer. Since I was no longer enrolled in school, I would have to start applying for jobs and enter the rat race of the work grind. I had not decided yet where I wanted to spend the next phase of my life.

After weighing several possibilities, I made a startling decision to many. I had decided that I did not want to come to the end of my life and have regrets about what could have been. I had not shared with any family my secret dreams of modeling and acting and thought this would be a good time to pursue them. I was getting no younger, and this seemed like the opportune time to go after it. I would pack my bags, rent a one-way U-Haul truck, and do the unthinkable.

With no job and about seven months' worth of living expenses at my disposal, I would be departing the great District of Columbia and be heading northward.

In my hand was a Big Apple, and I was finna take a bite!

# food stamps

"Eeeeeeey, Bernard!"

"Wassup, Zoe?" I saw her name pop up on my iPhone. "What's goin' on?"

"Nothin' much. Sitting here watching American Idol."

"Oh, okay. You inspired to try out for the show?"

"Not hardly. I just like it at the beginning of the season when they show all the people who sound a mess!"

"Yeah, that's 'bout the only time I watch it too." We laughed.

Zoe was my baby sister. Tam's daughter. She held a special place in my heart. She was much younger than I. Whenever I came home from college break, I would always go pick her up and take her out to eat or go buy her some shoes. Even though she and Keva had different mothers, they looked frighteningly similar. I guess my father's genes were pretty strong. She was getting a bit older now and had just recently had her first child, a son.

"So how's motherhood treating you?"

"It's okay. It's a lot of sacrifice. Them kids need you 24/7/365."

"Shoot, I bet. Well, just keep sticking with it. I know you'll be a great mother. You have a good heart."

"Thank ya, big bro! So what's this I hear 'bout you movin' to New York?"

I snickered a little. "Well, I guess news travels fast, huh?"

"You know it. And you know these people here in Durham can't hold water."

"You know I know. Anyway, yeah I'm staying in Brooklyn in an area called Bushwick. It's not too far from Bed-Stuy, one of the more popular areas. It's different up here. Everybody always askin' me where I'm from. 'Cause of how I talk I guess."

"Mm hmm. You prolly stick out like a sore thumb with that North Carolina accent."

"Tell me 'bout it."

"So what you doin' up there? You got a job?"

"Naw. I just needed a change. I moved up here to see how I'd do in the modeling and acting world. Something I always wanted to do."

"Wow. I actually do remember you saying somethin' 'bout that to me one time."

"Really? I can't remember, but I probably did."

"I can't believe you actually goin' after it. That's really good. I'm so proud of you."

"Thanks, Ms. Lady. It's fine that I don't have a job. I really don't want one right now. I have some money saved up, so I'll be okay."

"Well, you always been the kind of person to go after somethin' when you set your mind to it." She got a little sidetracked. "Wayne, stop!" She was upbraiding her son for something he did.

I heard him crying in the background and knew she needed to focus her attention on him. "Anyway, lemme let you go. We'll talk later. Thank you for calling me, though. I appreciate it."

"Okay, big bro! Stay safe up there. I heard it ain't no joke."

"I'll be fine. I'll holla at you later."

"Peace. Love ya!"

"Bye."

Zoe was actually right. I hadn't told anybody except Keva that I was moving. And I didn't tell her until I was literally driving northward on the interstate. I had decided that this decision was on me. I didn't want anybody discouraging me from pursuing what I wanted to go after. My grandmother probably wouldn't have approved because her rep was on the line since she had told virtually everyone she knew that I was going to be a doctor. Now, she'd have to eat her words. I was fine. Receiving a doctorate wasn't going to make or break me because I knew I'd get out of life whatever I was supposed to get, whether or not I had a certain degree.

So I drafted up some general announcements with my new address, printed them, and mailed them to family. This was how they caught wind that I was starting a new chapter. As expected, most were supportive and few were skeptical because of the lack-of-job situation. But this was another chance for me to stand on my own two feet. If I failed, I'd be man enough to admit it and choose another path. But for now, this was what I was going to pursue.

Brooklyn was indeed a different beast. Everybody was in deep survival mode. It was sink or swim, scam or be scammed. Every other person needed a quarter. Or a dime. Or a nickel. Or even if you could just spare a penny. Truth was, only the strong survived in that borough. And the sense of survival seemed to permeate every core of each block. I had once been distracted while walking home on Eldert Street. I was looking at my phone to see whose text I had missed. I hadn't realized that I had gotten too close to someone's property and soon heard some deep snarling from a beast that I had disturbed. Thankfully, it was barred behind a fence so it could do no one any harm. Once I looked up, I expected to see a ferocious Rottweiler, but to my amazement, I had been semi-attacked by a sharp-toothed poodle. Really? Even poodles went hard in Brooklyn. He was claiming his territory, and you could try him if you wanted to.

On another occasion, I had decided to take another route to catch the J train and decided to walk up Covert Street. In the distance, a guy was holding a leash and was walking his husky dog. I vowed to stay aware and made sure I had the appropriate distance between it and me. The closer I got to dog and owner, however, I was having trouble determining just what kind of dog it was. In fact, it looked less and less like a dog the closer I approached. When I got close enough to make out the mystery, I couldn't believe my eyes. This thug, donned in timbs, a wife-beater, and du-rag was out on the streets of Brooklyn, walking his cat. On a leash. In broad daylight. And he was doing it like it was an everyday event. And nobody questioned him. Only in Brooklyn.

I loved Brooklyn, though, especially around June because all the Puerto Ricans came from out the woodworks to represent their culture and heritage. They knew how to party and celebrate. They cracked me up by how they would speak Spanish and then start speaking English and then go right back to speaking Spanish, especially when they got excited. And the Puerto Rican Day parade was always off the chain. The second Sunday in June, I always made my way to Fifth Avenue in Manhattan and wore their version of the red, white, and blue. I blended in right with the rest of them.

The women were absolutely gorgeous, and their ethnic male counterparts never failed in letting them know it. Of course, there was nothing like my black sisters. They were in their own league. That was the good thing about it. There was no comparison between groups. Each group had its own beauty mark, different shades of *Lord, have mercy.* If I were given the opportunity to choose a second ethnicity, I would come out the womb asking for mofongo and asopao and screaming, "Boricua!" I guess that's what I loved the most about Brooklyn or New York period. Everyone celebrated their own heritage and ethnicity to the fullest and let you join in and be a part of their celebratory journey.

The city lived up to its other reputation too, however. It constantly was involved in hosting its own Olympics. Dozens of events abounded. But only a few seemed to contribute to city stress the most. There was *the seat rush*: where two or more people sprinted onto the train to vie for the coveted end seat. And then *the race walk*: where city-goers attempted to outpace those who were near, irrespective of where or how far either had to go. The thrill was only found in the simple act of passing. And its derivative, *the tourist dodge*: where those leaving work, drained after eight hours of earning wages, bobbed and weaved around oh-so-impressed visitors. With cameras in hand or around neck, the latter would increase the difficulty by stopping all of a sudden to take their version of a priceless photo. And the competition among competitions, *the mini-Indy 500*: where cars traveled at breakneck pace, jockeying for position in front of other roadsters. As walkers, we always knew who won the gold in that event because the winner's car was quiet. The silver and bronze medalists, however, always confirmed their defeat by the deafening honking of their horns. You had to use wisdom in dealing with people in the city because, of a truth, most people were only one tick away from a boom. And when the boom happened, there were fireworks everywhere. Indeed, it was a day-to-day Olympics, and, unless you put forth a concerted effort to march to the beat of your own drum, you were easily suckered into adjusting your rhythm to mirror the city's.

I finally managed to settle into the groove of the city and started securing a few modeling and talent agencies. I attended open calls and mailed in regular snapshots. I started receiving responses, and before I knew it, I had a handful of agencies and started attending casting calls. Some of them were cattle calls, and others were request castings, where they specifically wanted to see me. I was realizing how persistent people had to be if they wanted to succeed in this industry. You definitely had to have thick skin. For every job I got, there were hundreds that I didn't. You either had to be dedicated or crazed to keep moving forward, as if not getting the previous gig didn't affect you somehow.

At first, most of the "modeling" jobs I got didn't involve modeling at all. They were promotional jobs where I had to stand in the New York public and hand out flyers or free stuff. New Yorkers were brutal when it seemed like you were pestering them about some awful product, in their view. They had tunnel vision and weren't going to be distracted by you. You were just another obstacle in their way, like tourists. You were going to learn the lesson quickly that you had better move or be moved. On one occasion, a group of us had to stand in Times Square, wearing nothing but swim trunks in an effort to get people to buy Long Island beachfront property. I never before had felt like a piece of meat as people made catcalls and undressed what little I had on. I would remind them that the light had changed, so they could now cross the street. And all this for only $20 an hour. Another time, I had to dress up in a one-piece outfit that looked like an Excedrin bottle. We were handing out free samples of the pills. Since they were free, people literally bum's rushed me to get their share. These jobs were out of the norm for me, away from the predictability of some boring classroom. I felt alive.

I had finally gotten to a place where I had enough images to place in my modeling portfolio. I started going on castings for Izod, Sean John, and the like. Even though I didn't get a lot of these jobs, there was still an excitement I had because I at least felt one step closer to what seemed to be a closed-door industry. I had a chance to see where these key designers made their clothes, which was very cool. I bumped into a ton of high fashion models toting their portfolios from Ford, Major, Click, and Red agencies. And there I was, right there with them going after the same jobs. My agency was exploiting certain features I had that looked Asian to them. So they told me to say I was Black and Asian if asked my ethnicity, a far cry from my true, deep-south heritage. My friends in the city started teasing me and abbreviated my race to one word: Blackenasian. I hadn't realized just how competitive this industry was and what agencies did to try to get a booking. Admittedly, I was crazy excited whenever I got one. I knew that clients wanted my look, not a carbon copy or somebody who looked like me. For whatever reason, they wanted what I looked like and perhaps were drawn to my personality.

I was always instructed to carry my modeling book with me wherever I went. This was New York, and I never knew whom I would run into. These were the instructions given to me. So I obeyed this request. In one instance, carrying my portfolio caused me a bit of embarrassment as I went throughout the day.

I had decided that since I didn't have a job that it might be a good idea to apply for food stamps. I had no shame or pride in doing so. My funds were limited, so any assistance I could get from the government was welcomed. I went to downtown Brooklyn to the Hoyt-Schermerhorn train stop. Unless you got there by 7:30 AM, you'd have to wait in a line that snaked around the corner. Every day, the line was jam-packed with people trying to get what they perceived as their just economic due. So I arrived by 7:45. I had an audition I had to attend and was hoping this wouldn't take all day.

The line moved quickly. I was inside by 8:30 and signed my name on the waiting list. After sitting for about thirty minutes, a voice called my name to come forward: "Bernard Dillard?"

"Yes, I'm here." I got my stuff and headed to the front.

"Come right through here. You can have a seat." The lady pointed me to the chair next to her desk. On her desk was the all-too-common picture of her son, I guess, given how much both of them were smiling. No father in the picture. Typical. She started reading my application. "Let's see here. Okay. You out in Bushwick. Okay. Single. Okay." She was treating her gum in a strange fashion. Almost like she was putting it up against her teeth with a fake smile and squeezing air through the gum. It made a sound like those small paper bubble wraps when you get a grip and squeeze the life out of them. A series of quick pops. The sound was annoying, given that it was so early.

She continued. "Unemployed. Okay." She looked up at me as if she were calling me lazy in her head.

"Yeah, I'm just between jobs right now."

"Mm hmm." She sent me the translation of my statement via telepathy.

"I do a little freelancing on the side. I do a little modeling."

Her attitude changed quickly. "Eww for real? You a model?"

"Well, it's going a little slow now, but I'm sure it'll pick up. This is my portfolio right here." What did I say that for?

"Oh, okay. Let me see." Before I knew it, she grabbed my book and started looking through my images. I couldn't believe she was actually taking time to go through picture by picture while the rest of the people were waiting to be called for their food stamps. "Eww, I love this one right here. That one is sexy." She had even gathered an audience of her co-workers. "Shay Shay, look at these, girl. This guy right here, he a model. Here go his pictures."

"Wow. These are nice." Shay Shay had come over to her colleague's area, towering over me as I sat.

Before I knew it, two more co-workers had stopped working and were going through my book. At 8:45 in the morning. If I were white, my face would have been red. My light complexion still betrayed me.

"Y'all, he blushin'." One of them had called me out. I hated when people addressed me in the third person while I was present. "You gotta get used to people looking in your book. If that's what you want to do, you gotta let people see it wherever." I appreciated the two cents' worth of advice but tried to get them back on track.

"Man, I'm just trying to get my food stamps." I started laughing.

So did they. "I know das right." Shay Shay felt the need to co-sign. "He didn't come here for y'all to be goin' thoo his stuff. Give this man his food stamps." I shook my head at her "y'all" as if she too weren't a culprit.

The crowd finally disbanded and went back to its regular grind. The fourth worker drew her final conclusion. "Well, good luck. You'll probably get a lot of work with those. Keep doin' what you do."

"'Preciate it. Just trying to make it happen." That was all I could say.

I finally got processed. The lady helping me took my photo. She couldn't resist. "Give me one of them sexy smiles you got in yo' book." I smiled with a devilish grin. She took the picture and laughed. She told me the card would be in the mail within two weeks.

"Card?"

"Yeah. We use cards now with a pin number."

"Whoa. Really? Where I'm from, people used to have like a coupon book, and they ripped the food stamps out when they wanted to use 'em."

"Boo, we ain't used that system in I 'on't know how long. You gotta come on up to the twentieth century."

"Oh, okay. My bad." I didn't even correct her date reference.

I made my way out.  I felt several sets of eyes on me as I left, so I felt it necessary to say goodbye to the peanut gallery.  "Everybody have a nice day. Don't work too hard."

They were hoping I'd say farewell.  "Bye!"  They all eventually said it back.

What a day this was indeed going to be!

# a shot o' vodka

S oon, I started gaining some momentum with real modeling jobs. Most people I knew were saying they were a model but weren't receiving any money from it. I was actually getting real jobs. The focus and drive were paying off. It was one thing to go on an audition or casting, but when I would receive booking calls, I felt like I wasn't just running the hamster wheel of hope. I had done some work for a few magazines and clothing lines. One of the most fun shoots I had was with Temptu, a tattoo company based in New York. They specialized in temporary tattoos, which a lot of people loved. People didn't have to commit to some permanent body painting if they didn't wish. They could simply use alcohol to remove them. Apparently, a lot of costume directors used the product for movies.

My first editorial was with *King Magazine*. They got me dressed up and had me looking like a class act. Outside of modeling, I only really wore sweat pants and t-shirts. But when the client dressed me up, I always felt like a million bucks. They told me when the issue would print but forgot to tell me that, when all was said and done, my face would be retouched out of the actual ad. Great! My first editorial, and it wouldn't be obvious that I was the one in the picture. I showed people the ad and told them I was that person, and they looked at me like I was on crack. I was showing them a flyly dressed invisible being. It wasn't until I contacted the photographer to get the actual images that people started to realize I was telling the truth. I had to place the editorial ad on one side of my portfolio and then a blown-up image of the actual shot on the other side. Creativity was indeed necessary to stay ahead of the pack. Earl and I booked the job. He actually went on to star in Beyonce's *Irreplaceable* video.

I was also getting regular assignments with an online fashion company, based in Secaucus, New Jersey. There was a lot of modeling work to be had in Jersey. Clients set up shop there because rental space and workspace was cheaper than in New York. So a lot of models would book jobs and travel to get the across-the-Hudson dollars. Working for clients such as this was so tiring. There were several wardrobe changes, and they always wanted you to bring high energy. It was so far from the image of modeling that I had initially envisioned. When I flipped through magazines to teach myself certain poses, all I typically saw was just one image that the client eventually chose for its product. But behind the scenes, there were probably tons of images that were taken and several changes of clothes. I was definitely discovering that this was grueling work. After many of these assignments, I would go home and drop into a deep sleep. I was thankful for the work but clueless as to the commitment needed to thrive in such an industry.

I was also beginning to book commercials. I was learning that personality was key to booking jobs period, but this was especially the case for nabbing commercials. My southern accent didn't help much because they wanted someone who didn't sound like they were from a specific area. In order to reach the most people, they needed someone who didn't sound as if they were from a certain region. So I had to practice not sounding like I was from the country. This was difficult because I couldn't really hear it. I had grown up talking the way I did, so I had to step back and take an objective listen at how I sounded. On more than one occasion, I would start the audition with my non-regional tongue. By the time we had done five takes, I was back to my southern drawl and being told in so many words, "Don't call us, and we won't call you either!" Commercials were fun, though. In a *Sony Ericsson* gig I booked, I had to sing one of Usher's songs and dance at the same time. Every time I saw it on TV, I was floored. It was absolutely hilarious!

I had also started writing short articles for an online magazine. I was providing industry tips for aspiring models and those who wanted success in booking commercials. Although I didn't get paid for the columns, I got the byline credit and was able to keep my mind sharp.

As much as I was enjoying the work I was getting, the funds weren't keeping up with my expenses. The money was good, but it seemed to take forever for me to receive payment for services rendered. It could take up to three months for me to get paid, and the rent man wanted his money every month. A few of my friends suggested that I seek out teaching gigs, nothing major. They thought that since I had the education, I should use it. Very few models had the education that I did, according to them, so I should find a way to get creative and use it to keep bills paid while doing what I loved. I told them they were crazy and that I didn't want a full-time job. They rebutted that I didn't have to find a full-time job, just something part-time to keep bills paid. I mentioned to them that then I would have to give up my food stamps, the response to which they all said I was being shortsighted, not capitalizing on using all of my strengths to help me get to where I was attempting to go.

I eventually decided to take their advice. My savings were running out, and money from jobs wasn't coming in at a fast enough rate to keep me afloat financially. So I just took an entire weekend to get my CV together and send to the different colleges in the New York area. I'd only adjunct, so it wasn't like I'd be forced to work full-time hours. I must have sent out thirty-five resumes to schools like Brooklyn College, Baruch, BMCC, and LIU, to name a few. Part of why I did it was to shut up my modeling friends, who insisted that I follow through with it. The other part was that I realized they were probably right.

One day, I had to visit my agency for instructions concerning an up-coming shoot. When I left the agency's office, I was carrying so much stuff. I had my laptop, my book bag with a change of clothes for the shoot, my portfolio that I carried in my hand, and my Arizona tea. I couldn't carry anything else if I wanted to. Of course, since I was so bogged down, the unthinkable happened. My phone in my pocket started ringing. It always seemed like a set of invisible eyes watched to see how preoccupied I was with carrying things. Only then, like clockwork, did my phone always appear to ring. This time was no different. It kept ringing while I put down my tea and fidgeted for the phone in my right pocket until I discovered that it was actually in the left one.

"Hello!" I probably startled the caller because I yelled my salutation since the street noise was so loud.

"Hi! I'm trying to reach Bernard Dillard." The voice on the other end was making a request that I couldn't hear, thanks to the fire truck zooming by.

"Wait one second. A fire truck is going by. I can't hear you. One sec." I was convinced that there was no such thing as a quiet moment in New York. "Okay. It's gone by. Hello. Are you still there?"

"Yeah, I'm still here. Can you hear me?"

"Yes. This is Bernard. Who's calling?"

"My name is Rashida Starks. I'm calling from F.I.T."

"Where? What's F.I.T.?"

"The Fashion Institute. You sent your resume here."

I stood in the middle of the sidewalk and noticed how people looked at me in disgust. They wished I'd move to the corner. So I obeyed their stares and silent requests. "I did?" It was a shame I didn't remember all the places I'd sent my credentials. "Okay."

The voice continued. "The Chair here saw your resume and wanted you to come in for an interview on tomorrow."

"Oh, okay. That's cool. If it's not a problem, do you think you could call me right back and leave a message with the details? I'm literally out here on the sidewalk. I have all these bags I'm carrying and I don't have anything to write with and …"

"Okay, okay. I'll call you right back and leave all the information on your voicemail." She cut me off. I could tell she was getting annoyed.

"Alright, ma'am. Thanks a lot. Have a good one." I had better be nice before she conveniently misplaced my information.

About a minute after, I heard my phone ring again. I didn't bother to answer it. People in my vicinity wished I would, though. How rude, they thought, for me to hear my phone ringing and not answer it, polluting the airspace around me.

"Bernard! Where you?" She was talking to me on her cell phone and waiting by the baggage claim, not realizing I was standing right behind her.

"Right here behind you." I answered back quietly on my phone so that she would have to turn around to see if I was telling the truth. I was.

"Heyyyy baby!" She turned around and gave me a big hug. Her laugh echoed throughout all of the baggage claim area. Other customers glanced our way and smiled. Hurricane Vicky was in New York City and was ready to turn it upside down.

"How was the flight?"

"Boy, I was so scared." At sixty-five, this was my mother's first time flying. "You know I'm scared of heights. That lady on the plane that be helpin' you, what they call 'em?"

"Flight attendants."

"Yeah, her. She asked me if I wanted some'ta drink. I told her I wanted a shot o' vodka." She burst out laughing again.

"Mama, no you didn't."

"Yes the hell I did. And she gave it to me too. She said it was my gift since it was my first flight."

"Lord, have mercy." I couldn't believe it.

"Lord, have mercy is right. That was the only thing that was gone keep me calm looking down on all them houses and stuff. They look like ants. And they had the nerve to give me a window seat. And the lady next to me lookin' all past me so she could see out the window. I didn't wanna see nothin' out that window."

"Well, I'm glad you made it safely."

"*You* glad? Shit, *I'm* glad." More laughter. "I can't believe I'm in New York Citay."

I had decided to fly her up for a visit. I had never known her to take any type of real vacation and thought this would be a great opportunity for her to broaden her horizons. Indeed, she was like a kid in a candy store.

We did the typical New York things. Empire State Building. Broadway shows. New York Philharmonic. Outdoor movies by the Brooklyn Bridge. We made our way through the busy Times Square streets. Tourists seemed to incense her since everyone seemed so directionless. "Why 'on't they get the hell out da way? Why I got to be the one that move over all the time when we walkin'?"

"You don't. Just keep walking straight." It was nice to see her have fun. But she wore me out. By the time we returned home each day, all we could do was watch DVDs and whatever else was on TV.

My mother had her favorite. "Dat damn Madea a trip! She done slapped Brown. Look at uh. Look at uh. Look at. Look at. Look at." She spoke faster and faster, laughing in between breaths.

"Mama, I'm looking. I can't really hear what she saying 'cause you keep interrupting." By this time, she was already laughing wildly at the next scene. "Mama, I can't hear." So I had to rewind to catch it again.

Of course, she continued to interrupt. "And that light-skin big lady know she can sang."

"Mama, she not big no mo'. She lost a lot of weight."

"Really?"

"Mm hmm. In real life, she and Brown married."

"What? For real?"

"Yep."

"Well, she can sholl sang." By this time, the scenes had mellowed back down to the plot and allowed a break in the laughter. My mama always found a way to fill the silence, though. "Look at my baby, the professor. You know, you always were good at that math stuff."

"Thanks, but I'm not a professor. I'm what they call an adjunct. I'm only a part-time instructor."

She kept going with the bragging, not quite understanding my needless effort to distinguish between ranks. "All my chirren smart. Y'all take after me. Y'all daddy won't no dummy neither. Dwayne, Sr. was smart. He was real good in chemistry. All my chirren smart and pretty too."

"Mm." I tried to keep focused on the DVD's plot. She didn't get the hint.

"Hell, I might go back to school and get my master's."

"Mm hmm. You should." I thought that if I agreed, she'd be quiet. The opposite happened.

"Shit, I could get my master's in one year. When I got my bachelor's, your brother Dwayne was 'bout eleven and you won't nothin' but a little bitty ole' thang. I won't gone let nothing stop me. Baby or no baby. I remember my final recital, Dwayne, Jr. and yo' daddy were sitting right in that auditorium while I was playing that piano piece. When I got that music degree, I knew couldn't nothin' stop me." She paused. "What's in the frig to eat?" She made her way to the kitchen and rested her hand on my shoulder as she walked by. "Oh yeah, I washed those dishes for you."

"How you wash 'em and I ran out of dish detergent?" I had to brace myself for the answer.

"Oh, I just used some of the shampoo that's in the bathroom."

"Mama, you did *not* use shampoo to wash my dishes."

"Hell, it's still soap."

"But mama, it's not ..." I just let it go. "Thank ya for doing the dishes." It was the thought that counted. Or so I told myself to keep the peace.

She had gone into the kitchen and surveyed the frig. From the living room, I heard her say in a bragadocious tone of pride, ignoring my previous attempt at downgrading my title to what it really was: "My son is a professor."

Indeed, things had turned in my benefit in that regard. It turns out that I had been hired as a part-timer. After one semester, a full-time position opened up. I knew I wouldn't get it, but after one of the veteran professors kept prodding me to apply, I did. He kept saying he liked my work ethic. They strongly preferred someone with a PhD and would have around three hundred applicants for only two slots. I didn't want to waste my time. I would teach part-time to keep rent paid and keep pursuing why I moved to New York in the first place.

I went ahead and applied for the full-time position just to satisfy my curiosity. During this, my mother's first visit, I actually received a call for a final interview. So she had to accompany me to the campus.

"What's the name of this place?"

"Fashion Institute of Technology. They call it F.I.T. for short."

"Oh, okay. It's nice."

"Yeah. Tyra Banks' and Martha Stewart's show is just one street over."

"Oh, okay. What about Rachael Ray?"

"Nope. That's not over in this area."

"I love me some Rachael Ray."

We entered the building and made our way to the eighth floor to the Science and Mathematics office area. "Anyway, ma, you'll have to sit in this office over here until the interview is over."

"I'll be fine. I know you gone get it. Don't mind me."

That would be easier said than done. The interview was somewhat intimidating. There sat a panel of twelve in a U-formation around a huge table. And I sat in the hot seat. I saw no African-Americans. One young like me. Mostly white. Older. Males. Some females. PhDs. I was honest with them concerning how close I had gotten to getting the PhD and what prevented it. I had done all the coursework and had done what I thought was cutting-edge research. Still, I had failed in that regard. Even so, I fielded an avalanche of questions. "So how do you like New York? Why do you think you'd fit here at F.I.T.? Have you taught online before? What new courses do you think you'd be more inclined to develop? So we hear your mother's here. How does she like the City? How would you maintain discipline in your class since you look so young?" And on and on and on. It was finally over and they said they'd let me know if they were interested. I said okay and thought nothing more of it.

I went to my office to get my mother, who was sitting as calmly as I left her. "Alright, you ready?"

"Yeah," she said. "I gotta pee, though."

We eventually left the building and got on the C train to West 4th. I wanted to go by Westville Restaurant for a turkey burger. When we came to the street level, I saw that someone had left me a voicemail message.

"Who in the world done called me now? Seems like people be watching to see when I go down into the train and only call me then."

I listened to the message with a sense of unbelief. By the time we got to Westville's, mama inquired. "So who was that?"

"It was the people who just interviewed me. They want to offer me the job as a full-time math professor."

"See, I told you. I told you. It's because I'm here! I know what I'm talking 'bout! I knew they were gone hire you. I got some smart chirren. You, Keva, and Dwayne, Jr. All y'all smart." She went at it again. It made no sense to attempt to derail her logic. At the end of the day, whatever the logical reasoning was, the matriarchal prophet was correct. Her calling me "professor" would no longer be erroneous.

"Yep. I guess you right, ma." No PhD. No laundry list of publications. No real connections. But here I was. One of two selected from hundreds for a coveted full-time slot, where I'd have a great chance to mold young minds, and I'd have summers off with pay. I could say farewell to the choppy income stream that went along with trying to solely make it in such a fickle entertainment and modeling industry. God had granted me favor beyond measure, and I was excited about it. From food stamps to full-time professor. What a transition!

And soon thereafter, I got tenure.

# where i was on that day

I sat in front of the TV mesmerized and watched the scenes progress. I would barely blink as I tried to figure out whodunit. Even if I had to use the restroom, I waited until it was time for a commercial. I was hooked on *Criminal Minds*. If there were ever a show I wanted to be a writer for, this was the one. The tension in each scene was palpable. I often wondered if they actually used real historical crime scenarios to stage different episodes. The way they seemed to pry into the minds of deranged individuals was amazing. All of these different types of crime shows seemed to be surfacing after the infamous O.J. trial. There was a certain fascination with analyzing bloody crime scenes and putting pieces together to solve a murder.

This episode was building like no other. And as the last few minutes were about to reveal the killer, the phone rang. I saw it was my mother and knew I needed to answer it. Her visit was complete, and her plane had made it back to North Carolina. She wanted me to know she was fine. I'd hurry and answer and get right back off.

"Hey. So you made it?"

"Yeah, son, I made it back. I'm waiting right here at baggage claim, waiting for Keva to come get me."

"Oh, okay. Good." I tried to keep it short so she'd get the hint. No dice.

"Thank you so much, son, for a wonderful vacation."

"You welcome. Glad you had a good time. Did they help you alright with the wheelchair?"

"Man, I only sat in that wheelchair so I could skip them people in the security line. Hehehehe!"

She had played the system. She acted so crippled and lame the entire time she was going through the checkpoint area. Since she had a hip replacement, she always reverted to using that as an explanation for why she needed so much help. "If the thing starts beeping, it's because of this replacement. Here's the card they gave me to show you." She'd inform those working security and pulled out her hip-surgery card to show the airport personnel while being wheeled through the scanner. Once she had gone past security, she would hop out of the wheelchair and start walking beside the employee, who kept pushing the empty chair. Security staff was dumbfounded.

"Mama, those people gone lock you up one day for getting over on them."

"Shit! I ain't got time to be standing in that line that go on forever." She would catch herself. "Oh 'scuse me. I forgot you a preacher. I'm trying to stop with all this damn cussing."

She was doing well. She had stopped smoking for about a year. I believe it had a lot to do with her not having to deal with as much stress now as compared to her earlier years. Maybe she was calming down a bit and learning how to conquer this thing called life. She was doing her best now to kick her cursing habit to the curb. She fueled her desire by deferring to what she thought I represented.

"Oh, here come Keva. I'll call you when I get home." By this time, *Criminal Minds* was over. I missed the plot's ending. I'd have to catch a rerun.

Keva had arrived to pick her up. My mother felt the need to tell Keva every detail about the visit. She would try to talk about every single event we had experienced as they rode home. Keva admitted to doing about 80 mph on the highway to hurry and get her home. She didn't want to hear a blow-by-blow account of the trip. She was tired and just wanted to hurry and get back to her own house to rest.

"Keva, slow down! You going too fast." My mother wondered why Keva was speeding so. She had no idea she was the reason. Keva ignored her and kept up the same speed. She would drop mama off, help her get her bags in, and jet.

"Bye, ma."

"Thank ya baby for picking me up. Love ya." She always managed to end conversations with that. Keva's personality was the way it was, and she would have nothing of this talk.

"Mm hmm. Bye."

292

"Moi, mitä ukko?

–

Ootko tulossa pelaamaan perjantaina?

–

Hyvä. Tulee varmasti tiukka matsi. Viime kerrallahan me voitettiin, mutta nyt niillä on kuulemma jotain uusia jätkiä.

–

No ei se mitään, eiköhän me klaarata. Ainakin yritetään.

–

Jes, palataan. Moi."

I sat in the passenger's seat, listening to what was completely indecipherable. It turns out that it was actually Finnish, and Toivo was rolling it off his tongue like nobody's business. We both were professors in the same department at F.I.T. and often grabbed a bite to eat at Dinosaur BBQ in Harlem whenever we felt the craving for southern food. He grew up in Finland but later moved to the States for college, attending Rice and eventually getting his PhD from Columbia.

We were on our way now to a geometry conference in Upstate New York. We rented a car and just agreed to half the expenses up. As he drove, I resisted the urge to tell him not to drive and talk on his cell. The language he spoke was so intriguing and otherworldly that I just listened to his monologue with its sporadic pauses. I assumed the person on the other line filled in the pausal gaps. He finally hung up.

"You know you can get a ticket doin' that." I tried to act concerned.

"Yeah, I know."

"Who was that, Kyong?" I thought he was speaking with his fiancée. Then, I realized she wasn't Finnish, so there was no point in speaking his native tongue to her.

"Nah. Just a hockey teammate. Got a big game comin' up, and I wanted to see if he was gonna show up. The other team's really good, and we need all the help we can get." Toivo played the game as an extra-curricular activity to decompress from the rigors of his real job.

"Oh, aight."

After about five minutes, I had almost drifted to sleep until he broke the silence again. "So, what you think about Obama?"

"I think he's pretty good." I hadn't researched his politics or views, so this was my safe answer. "He's supposed to be visiting the city on next week for a rally. He'll be over by NYU. I'll probably go hear him to see what he's about. What about you?"

"I haven't really done a lot of research on his views either. I watched some of the debates. Hillary goes toe to toe with him. I just hope they don't damage each other's credibility and give the Republicans too much ammunition by the time the general election comes."

"True. Hillary ain't no joke. She acting like it's now or never. Her and that husband o' hers going for broke and ain't 'bout to let no black man get in there that easy."

We both laughed. We both knew it was a true statement.

"Yeah, politics ain't really my cup of tea. I may help out with his campaign in Pennsylvania being sponsored by our Union. You should go too, Professor Dillard." Over the years, that was just the adopted name he settled on when addressing me, which I just ignored. I was used to it from him.

"I may. I try to stay out of political stuff too. I vote and everything, but that may be a bit much goin' out to knock on doors. From what I hear, it's a pretty heavy Republican area they are going to. I ain't tryna get shot, especially if they see a black man and white man walking together, talking 'bout they out campaigning for Obama votes." I laughed a concerned laugh. "We might leave the bus as a pair, but you might come back solo." We chuckled again. "Anyway, I'll let you know."

"Okay, Professor Dillard."

After about ten more minutes, I was out like a light. The next thing I knew, Toivo was pulling up onto SUNY-Binghamton's campus. We both got out, stretched, and put on our math hats, anticipating a great day of learning.

Afterwards, we made it back to Manhattan and went our separate ways.

My phone rang again.

"Yep." I knew it was my mother.

"So thank you again baby for everything you did for me on last week when I came up there. I really appreciate everything you did for me." She would begin to cry on the spot.

"Mama, I told you that you could win an Oscar if you went into acting. I don't know nobody who can cry on the spot like you can," I reminded her again.

"These tears ain't fake. I mean what I'm saying."

"Okay." I changed the topic. "Yeah, I'm supposed to go down by NYU today. This guy running for president is supposed to be speaking there. He from Chicago."

"Oh yeah, Oback or Barama or something like that. I was listening to him on TV. Sounds like he got his head on straight."

"Mm hmm. Barack Obama. He seems real cool. He's speaking outside at Washington Square Park. I'll probably go see what he's about."

"I hope he can do something with this country 'cause it's shonuf in terrible shape."

"I know. Anyway, lemme go. I gotta get myself together."

"Okay, baby. I'll talk to you later. Mama love you."

"Kay. Bye. Love you, too."

Obama was indeed speaking in town. I had learned not to put my faith in any politician, even if he or she was black. I hadn't become cynical, but I knew that the state of the country depended on more than just what a group of Republicans, Democrats, Independents, or Tea Partiers did. Ultimately, I knew God was in control of the world. Or at least that was the attitude I adopted to help keep myself sane as I watched politicians bicker over Iraq, Afghanistan, and the economy. Congressional meetings I saw seemed to turn into circus meetings, but hopefully this new guy could emerge as some voice of reason amid a national freak show.

When I arrived at the park, I decided that it was way too crowded to stand and wait for an hour. So I found some Italian restaurant, ordered dinner, and sat outside within earshot of the gathering. The perfect seat. Nice weather. Nice food. Nice crowd.

When he took the stand, it was amazing to hear how he mesmerized the crowd. It seemed like he couldn't get a word in edgewise because the crowd kept drowning him out with their cheers. This man couldn't do or say anything wrong. For all the crowd cared, he could have been saying, "One, two, buckle my shoe! Three, four, knock on the door!" To the crowd, those would have been nuggets of truth to live by. It would have been gospel. Thankfully, he had education to back up his rhetoric. He really seemed to be a smart guy.

As I ate my lasagna, I listened to his comments that kept the crowd in a trance. "It is not enough just to change parties in the White House if we have the same kind of politics. It's not enough to change parties if we continue to see the country divided. We have the red states and blue states, and we end up fighting the same petty, partisan battles over and over and over again." That was true. He was right. As I sat and pondered, it finally clicked. This man sounded like Martin Luther King, Jr. Not just with the type of imagery and forward-looking message. But he actually sounded like Dr. King to me. The timbre of his voice was so unique and undeniable, reaching out as if it were King's echo that had traveled through the decades. Sort of like a continuation of *I Have a Dream*. It was magical but still a little eerie. I had zoned out and hadn't realized I had fallen into the same trance as the audience, failing to realize the waiter's presence.

"Anything else?" The waiter cleared my plate.

"Nah. That'll do it."

"How was the meal?"

"Oh, it was great. Actually, I think I *will* take some coffee."

"Cream and sugar?"

"Please."

"Looks like you got one of the best seats to hear Obama, huh?"

"Yeah." I exhaled a small laugh. "He seems pretty cool. I haven't done that much research on him and his views, but he's a great speaker."

"I know. There is a lot of buzz swirling around him and Hillary. That will be a good match-up. Anyway, be right back with your coffee."

"Thanks."

As I sipped on the decaf, the crowd dispersed. They walked past my table in such a state of euphoria over this man. They wore Obama t-shirts and passed out Obama pamphlets. One shirt even ended up on my table. They were passing them out to anyone who'd take them. Students made their way back to their safe and secure NYU dorms. He was appearing to motivate a group of young people who were otherwise cynical and detached when it came to things political. You could hear the cheers from a distance and up close: "O-ba-muh! O-ba-muh! O-ba-muh!"

He was a smart player. He had figured out how to tap into using technology to secure such a wide base of supporters. I would eventually join the online community that pushed his political agenda. Here, I'd receive periodic email messages from his campaign camp. He had gone viral, and my gut feeling was that he'd be around for a while.

In fact, he did confirm everyone's suspicions. After winning the primaries, he went on to vie for the general election win, up against John McCain. There would be a huge rally on 125$^{th}$ Street by the Adam Clayton Powell State Office Building. City officials had set up a big screen television in the plaza and would show the results live. I had moved a couple of doors east of Abyssinian Baptist Church, so I decided to walk the ten or so blocks to watch what I believed would be history. I wanted to have a good answer to the question, "So where were you when it was found out that Barack won?" I didn't want to have to say, "Chillin' in the bed, eating some leftovers from Dinosaur."

When I got to 125$^{th}$, it was mayhem but in a good way. All kinds of celebration were going on. African people were playing drums. There were people rapping. Of course, business owners were passing out flyers, promoting their respective businesses. Cars were pumping music. It was magical. And then the results started pouring in. The map on the screen kept turning bluer and bluer. Obama was winning tons of states. He even won my state of North Carolina, which had a long-standing history of being red. Finally, it was announced that this man, this African-American man, would be the forty-fourth President of the United States of America. Immediately, people started cheering senselessly. I kept watching the big screen outside to see if it was real. The famous image of Jesse Jackson's shedding tears popped up, and it started waterfalls around me. Both men and women were bawling.

I tried calling Olivia in Atlanta, but the calls were dropped each time. I couldn't get through for a good twenty minutes. All cell phone lines were tied up where we were. I finally got through. "Mama, can you believe it? He won!"

"Yes, son, he . . ."

I had lost the call again. So I decided just to wait until the initial shock wore off before trying again.

The sights I saw were unique, to say the least. Never again would this scene be repeated. Even after he would defeat the Romney-Ryan ticket for re-election in 2012, it wouldn't drum up this type of commotion. I observed quietly, laughing inside at the different scenes of the moment:

- A crawling MTA bus with passengers hanging out the window as they shouted expletives and pointing at the big screen television in amazement at the outcome.
- Groups of rival gang members with bandanas covering half of their face, shouting: "Get them O's up. Get them O's up. Get them O's up. Get them motherfuckin' O's up." They were real thugs, so they didn't mince words. As they chanted, they made the letter O with their middle finger and thumb on both hands.
- A drag queen, who used part of the sidewalk as a runway, scream-ing, "Yes, girl, yaaaas! Yes, girl, yaaaas!" The crowd egged him on as he posed at the end and then repeated the ritual.
- Executives, who had just gotten off work, walking in the middle of the street with their ties partly undone and briefcases in hand. Traffic had virtually come to a standstill.
- African dancers breaking out in an extemporaneous routine, accom-panied by drummers. Each of the dancers freestyled to the beat, reaching to the heavens, kicking up feet, and bowing toward the ground.

This new president was puttin' it down. For that moment, it didn't matter where you were from, where you worked, if you worked, or which group you most identified with. This was a new day! Singlehandedly, this man was making the lion lie down with the lamb. This Harlem scene was a pseudo-New Year's, mini-Times Square celebration. And I'm sure it was the same all over the world.

I decided to call it a night and head home, taking the more scenic route past Sylvia's. I'd just retreat tonight and watch *The Wiz* again. As was my habit, I'd continue to rewind the instance where Nipsey Russell, playing the Tin Man, would cry for fifteen seconds, lamenting Teeny, his wife, who was anything but. His wail of misery simply was a repeat of his wife's name: *Teeeeeny ... Teeeeeny ... Teeeeeny*. I roared like it was my first time watching it. Tonight, that laughter was made sweeter by the thought of this moment. Whether you agreed with him ideologically or not, Obama had in fact made political history. Thankfully, I would have a pretty good answer if anybody asked me where I was on that day.

# still laughing

hat!" Keva was calling. The caller ID gave her away. I gave her a taste of her own medicine by answering the phone as she did when she knew who was calling.

She started laughing. "Boy, don't be saying 'what' when you answer the phone."

"*You* do it, so why can't I? What!" I said it again.

She laughed again. "Well, just wanted to let you know that daddy in the hospital."

"Really?" I got a little more serious. "For what?"

"He having some breathing problems."

"He been in there for 'bout two days already. I've been going back and forth there between his room and Raleigh." She was married now, living in the state capital.

"Oh, okay. I'll see if I can get there this weekend and help out."

"That's fine. If you can, that's good. That'll help out a lot. Dwayne, Jr. livin' in that house wit him and ain't thought about comin' to the hospital to make sure daddy okay. A shame." Dwayne had since moved back in with my father, along with the other boarders, who were residing there.

"Mm hmm. I'll let you know what I'm able to do."

I went ahead and got a last-minute ticket. He hadn't been the best father, but he was my father nonetheless. As I got older, I understood how fleeting life was. At the end of the day, this could be life or death. As I headed toward the hospital, my phone rang. I didn't know why I thought my entry into the city would remain a secret.

"You in town?" My mother had caught wind of my arrival.

"Yes, I am."

She gave off a hearty laugh. "Okay. You here to see your daddy? I called him and he sound bad."

"Okay. Well, I'll see for myself. I'll probably spend the night in the hospital and come by during the day at your place to shower and change clothes."

"Okay, baby, that's good. I'm glad you made it safe."

"Bye."

When I entered the hospital room, his TV was blaring but he was asleep. His typical thing. I decided not to wake him. I turned down the volume and adjusted the window shades. In the line of sight across from his room was Durham County Stadium, where our band had played during many high school football games. The view brought back many memories of Keva's and my bumming rides home with friends because no one was coming to pick us up after the games. I left the window and started straightening up the room a bit.

He started stirring, opened his eyes, and caught a glimpse of me. He seemed so happy to see me. "Hey, Bernie Wernie. I didn't know you were coming." His usual greeting. I'd be fifty years old, and this name would always stick.

"Hey." I adjusted his covers. "Yeah, I finished teaching and just decided to come see how you were doing. How you feel?"

"Hangin' in there." He started making a strange breathing noise. It wasn't a wheeze or faint shortness of breath. He was producing a humming, deep-seated continuous grunt as a breath. I had never heard anything of the sort. It sounded like an idling engine. "Hard to breathe." Pause. Engine revving. "But I'm here."

"Okay." I sat in the extendable chair beside the bed. "Keva told me you weren't doing too well, so I came for the weekend to help out."

"I 'preciate it, Bernie."

I looked on the bed railing. Attached to it hung a plastic container with an opening at the top. It contained a yellowish liquid. I'd soon discover its purpose.

I leaned all the way back in the chair. My feet elevated. "No problem." He looked and sounded terribly. Here was the man who seemed to be monster-like to me when I was a kid. Now he could barely talk and move, depending on somebody else to get him through this.

301

He kept explaining. "I didn't realize how much I was having problems breathing." More revving. "'Til Joey heard how bad I sounded and called . . ." He stopped mid-sentence and reached for the container. He started relieving himself in the container as I sat aghast. His bladder was to the point where the urge to urine would hit him without warning. It was so strong that he had to lie in bed and use the restroom there. He then dabbed himself with tissue, returned the container to the railing, and continued the story. "Joey called the ambulance." Joey was a boarder who lived at the residence along with Dwayne, Jr. and Samantha, a woman boarder. Although all were supposed to be paying rent, none of them was consistent.

"Oh, okay, I see. Well, I'm glad you made it safely to the hospital." The nurse came in for her rounds. She gave him some steroids and other pills. Then, she gave him a nebulizer treatment, which supposedly opened up his airways. The clear mask smoked and covered his nose and mouth. I could tell he felt relieved. It seemed to be a psychological cure, though. The noise from the machine and the visible smoke would convince a dead man that he was breathing appropriately. I was just happy he was getting treated.

I barely slept during the entire weekend. When he woke up at night barely breathing, I made sure he was okay. And when he woke up and had to go, I just grabbed the plastic container, gave it to him, and hung it again at the edge of the bed when he finished, noticing the warmth of the container's bottom. I kept tissue handy too for him to dab himself since he couldn't do the normal manly shake after finishing. It wore me out. I couldn't imagine situations where people had to take care of invalid, sick parents day in and day out. I developed a new respect for those caregivers.

I waited on him hand and foot, alternating shifts with Keva to make sure he was fine. I knew I had to head back northward and didn't know how I'd survive teaching on Monday since I was so tired, but I was sure I'd figure something out. I was glad I had it in me not to hold any animosity toward him. I was grateful to God that I had grown and not adopted the attitude that said, *Good, this is what he deserves for all the hell he put my mom and us through*. He was still human and was hopefully realizing the beauty of life. Whether I had vengeance in my heart or not, it was true that one still reaps what he sows. So I didn't have to add any extra difficulties on my end. I chose just to show love and be a good son.

He finally got to a point where the hospital had to assign him his own portable oxygen machine that he would have to tote around for a while wherever he went. Through exercise, healthy living, and the use of this machine, he could regain some sense of normalcy to his life. This temporary change would be something he wasn't accustomed to, but he would grow from it, I hoped.

During one of Keva's shifts, I made it to my mother's house to change clothes and relax a bit. Her viewpoint on the matter was a little different than mine, and she had no reservations about voicing them.

"See, that Dwayne Dillard, Sr. better start listenin' to what the Man Upstairs saying. He tryin' to get him to see he didn't do me right all dem years ago."

"Mama, what any of that got to do with it?" I pulled off my pants. I didn't have anything to hide from her.

"Shit! Don't nobody in the family believe me when I tell 'em that Dwayne, Sr. did me wrong. He had Denise in that damn house layin' in that damn bed wit her. And it was *my* damn name on that deed wit his. She layin' up in there like her name on the deed."

"I know." That was all I wanted to contribute. If I said that, maybe she'd be quiet. Wishful thinking. I figured that the other story she was used to telling me was next. I was right.

"Just like that time I came to check on y'all to make sure y'all was alright. I walked in that house and went to the back room. Dwayne didn't know I was comin'. I opened that door and saw Denise standin' over top o' him holdin' a damn needle in his arm. Like she was a damn nurse! Lord, help me to stop cussin'!" She was catching herself again.

"Oh. Well, mama, why you lettin' yourself get worked up over that all over again?" I was trying to calm her down in my own unobtrusive way. I grabbed a towel and placed it around my waist.

"It's just the memories, baby, the memories." Then, she thought she'd informed me of something else she had forgotten to tell me. "Oh yeah, you know they found her up in that house dead, right?"

"Who?"

"Denise ass. Layin' up in there like she own that damn house."

"What you mean 'dead'?" I was enrapt in the conversation now.

"As a door knob. Your daddy got up and saw she won't moving for a couple of hours. He called Dwayne, Jr. in the room and they saw she won't movin'. Just layin' there stiff as a damn board. She had that rigum ... real-go ... what's it called when you can't move?"

303

"Rigor mortis."

"Hell yeah. Them people came to take her body out and she was laying in the same position when they carried her out as she was when she was sleep. Her arm bent under her head and everything. Locked in place."

"Mama, you lyin'. She died right in his bed?"

"If I'm lyin', I'm flyin'. And I ain't got no wings. At least not yet. She died right in his bed." She started laughing.

"Mama, it's not nice to laugh at that." I headed for the bathroom.

"Shit. Whatever! God don't like ugly. God don't care nothin' 'bout how important you 'posed to be. Or what yo' last name is. Or how you try to hide stuff. Throw rocks and hide ya hands. He see erthang, and He ain't 'bout to let you get away with stuff, especially if you do people wrong. It get to a point where He gone say, 'Enough is enough.' He tryin' to tell your daddy that. God done kill't Denise. Now your daddy can barely breathe, layin' up in somebody hospital. He need to open his eyes and see what the Man Upstairs tryin' to tell 'im. He tryin' to get his attention. Done carried me and my chirren through hell and act like he ain't done nothin' wrong. 'Scuse me fuh cussin'."

"Mama, I think he knows. Whether he admits it or not is another thing. He ain't crazy. And he has plenty of time now to think about what he did. We just have to be sure we don't stay trapped in the past and let it control *us*." I closed the door to the bathroom and crept into the shower.

She walked up to the door and made sure I heard her voice. "Yeah, you right. He damn sholl got plenty of time to think about it now." She always had to have the last word. This time was no different.

After that weekend, I said my goodbyes and headed back to New York. A key lesson that rang true to me was that you'll have to deal with the effects of getting old if you don't die early. No matter how immortal we feel in our young age, we will have to deal with our decisions and choices as we get older, good or bad. Hopefully, we stay humble and treat people right, especially our children or mentees, because they may be the ones who have to care for us as we age. That weekend of caring for him and helping him make it over that hump shed a lot of light on my own perspective on life. I wouldn't want to act carelessly in my younger years and be left standing alone as I went through low moments in life. Thankfully, I was able to get to a point where I grew as a man, let my bygones be bygones and my "my-gones" be "my-gones."

In fact, that's what my life had become: one big classroom filled with all kinds of life's lessons. I had been exposed to some good, some bad, and some ugly, all having significant influences on whom I had become. Some days, I wondered if I had some form of autism since I had sometimes been so prone early on to looking inwardly often and evaluating where I was in life at the moment. I had discovered that autism literally came from the root word "auto" or "self" and had to do with people whose behavior was so "self"-centered or introspective that they lacked a great deal of social know-how. At one point, one of my grandmother's sisters even asked my grandmother, "Girl, is Bernard okay? He sholl don't talk much. He keeps to himself a lot."

What many failed to realize was that early on I had learned the benefit of reflecting on situations that involved me and mine. How could I encourage someone who had to endure the pangs of sexual molestation? How would I help to convince someone that they didn't have to follow the same path of domestic abuse just because they witnessed it themselves? How could I make someone understand that they could bounce back from failing a class or an entire program altogether? What would I say to a son who considered Father's Day as just another day on the calendar, having no real meaning behind it? Or what would I say to someone who went out on a limb to pursue their dreams and passions, despite little resources, networks, and connections?

The unifying response to all these questions and more, the answer I would give concerning all of these challenges, after having an opportunity to sit back and reflect on these minor setbacks that have found themselves into my world is that you can survive all circumstances. When the smoke of life clears, you can still stand and not just survive but thrive. With the help of the Lord, there is nothing that can impede your forward movement, except you. The only real force of opposition will come from yourself and allowing yourself to stand in your own way. You're more prone to fail by internalizing other people's opinions of you and by operating within a box that others, be they family or friend, try to put you in. The challenge becomes to break free of the box and reach for the standard the Lord has set for your life. After all, He's the one Who created you. Why base your purpose and destiny on what others, who are simply a part of the same creation that you are, say about you and not what the Creator says? This is perhaps the biggest hindrance that you face on the road to greatness, of shrinking to appease others' limited estimation of who they think you are and are not, of hiding your light under a bushel.

If you adopt an I-can attitude, you will arise like the proverbial phoenix, in spite of the pains and disappointments that you have to stomach. I discovered that Jesus has the ability to turn your scars into stars, all for the purpose of bringing glory to God's vision and purpose, and He can make you, like the star, shine brightly. The good thing I've learned about life is that the next day always holds a new sense of possibility and opportunity. Twenty-four fresh hours. No matter what I've experienced today, I have a chance to try again on tomorrow. And no matter what negativity has entered my world on today, it doesn't mean that it will exist tomorrow. Thank God for a new sense of hope that tomorrow brings.

So if you are struggling with your today moments and are trying to figure out how you will make it, know that your tomorrow will pull you through. Your todays are actually your past tomorrows manifested. And just like you didn't think you'd made it to today, you got here because your tomorrows kept on coming. So rest in the knowledge that your tomorrows have a way of taking you by the hand and ushering you into your place of purpose. It makes no difference where you start or how much you don't have or what struggles you face at present, tomorrow has a way of making all things right. If you keep the right perspective and attitude, the scales of life have a way of becoming more and more balanced. And while you don't have to become paralyzed today by being transfixed on tomorrow, wishing for it to hurry up and come, you can through prayer and faith solidify your victorious slot in tomorrow's bosom.

Learn the lessons and keep the right attitude on today! It is only then that your real tomorrow will take form and meaning. You will be able to mentor and encourage someone else who is struggling with their own today en route to their own tomorrow.

"Woo, chile! These legs givin' out. I need to take me two Excedrin. Mama ain't as young as she used to be." My mother was visiting me again during the Christmas season and was struggling to climb the stairs leading out of the D train by 135th Street. There were twenty-eight steps in total. I always subconsciously counted the stairs whenever I went up or down a set as I made my way through the city. It was part of my math mind, I guess.

"I hear you." As we walked home on 133rd Street, she took her sweet time. Her recent hip-replacement surgery was fine, but it caused more pressure on her knees for some reason. She was already pigeon-toed. So the extra stress on her knees was undeniable as she negotiated the steps, and it seemed that her body was reaching its tipping point for the day. She had to catch the bus to pay bills back in Durham, and her body was falling prey to basic wear and tear. She was indeed right. She wasn't as young as she once was. It was my goal to be able to purchase a car for her. I had already saved about $500 and cut spending, so I'd be able to surprise her one day with one. Until then, though, she'd just have to deal with it. "Just take it easy. My apartment ain't goin' nowhere. Thankfully, you ain't got to climb no steps when we get to Abundant Life Tabernacle on tomorrow."

"What's that, that church in the Bronx?"

"Mm hmm."

"Oh, good! I like dat li'l church. Dat man know he be preachin' from his gut."

"Yeah, he real good." I was actually tiring of Harlem and its rent gouging. I decided that I wouldn't be renewing my lease in January. I'd be searching in the Bronx area for a new place, perhaps by the Yankee Stadium area. I knew I could get more bang for my buck there with respect to apartment space.

We arrived at my building and finally made it inside the apartment. "I don't see why they got to be sittin' right on the steps in the damn way. We can't even get by. They so nosy, watchin' what you doin' 24/24." She meant 24/7. She was talking about the people who lived in the building and hung out on the stairs leading to my apartment. They congregated there to pass time and often had to move whenever people had to get in the door. "That don't make no sense. Can't even get home in peace."

We finally got settled, and I started dinner. I got out the pork chops, the corn-on-the-cob, the beans and rice, and broccoli. She plopped on the sofa and started flipping through different channels. "Oh, yeah, I forgot to tell you. I think I heard your aunt is thinkin' 'bout selling the restaurant." She was doing her job in keeping me up to date concerning things on the home front. Facebook and Twitter didn't have anything on Vicky Dillard. She owned no computer, but she still got her news somehow before the news seemed to happen.

"Really? It's been around for such a long time. But come to think about it, it just might be time to let it go."

"Yeah, but it's sorta sad. I remember workin' in there way back when. You would think maybe she'd find somebody to rent it out or somethin'."

"Yeah, but it just may have served its purpose. That was granddaddy's vision, not hers. Sometimes, things change with time. Plus, she ain't gettin' no younger. She done put her life on hold for a long time. And ain't nobody really helpin' her wit it. Her brothers sholl didn't do nothin' with it but create headaches for everybody involved. I 'on't blame her."

"Ewww. I got me a dress like that." The meteorologist on the news station was dressed to the nines, and mama quickly shifted the conversation, as was her custom.

"Mama, you ain't got no dress like that."

"Yes I do, too." Then she changed the subject as she switched to the Food Network. "That Paula Deen know she some'm else. She can cook."

I rebutted, "She can cook, but I think she be tryin' too hard when she talks. She acts like she more country than she really is." I wasn't impressed with her too much. I thought she gave southern people a bad rap by trying to be extra-southern.

"Nuh uh. That's just how she talk."

"I guess. And she ain't thinkin' 'bout making no kinda healthy dish either. She told Oprah one time that she was your cook, not your doctor. I couldn't believe she let them words come out of her mouth on nationwide TV."

"Well, what you see is what you get wit huh. You ain't got to wonder 'bout nothin'."

My mother changed the subject on a whim again as I sat down to check my messages online. "You know your daddy started going back to church again." She was dropping more knowledge and information.

"Really? That's good. I guess that hospital experience got his attention. Maybe he realizes that he better get himself together."

"Mm hmm. Singin' in the choir and erthang. But I'm staying right where I am, living by myself. I just don't feel the same way 'bout him like I used to."

"I definitely hear you on that. Don't nobody expect you to move back in with him. Anyway, you doin' pretty good on your own. I guess there is hope for him after all. That man done took us through a lot o' stuff. If God can change him, He can change anybody."

"Ain't dat the truth. I tell you. People don't know the half of it. People wouldn't believe the kinda stuff we been through. I could write a book. I tell you the truth, I could write a damn book!" She didn't apologize for the cursing this time and didn't have to. It probably needed to be said just like that. She instead let herself go into a hearty laughter as she kept switching channels. As she continued laughing, she strangely said it again in the midst of her own uncontrollable humor-filled sideshow. "I *know* I could write a damn book!"

I had been seated for a while and didn't realize my leg had fallen asleep. I accepted a few friend requests and got up from the computer so I could finish preparing the meal. I got up and felt that weird tingling feeling as blood flowed through the leg again. Her laughter made me laugh to myself. Giggling, I placed the broccoli into the pan, covered it, and stared at the boiling water through the clear cover and just waited. Although she was in the other room, I could still hear her laughing and decided to confirm her prophetic unknowing.

"Yeah, you could. You *really* could." She had no clue that *Lemonade* was three-quarters finished, but she always seemed to say things out of the blue that signaled a mother's intuition.

Almost choking on her own saliva, she managed to find a way to keep on laughing.

# bring bernard

Bernard has dedicated himself to inspiring others to reach their potential in several areas, especially *personal growth*, *education*, and *personal finances*.

Bring Bernard to your church, organization, or group. He is available for:

- Motivational speaking
- Seminars and workshops on personal finance and budgeting
- Seminars and workshops on college preparation and navigation
- Modeling and acting assignments

To book, contact, and stay up to date with the
latest concerning Bernard, visit:

www.bernarddillard.com

Or email:

bringbernard@gmail.com

Proof

Made in the USA
Charleston, SC
17 September 2014